Potentia of Poverty

Historical Materialism Book Series

The Historical Materialism Book Series is a major publishing initiative of the radical left. The capitalist crisis of the twenty-first century has been met by a resurgence of interest in critical Marxist theory. At the same time, the publishing institutions committed to Marxism have contracted markedly since the high point of the 1970s. The Historical Materialism Book Series is dedicated to addressing this situation by making available important works of Marxist theory. The aim of the series is to publish important theoretical contributions as the basis for vigorous intellectual debate and exchange on the left.

The peer-reviewed series publishes original monographs, translated texts, and reprints of classics across the bounds of academic disciplinary agendas and across the divisions of the left. The series is particularly concerned to encourage the internationalization of Marxist debate and aims to translate significant studies from beyond the English-speaking world.

For a full list of titles in the Historical Materialism Book Series available in paperback from Haymarket Books, visit: www.haymarketbooks.org/series_collections/1-historical-materialism.

Potentia of Poverty

Marx Reads Spinoza

Margherita Pascucci

Haymarket Books
Chicago, IL

First published in 2023 by Brill Academic Publishers, The Netherlands
© 2023 Koninklijke Brill NV, Leiden, The Netherlands

Published in paperback in 2024 by
Haymarket Books
P.O. Box 180165
Chicago, IL 60618
773-583-7884
www.haymarketbooks.org

ISBN: 979-8-88890-213-4

Distributed to the trade in the US through Consortium Book Sales and
Distribution (www.cbsd.com) and internationally through Ingram
Publisher Services International (www.ingramcontent.com).

This book was published with the generous support of Lannan
Foundation, Wallace Action Fund, and the Marguerite Casey Foundation.

Special discounts are available for bulk purchases by organizations and
institutions. Please call 773-583-7884 or email info@haymarketbooks.org
for more information.

Cover art and design by David Mabb. Cover art is a detail from *Construct
67, William Morris, Fruit/Kazimir Malevich, Square,* acrylic on wallpaper
(2012).

Library of Congress Cataloging-in-Publication data is available.

Contents

Preface to the Italian Edition

It now seems to be a given that the history of modern philosophy recognises a line of thought that links Machiavelli to Spinoza and Spinoza to Marx. Even though this line does not represent itself as anti-modern, it does seem to prefigure and to empower the tensions, dynamics, and mechanisms of 'alter-modernity'. That is to say, this line expresses the development of a humanistic ontology and a radical immanence at the same time as it stands in conflict with the genesis of the capitalist organisation of society. In its twisting path, this line opposes the values affirmed by the victorious modernity with ethical alternatives and a different conception of the human – that is, of the constitutive relation between the singular and the common.

The Machiavelli-Spinoza relationship has been widely explored within this framework. The great interpretations of both these authors that followed one after the other across the second half of the twentieth century emphasised the continuity of this line of thought. But moreover, within this continuity, they identified an irreducible alternative to the lines which configured the hegemonic ideology of capitalist modernity and sovereignty from Descartes to Hegel. Even today, when frequent objections are levelled against this continuity, with the indecent digging up of idealistic or naturalistic positions, the centrality of Spinoza's materialism (in its relation to Machiavellian thought) is still considered essential. The theories prevalent today that rely on a negative interpretation of ontology, do not succeed in breaking up this awareness. And if, as is well-known, Heidegger never considered Spinoza a philosopher who could be considered a part of modern metaphysics, this sectarian underestimation not only deserves no response, but serves as a condemnation of its author.

The Spinoza-Marx line has been instead very little studied in the history of contemporary philosophy. When this has been done, it has been done starting out from the supposed continuity of an objectivist and progressive 'revolutionary materialism' – a continuity which presumed specific political options, in this particular case meaning *diamat*. The Spinoza-Marx relationship was not set on a line of altermodernity but on the line of progress. Despite and against all this, today the Spinoza-Marx theme assumes renewed present relevance [*attualità*], which is to say, it again becomes fully theoretical. Pascucci centres on this crux of present-day thought. The subtitle of the book is 'Marx reads Spinoza'. The proposed themes are the virtuality of *potentia* in Spinoza; the *potentia* of poverty in Marx; the definition of the 'common notion' in Spinoza; and the definition of the 'law of value' in Marx. The thesis is that the *potentia* of poverty sets value free.

The volume articulates three moves. In the first, the Spinoza-Marx relation is established starting from the juxtaposition, in the development of the immanentist mechanism, of the definition of common notion in Spinoza and of value in Marx. The second highlights the faithfulness and fruitfulness of Marx's reading of Spinoza in the 1841 *Cahier*. The third develops the theme of the virtuality of labour-power, that is of the *potentia* of poverty, through an attentive comparison of Spinoza's and Marx's writings, as well as of their most recent interpretations.

The questions that Pascucci poses, starting from the 'poor' virtuality of labour-power, are precise ones: can production be imagined, on such a basis, as a liberation of value from the abstraction which it is forced into? Can the *potentia*, recaptured from within the time of capital, be liberated and constructed as the time of our lives? Can Marx's transformative praxis materially organise the *potentia* of Spinoza's imagination? Steering clear of any economistic conception of Marxism, Pascucci believes that it is possible to oppose the 'surplus-value of capital' with 'a surplus-concept of life: an excess of being, a dismeasure[1] which annuls capital within its own production mechanism and overturns it into non-sense, which lets it vanish in the void that it is'. This thus again proposes the value of the world as a production of the poor.

I will leave it up to readers to evaluate Pascucci's refined research, through which, throughout her entire book, she outlines the abstraction of value, the disproportion of labour, and the *potentia* of transformative praxis. I would like to insist on the characteristics of the *potentia* of poverty and on the way in which poverty can be read as *potentia*. We can thus say that the production of the subjectivity which emerges within capitalist development reaches its own truth only when it stands on the basis of the liberation of labour-power. That is to say, when it rests on the freedom and the infinite potentiality that labour-power has inasmuch as it originally consists of poverty. The production of commodities and the construction of life enter into contradiction and open up into a process of metamorphosis, or rather of practical transformation, when the *potentia* (of poverty) succeeds in expressing itself. Poverty cannot be defined in the restrictive terms of misery to which capital would like to reduce it: rather, it constantly rises up against this, continuously revealing common potentia and capacity to give rise to joy. If virtuality opens up to time and coordinates the tendency of the real, poverty is the site of both the knowledge of the capitalist violation of the common and of the revolutionary praxis that is thus necessary. Poverty is never lack, it is not a state of need; rather it is a

---

1   The Italian is *dismisura*.

potentia which expresses itself incessantly in the time of life. It is impossible for capital to handle it. It is constitutive of new life.

How paradoxical it seems, to identify the origin of wealth and joy in poverty! Yet, it is this relation which realises Spinozist virtuality in praxis. The movement of this poor virtuality and its metamorphosis mark, illustrate and enhance the theoretical path which defines poverty as *potentia*.

In the present renewal of communist thought (which runs against the further abstraction of capitalist power), more and more voices are powerfully rising up to refer to poverty as a productive force. Indeed, we have learned to read poverty as the virtuality of a common *potentia*. On these foundations it will probably be possible to renovate the communist experience. But how can we do this, if not by plunging our thought and our lived existence into the experience of poverty (and of its creative potential), of exclusion (and of the resistances that it produces), of the refusal of command (and of the imagination that it liberates)?

Margherita Pascucci's book is easy to read when we follow the Ariadne's thread which leads our intelligence and our *potentia* into conflict with the capitalist Minotaur. In this panorama of legends, we find other, similar ones which do not however likewise stimulate our imagination. Neither does Icarus do so, with his utopian will to fly away from the misery that capital imposes, and nor does Hercules, who as a good reformist thinks he is always stronger than the adversary, right to the point when the illusion turns into defeat. No, here our ethical and revolutionary responsibility pivots knowledge toward poverty – neither to utopia nor to the arrogance of realism – but indeed to the experience of poverty. The poor is the powerful, Pascucci tells us. She interprets Marx as a reader of Spinoza; however, maybe there is something more here than there is in Spinoza and Marx themselves. A further passage is necessary to grasp this 'more': namely, to tie the experience of poverty to an ontology of '*cupiditas*' [desire], that is, of '*amor*' [love].

Antonio Negri

Author's Preface to the English Edition

When this book was published in Italy, almost twenty years ago, my assessment of Marx's reading of Spinoza produced a short circuit between *potentia* and the virtual, of which I gave an account in the monograph which followed: *Causa sui*.[1] Here I have added a Chapter 4, which bridges the content of both texts and continues my reflection, expanding it to include immaterial labour and the construction of the 'plus' of being.

This short circuit contained a theoretical product, already implicit in this earlier text, which emerged more powerfully and was explored further in *Causa sui*. This was the planning of *potentia* – how *potentia* is production, a prospective virtue, a creative texture and free force of our self-causation.

In these twenty years, many works have been written on poverty, conceived from a philosophical point of view. Universities around the world have organised seminars, conferences, and classes; academics have united against the increasing misery which we witness on a world scale.[2]

Yet that political ethics of which the *potentia* of poverty is the expression has still to be materially constructed.

I would like, in this preface to the English edition, to resume the discourse by starting out from the last sentence of Negri's preface to the Italian text: that is, the need for a further passage 'to tie the experience of poverty to an ontology of "*cupiditas*" [desire], that is, of "*amor*" [love]'.[3]

In the trajectory that these last twenty years wrote on our common body, world society, two experiences of mine embodied the tying of the experience

---

1   *Causa sui. Saggio sul capitale e il virtuale*, ombre corte, 2009.
2   See footnote 11 to chapter 4.
3   Negri 2012 summarises this constitutive process of *potentia* in the articulation from *conatus* to *cupiditas* up to expressing *amor*, love. See Negri 2012, pp. 14–15, 30–1, and 42–5. On a new form of the political see p. 15, for the production of subjectivity, the 'powerful virtuality' of the productive forces, see pp. 30–1, 43–5. Among Negri's works, we should bear in mind the milestone Negri 1991 and Negri 1992, together with Negri 2013a; 2013b. Meanwhile there has appeared Negri 2017, where in II. 6, the conceptualisation has affinities with the conceptualisation that you find in *La Potenza della povertà*. On the concept of political love, see Michael Hardt's work, including his online courses at European Graduate School, *About love*, 2007, (https://www.youtube.com/watch?v=ioopkoppabI); as well as Hardt 2012, mainly pp. 4–5, 6–8, 9–12, and the passages on love in Hardt and Negri 2009, pp. 179–98; 316–18; 379–80. As regards the conceptualisation of poverty, affinities can be found between *La Potenza della povertà* and some passages in *Commonwealth*. On the reference to Heidegger's 'Armut' in *Commonwealth*, please allow me to refer also to my 'Privilegium Paupertatis. On poverty and potentia', in *Millepiani*, Mimesis, Milan, no. 26, 2003.

of poverty to love, to the political concept of love. The first was the experi-ence of extreme misery in Bangladesh in 2006, the second the experience of the oppressed people of Palestine in 2013. These two experiences profoundly challenged, and thus reinforced, the need for the construction of that political ethics, or economic ethics, which is the object of this book. These two experi-ences reaffirmed how far we are from an adequate knowledge of our common world. And they were, indeed, the experience of the *potentia* of poverty and the experience of the political concept of love: both forces striving against all undue appropriation of life, be it the misery of Dhaka, the direct product of the mechanism of Capital, or the still ongoing occupation of Palestine, the clear effect of a similar mechanism.[4]

While Dhaka cried out with the crude, impotent, inhuman experience of misery, there seemed to be neither space nor opportunity for a *potentia* of poverty. Yet living there, sharing knowledge with university students, cross-ing through the slums every day, every day a new line of actualisation, a new instance, a new voice surfaced, challenging misery and its causes. This voice seemed to say that *there is a nature of the material which can be met only if it is common. And there is a common which is only material, it is desire. The common is desire. Poverty is the common which becomes desire, it is desire of the com-mon. We are its* potentia. In its sometimes violent internal clash with Dhaka's slums, its children, its workers engaged in both material and immaterial labour, its strikes, its humanity reduced to nothing, in the overwhelming misery that crushes bodies and minds, the force of the struggle for life pierced through this very misery. In the intensity of material labour, this struggle against misery presented itself as a *potentia* of poverty, a rhizomatic virtuality seeking the lines of the actualisation of an adequate production, a just life.

> *We are wild as the storm*
> *We are restless as the spring* (...)
> *We are free as the sky*
> (...) *We know no king*
> *nor any king's laws*
> *We submit to no rule or regulation,*
> *We are born free with the mind*
> *open as the blossoming lotus.*
> *We are the murmuring flood tide of the sea and the warbling waters of the*
>   *mountain spring*

---

4   See Deleuze 1984 (English translation in Deleuze 1998), and Deleuze 2006.

(...) We are flying birds with outstretched wings
We are bubbling laughter and gay songs.
(...) We are the gushing river of life
We are the flowing waters of mountain brooks
warbling singing roaring
always restless and ever on the move.
kol kol kol, chol chol chol chol chol chol

NAZRUL ISLAM, A Mountain Song, *Panari Gan*

'Intensity affirms even the *lowest*, it makes the lowest an object of affirmation. The power of a waterfall or a very deep descent is required to go that far and make an affirmation even of descent. Everything is like the flight of an eagle, overflight, suspension and descent. Everything goes from high to low, and by that movement affirms the lowest' (Deleuze, *Difference and repetition*).

In Bethlehem I experienced for the first time the violence of the state and the nonviolence of a people. The violence of an occupier state and the nonviolence of an occupied people. The power of the lowest, those on the ground, to think *differently*, to conceive the other and herself in the *difference*, to empower this thought and praxis of difference, this affirmation of life against death as the inner power to be free, where depth and intensity produce individuation and love, free singularities and political love. 'A free man thinks of death least of all things, and his wisdom is a meditation of life, not of death' (Spinoza, *Ethics*, IV, LXVII). The Palestinian and Israeli men and women who make the choice of nonviolence in today's occupied Palestine, every day risking their lives, are the free men and women of Spinoza's *Ethics*. They think of nothing but death: every morning when they wake up, on Fridays before they go to peacefully demonstrate, every night when they go to sleep, they know that it – the occupation, death – can suddenly disrupt their intimate life. It is like this for them just as it was for their fathers and mothers, and still is for their children. Yet they know, because they are free, that their greatest wisdom, the greatest act that they are doing, day after day, night after night, is that which meditates not on that death which comes from the outside, but radically, affirmatively, on the life that comes from within.

'Revolution never proceeds by way of the negative'. 'Revolution is the social power of the difference'. 'Depth is like the famous geological line from NE to SW, the line which comes diagonally from the heart of things and distributes volcanoes: it unites a bubbling sensibility and a thought which "rumbles in its crater". Depth and intensity are the same at the level of being, or vice versa. The vectors or vectorial magnitudes which occur throughout extensity, but also the scalar magnitudes or particular cases of vector-potentials, are the eternal witness to the intensive origin: for example, altitudes' (Deleuze, *Difference and Repetition*).

Nonviolence runs like a volcano underneath the violence of the State. Its act of political love is depth and intensity, the vector-potential and vector-magnitude of that altitude of being which is steadfast affirmation against any negative, against all erasure of individuation.

These two experiences deeply marked, and radically changed, my way of thinking and doing philosophy.

In the first experience, commodities needed to become a common notion and the people needed to know their *potentia*. But the decisive thing in the second experience was the concept of political love that nonviolent activists were striving to realise through their *causa sui*, their common power to produce themselves as free singularities and affirm life through difference.

Love is the power to conceive the other and to be conceived through the other. For it is the immanent construction of a surplus of being, whose freedom, whose adequate plane, cannot but be a common one. This is also the essence of adequate labour (commodity as common notion) – the adequate production which is the production of true wealth. This, too, cannot but be common.

As with the *potentia* of poverty, the path runs from commodity-imagination to common notion-adequate relation of production to the adequate knowledge and cause of production, which is the production of true wealth. With the labour of love we increase our capacity of acting and our capacity of knowing, we increase the *potentia* of the mind and the *potentia* of the body, through the very foundation and movement of the *potentia* of poverty. Being conceived through the other, the power to conceive through the other, their coming together: this is the construction of the common, when the free expression of individuation produces a common texture.

Love is something concrete, difficult, it is a labour. That is, a labour to construct all the places and times where virtue and *potentia* are the same thing.

That the worker's labour could become love is extremely difficult too, but when it does occur, we are truly happy beings.

'All things excellent are as difficult as they are rare' ends the *Ethics*. I thus dedicate this book to the adequate love, and the adequate praxis of love; to the adequate knowledge of love, and the adequate cause of ourselves which will allow us to be happy through labour and the construction of the common being which is love; to all those who make of poverty, potentia – all excellent things, which as difficult as they are rare, however continuously, steadfastly, joyfully constitute our life.

Introduction

1   To Define Poverty as *potentia*

The object of this study is the definition of a field of reflection on poverty, the theoretical apparatus for which is found in the elements of Marx's system which derive from his youthful reading of Spinoza.

Spinoza's conceptual apparatus, from the *Ethics* to the *Tractatus* to the Letters, is the foundation of a theory of praxis which we rediscover in the Marx of *Capital* and of the *Grundrisse*, and, above all, in the Marx of the concept of value. At the core of this theory of praxis is the figure of virtuality.

This study's hypothesis holds that in the Marxian notion of virtuality we find the kernel of the elements of the young Marx's reading of Spinoza: Marx's 'according to potentiality'[1] [*dunamei*] has a much more than just semantic affinity with the Spinozan concept of *potentia*. The familiarity is an ontological one: what the *potentia* is for Spinoza's ethics, virtuality is for Marx's materialism.

The 'virtually poor' in Marx and the conception of history *dunamei* have in common with Spinoza's *potentia* the character of revolutionary praxis – *umwälzende Praxis*.

This study thus starts out from Marx's 'free worker, virtually poor' to investigate the role that virtuality has therein. It seeks understand the links between this and Spinoza's system of thought and, lastly, to arrive at a definition of poverty that binds it with the Spinozan concept of *potentia*.

If we do succeed in defining poverty as *potentia*, we can perhaps make an opening to a material understanding of those abstract relations which Capital creates. And only by disclosing the aconceptual relations that Capital fabricates – that is, by focusing on the role of fixed capital which knowledge, and life, have today assumed in the economic system – can we give back to the worker, the virtually poor, her *potentia* as her real freedom.

Often in history, reflections on the concept of value are accompanied by specific reflections on the concept of poverty. Some instances are of particular interest for the reading of poverty as *potentia*: Petrus Johannes Olivi, with his theories on value, on capital and on the *usus pauper*, before which Francesco

---

1   In the Italian it is 'virtuality'. Throughout the book we will explain the coincidences and passages between potentiality and virtuality.

and Chiara required the *privilegium paupertatis*; Shakespeare, with his ironic figuration of Money and the first Poor Laws; Spinoza, the new Ethics, and the concept of *potentia*; Marx, the 'virtual *potentia*' of history, revolutionary praxis, the second Poor Laws; and today, cognitive capitalism and the growing poverty on a global scale.

These moments in history, when value and poverty unite, are thresholds: a threshold for knowledge, a threshold for the senses; a threshold for thought, for custom, for sensation.

They are thresholds but also planes: a plane of immanence, where the thinkable and the sensible meet and discover a new dimension; that time which escapes expropriation; a plane of creation, where the new is born, because the virtuality actualises itself therein; a plane of conceivability, where knowledge exposes its immaterial aspect to praxis: immaterial labour as the site where a new praxis has its maximum grasp on life.

The following is a small glossary of the meaning given to the different terms:

Abstraction = the act of the separation of thought from body, of existence from essence, of matter from its concept.

Actualisation = the reality of virtuality, which is totally new.

***Causa sui* (cause of itself)** = for Spinoza 'that whose essence involves existence; or that whose nature can be conceived only as existing' [*Ethics* I, Definition 1]. Together with which I read the concept of substance, 'that which is in itself and is conceived through itself' [ivi, Def. 3].

***Causa ab alio* (cause from other)** = that which is 'in the other' and can be conceived only through the other.

Caesura of history = revolutionary praxis (crisis, revolution, strike, civil war) or its exploitation, its violation (war). To this is made to correspond a

Caesura of knowledge = the imagination is such a type of caesura: it can be productive (material, creative imagination) or the site of an illusion (phantasmagoria, 'regress').

Chiasmus = place where an exchange occurs, and where an illusion can be produced: something material is defined through an act of abstraction, something abstract is achieved through the impoverishment of what is material.

Clinamen = *parenklesis*, the movement or the 'deviation' of the atom in Epicurus and Lucretius. There, virtuality and actualisation meet.

Commodity = what is produced to satisfy a need. It annexes a principle of equivalence and defines something as 'common'. Through the exchange it loses its free modality.

Common notions = second degree of knowledge in Spinoza, when ideas are clear and adequate. Common notions [*notiones communes*] are the knowledge of what is common to a body and others.

Concept = true and adequate knowledge of itself, which is also the true, adequate, immediate cause of itself. Plane of an immediate co-implication of essence and existence (plane of immanence). **Knowledge** = gradation in the Spinozan system: imagination – common notions – beatitude/intellectual knowledge. A similar gradation can be applied to the material and abstract knowledge in Marx; to the contemporary definitions of material and immaterial labour.

Crisis = threshold and temporal point of change.

dunamei = term used by Marx in some passages to define the movement of history; or, better, its reception. Marx quotes Aristotle's concept of *dunamis*. Here the concept implies the idea of virtuality, of potentia and of revolutionary praxis.[2]

Force = *conatus*, desire, always actualising itself, to produce one's own life.

Lack of concept = privation of the plane of immanence produced by the concept.

Mode = expression of the substance and *causa ab alio* [cause from other]. The Marxian commodity is a mode – expression of *Natura naturans* [creating nature] and *causa ab alio* [cause from other].

Potentia = expression of the actualising force of life; expression of the *conatus* [desire to be], its space and time.

Poverty = there where the expression is taken away from the *conatus*; where *conatus* and expression are separated from one another. Poverty is *potentia* without concept.

Revolutionary praxis = man knows his nature as essential 'practical *potentia*'. He achieves an adequate knowledge of his composition in relation *to* the world and an adequate knowledge of his activity *in* the world.

Substance = *causa sui* [cause of itself] in Spinoza. In the young Marx, who studies Democritus and Epicurus, it can be compared to the atom.

The material = the reunion of the divided parts (of the matter).

To become *causa sui* [cause of itself] = that which, thanks to its being conceived through another, becomes *causa sui* [cause of itself]. It is an adequate cause of itself; it has, that is, an adequate knowledge of itself.

---

2 In this book I try to show the possible theoretical path connecting pre-Socratic *dunamis* to contemporary poverty, including the transformation Aristotelian *dunamis*-Spinozan *potentia*.

To be conceived through another = that which is conceived through another and in this sense is a 'common concept'.

Virtuality = a concept which we find in Deleuze (taken from Bergson). Here it is understood and used as the actual translation of the concept of *dunamis* (potency) in Aristotle, already in Spinoza delineated as, and further transformed into, *potentia* or life of the mode.

2   Marx Close to Spinoza

The commodity in Marx and the *common notion* in Spinoza are both defined through an other. This 'other' which defines them is the 'common' among two or more things. In the case of the commodity, this common has a character of abstraction – it disappears at a certain point;[3] in the case of *common notions*, this common is something material, that which, common to a body and other bodies, brings the trace of the relation and allows for its knowledge. Both these concepts, the concept of commodity-value and the concept of common notion, have their origin in Aristotle – Aristotle is the first commonality.

Thus in the analysis of the quotations which Marx transcribed in 1841 from the *Theological-Political Treatise* and from the letters (the so-called 'Heft Spinoza') there are two further characteristics which draw Marx close to Spinoza: a) the order of Marx's quotations from the *Theological-Political Treatise* proves to be an index of the comprehension of the mechanism of the intellect and of the nature of knowledge: we can understand the nature of the intellect from a situation like that, for example, which appears in miracles; b) in 1841 Marx transcribed the quotations from Spinoza and composed his dissertation on Epicurus. The analysis of Epicurus and the theory of the *clinamen* present themselves as a red thread: time is the central mechanism of the encounter of the atoms in that deviation from the rectilinear movement that is called *clinamen* and which represents the 'actualization of the virtuality of their being single'. This time is later explained by Marx as the mechanism of capital and heart of surplus-value.

2.1   *The Practical Structure of the Intellect*

We know that Spinoza's system of knowledge consists of three degrees:[4] imagination – *common notions* – intellectual knowledge. In the almost impercept-

---

3   Given A = B, B = C, we have A = C where B, common element to A and C, and which allows for the comparison, disappears.

4   Spinoza calls them kinds of knowledge, I read them as degrees.

ible ordering of Marx's quotations from Spinoza, we perceive in filigree the structure of this system of knowledge and the concept which Marx derives from it: the practical structure of the intellect.

In the order of Marx's quotations, the Spinozan imagination becomes the first element of that process of temporal anticipation which is at the heart of the mechanism of the production of surplus-value. The imagination in Spinoza, which virtualises a presence which is not there, becomes, in Marx, the focal point of capital's fiction: the time of life which seems to be actuated by labour, comes to be, in this same labour, violated and suppressed. But – and this is the hypothesis we will base our work on – if imagination stands in relation to the commodity legislated by value as common notions stand in relation to the commodity as poetic object, intellectual knowledge can and must produce a new element at whose centre is the liberation, thanks to the economy, of the time of life. A gradation exists (like the imagination-common notion-intellectual knowledge gradation) also in the commodity known as value and as a poetical object (the phantasmagoria). This requires a third element – that is, the commodity as a production of time of life (commodity as political object).

The imagination is the first knowing object from which we move, because it allows us to bring the commodity and common notions onto the same level. Imagination is made of abstraction and materiality; it drives us toward a true knowledge, to be the adequate cause of the self, in the moment in which its structure is understood as the *first degree of the composition of the intellect*. Imagination is near to the truth, that is, to its plane of reality, when it frees itself from the abstraction. This process of getting up closer to the material is what Marx defines as the 'point of combustion' of value: value is released from its own abstraction if and when it can be understood as principle of equivalence. When we understand value as principle of equivalence – when we grasp it, that is, as an act of abstraction – then its similarity to the structure of imagination becomes clear.

The knowing system of the commodity is: value – poetical object – production of a free time of life. Value is the most abstract, the production of free life the most adequate and concrete.

It thus becomes clear how we can liberate value from its own abstraction: we have to find a 'focal' point through which value can turn itself toward the material. For the imagination this point is the level of reality, the plane, that is, of an adequate knowledge. For value, this point is the dissolution of the principle of equivalence, achieved in the moment of self-combustion of value, that process for which the principle of equivalence collapses under the inequality which it has itself established: it is the liberation of the space of incommensurability.

When, in the imagination, we understand that what we believe to be present, is not, or is no longer, the imagination then becomes productive, it sets in motion toward true knowledge. Likewise, when in the system of value we understand that the equivalence which it represents is made of inequality, value 'self-combusts' and liberates from itself that same inequality which it had hitherto produced.

2.2   *Marx Who Reads Spinoza*

The time of the theory of the *clinamen*, the central mechanism of the encounter of the atoms, which Marx would explain as the mechanism of capital and heart of surplus-value, seems to be the thing that arises in common between imagination and surplus-value. It seems to constitute the weft of the relation between Spinoza and Marx, the place of Spinoza in Marx's construction: the *Ethics* of Marx.

But what can the Marx who reads Spinoza mean for us when he is reading Democritus and Epicurus, with Aristotle as a secret focal point? Is this a cascade of conceptual metamorphosis: the *dunamis* of Aristotle translated into the time of the deviation of the *clinamen* in Epicurus, in turn translated into Spinoza's *conatus*, lastly translated by Marx into the time of Capital? Or, rather, is it the exposition of this cascade of translations: is what is anticipated and violated by Capital the *dunamis*, the potentia, the *conatus* of history and the time of our life? Is what Capital takes away from us that virtual time of each, which is definition through another, through the world and through becoming? Can poverty, virtually connected to freedom, actualise itself in potentia? To try to answer this requires a revolutionary action, *Umwälzende Praxis*, and a Marx who reads Spinoza.

3   A Surplus-Concept of Life

The relations that Capital produces are relations that lack the concept. In order to be able to exercise its sole dominion and to take away free time, Capital needs to take away that aspect of being which can be conceived through another. Capital must, that is, isolate the relations of labour which compose it, so that it can become the only relation that exercises a grip over the whole. This 'hold on the whole' is what is indicated here as *dunamis*: the virtuality of each thing, its force of becoming, the time of producing its own actualisation, ultimately, its self-definition in relation to another thing.

This virtuality is contained as something inconceivable on the plane which Capital produces. It can be understood only in the ruptures of the plane of the immanence of production, in its abysses and the holes in its web. These ruptures are the places where poverty is, and where it reflects the grip on life itself.

Marx writes in the *Grundrisse* that as long as the worker is capable of work, labour is the new source of exchange [*'solange der Arbeiter arbeitsfähig ist'*], and explains that labour is to be found in the very definition of the concept [*'Begriffsbestimmung selbst'*]. For 'he, the worker, sells only his temporal disposition over his capacity to labour' [*'dass er (der Arbeiter) nur zeitliche Disposition über seine Arbeitsfähigkeit verkauft'*], in order to be able to reproduce his own living conditions [*'Lebensäußerung reproduzieren zu können'*]. There thus becomes clear the nexus which links the capacity to labour, the definition of its concept and the temporal disposition – the relation, that is, between the time of a life and the production of the conditions for its reproduction, expressed by labour as source of exchange. Indeed, so long as the worker is capable of labour, this is his source of exchange, this capacity is his time of life and this activity is his 'conceptual' definition, that is, his self-definition in a relation of production.

The relation between the time of life and the production of the conditions for its reproduction, as effected by labour, plays out within the thread of the composition, or decomposition, of the capacity of man's labour with the definition of his concept. It plays out, that is, through each person's virtualities being set into productive relation with their own actualisation. Where virtuality and actualisation, imaginary and true knowledge, temporal disposition and the time of life do not come into composition, that is, do not find the bridges for transforming one into another, there occurs a rupture of the social plane.

The hypothesis of this study is that life's force explodes exactly in these ruptures of the plane; or, in other words, there lies a sometimes violent, but affirmative, force precisely where life bursts into ruptures. Nothing affirmative can be achieved with violence alone. But if violence contains in itself a further aspect, naturally different from destruction – perhaps a secondary aspect, but certainly a powerful one, which manifests itself in the ruptures of the plane – this aspect expresses violence as a force which affirms and interrupts, and which produces new spaces and times through this interruption. This interruption is the 'plane' where today wealth and poverty are situated. Wealth is Capital's hold on life: '*der Kapitalist nicht mehr wünscht, als dass er seine Dosen Lebenskraft soviel wie möglich ohne Unterbrechung vergeudet*' ['The Capitalist does not desire anything else other than to waste as much as possible his doses of life's force without interruption']. Poverty is the comprehension of this hold on life as the first act of Capital; it is the concept of life's force which is 'beheaded' by Capital. In this, it becomes a place of crisis and potentia of change.

We can, without doubt, oppose to the surplus-value of capital a surplus-concept of life – of the worker, of the non-worker, of the poor, of the rich: an excess of being, a dismeasure of being, which undoes capital with its own mechanism, turns it into a non-sense and leaves it vanish amidst the void that it is.

CHAPTER 1

Self-Cause and Cause through an Other [*causa sui-causa ab alio*]

1.1 Value and Common Notions

The object of this first part is to demonstrate that the Spinozan 'common notion' and the Marxian 'concept of value' have a common origin. The Marxian 'concept of value' goes back to the Aristotelean definition of what is commensurable. The Spinozan common notion is a combination of the common notions in Euclid and the concept of axiom in Aristotle. Both are broken down to arrive at their basic constitutive element: the common notion concerns the relations of proportionality among equal figures (Euclid) and their knowability (Aristotle): what is common can be set in relation, and in the relation it can be known. The concept of value concerns the commensurable, what can be made equal and, in this equality, exchanged (Aristotle).

The basic element of value is the 'definition through an other' for exchange, as in the case of 1 house = 5 beds.

The basic element of the common notion is the proportional relation between two elements, the idea of what is common to them and allows them to be set in relation.

Commodity and common notion are thus both defined through an other (what it is here called *causa ab alio*, cause through an other). In common notions, this definition through an other leads to the knowledge and the definition of the self, to the self-cause in life (*causa sui*). But in the case of the commodity, the definition-through-other of the concept of value serves exchange, an abstract knowledge, and escape from a material relation. The commodity and common notions depart from a common origin – one to serve abstract knowledge, the other to serve material knowledge. For us they constitute the two coordinates by which we can go on to understand capital and poverty.

1.1.1 Value and *Common Notions*

'Those things that are common to all things and are equally in the part as in the whole, can be conceived only adequately' (Spinoza, Ethics, 11, P 38). A common notion is a notion of something common to all bodies; as such it is a 'clear and distinct' idea.

Marx takes the concept of value from Aristotle's *Nicomachean Ethics* (book v). Aristotle states that the *commensurable*, the exchangeable, is that which is 'equivalent' – that which can be compared. In Marx, this is the basic element composing the general concept of value.[1]

The Spinozan concept of the 'common notion' has different sources: Aristotle, Stoics, Descartes, Euclid.[2] We analyse here that aspect of common notions which derives from Euclid (*Elements*, I, Common Notions, and VII, 19) and from Aristotle (*Posterior Analytics*, I, 2, 71b–72a). In Euclid, the definition of common notions [*koinai ennoiai*] concerns the relations of proportionality between equal figures; it defines a kind of 'axiom of congruence'.[3] 'Things which are equal to a same thing are also equal among them' (Euclid, I, Common Notion 1). Spinoza combines the definition of common notion in Euclid and the definition of 'axiom' in Aristotle, for whom the 'axiom' or demonstrative reasoning must start with premises which are 'true, immediate, more known than the conclusions, to them prior and of which they are also the causes' (*Posterior Analytics*, I, 2, 71b–72a).

Through the equivalence, *qua* middle element of proportionality, an identity is 'produced' (Euclid) – an identity which is a true axiomatic premise (Aristotle). This element common to all bodies, which can be known as the common notion (Spinoza), is the element at the basis of the concept of commensurability (Aristotle) and of the concept of proportion (Euclid). Both the concept of value, which Marx takes from Aristotle, and the concept of common notion, which Spinoza takes from Euclid and Aristotle, have to do with this element common to two or more things in a relation of proportion.

In the case of value, the 'common element' is what is commensurable and from here made equivalent; in the case of common notions, the common ele-

---

1 In the case of the passage from *Nicomachean Ethics*, what can be comparable, the commensurable, is the 'just' (*to dikaion*). From the extensive literature on this theme, I refer here only to deGolyer 1992.

2 See Spinoza 1992 (for the Italian edition with its commentary, see Spinoza 1988, p. 384). Giancotti refers to Gueroult 1974 for the distinction that Gueroult makes between the 'universal common notions' (pp. 37 and 38 with corollaries), the 'proper common notions' (p. 39) and the 'notions which are deduced from the common notions' (p. 40). Giancotti refers also to Wolfson 1934, II, pp. 118–22 for Euclid and Maimonides; and to the edition of the *Ethics* [Laterza, Classici della filosofia moderna, XXII, Bari 1915, pp. 754–755] edited by Giovanni Gentile where the *Manuductio ad Stoicam philosophiam* of Justus Lipsius (1604) is quoted as a possible source. Here we refer to Deleuze 2001 and to chapter 2, of Deleuze 1969.

3 Euclid, *Elements* [ed. Heath, vol. 1] 225: '*It seems clear that the Common Notion, as here formulated, is intended to assert that superposition is a legitimate way of proving the equality of two figures which have the necessary parts respectively equal, or, in other words, to serve as an axiom of congruence*'.

ment is the idea of something common to two or more bodies. The first serves the exchange, the second serves knowledge. Both the concept of value and that of the common notion, can in fact be referred to a common origin: the **element** which defines the commensurability of the 'commonality' between two or more things, two or more bodies. *In the case of value, this element is the concept of 'equal'*, which will become first in Aristotle, then in Marx, the equivalent form of, and for, exchange. *In the case of common notions*, in Spinoza, it is *'what is common to all bodies'*. In the Spinozan common notion, the 'equal' in the Euclidean common notions is translated into 'what is common to all bodies'.[4]

From this common origin, the two concepts part ways. Whereas the basic element of the concept of value, the 'equal' (which in Aristotle is the commensurable, in Euclid the motor element of proportion) serves a function of abstraction, the basic element of the common notion, 'what is common to all bodies' (Spinoza) serves the knowledge of the concrete.

In exchange, for example, which is an instance of the function of abstraction, things are made into equivalents to be exchanged. This can be done only if we abstract from their differences. In the case of the knowledge of what is common to my body and to another with which I enter into contact (which is the second case, that of the practical function of the common element), this knowledge is possible because *all bodies agree in some respects* and it is in virtue of this 'element common to all bodies' that a concrete knowledge can occur, not only in the differences but also of the differences.

The concept of the equal, the basis of value, will develop into the equivalent-form, an abstraction-form. The concept of 'common to all', the basis of the formation of common notions, will develop into a praxis of a knowledge of things and of their causes in an adequate and distinct way.

There are spaces where the equivalent-form and the commonality between things are mixed – they overlap: this is the case, for instance, of the imagination in Spinoza; or of the notion of the fetish character of the commodity in Marx, with the relative notion of phantasmagoria in Walter Benjamin.

In these cases, the abstraction-form takes the lion's share with respect to the concrete element of which it is the form. At the same time, though, the concrete element that this form hides, from which it abstracts, pops out from every side.

These areas of indiscernibility between the abstraction-form and the concrete aspect of the commonality between things are made of both a process of

---

4 'All bodies agree in certain respects' [Spinoza, *Ethics*, II, Lemma II]. 'All bodies agree in this, that they involve the conception of one and the same attribute (Def., 1, II)' (ibid. Proof).

abstraction and a concrete knowledge. Given this double aspect of their constitution, they are the privileged places for the attempt to draw events away from
the abstraction they are pitched into, and for knowing them adequately.

To take just one example: imagination in Spinoza is a knowledge of things
as contingent and not necessary. It is knowledge of something which is not
present, as present. Given these definitions, we could say that imagination
knows things 'abstractly', by thus abstracting from their necessity or presence.
But then we discover that the objects of imagination are bodies and their constitution; that the imagination is mistaken in thinking an object present when
it is not, or is no longer. It is mistaken, that is, in thinking things as contingent
when they are, instead, necessary.

We discover that the images of which the imagination is composed are the
traces left by the encounter of our body with other bodies. Thus, the imagination is a concrete knowledge, a knowledge of concrete forms of being, of bodies
in their encounters. It is knowledge of elements of commonality, only in an
uncertain state: the imagination does not know that everything is necessary:
it thinks that things could also be contingent. The imagination does not realise that things which once were present can no longer be. It makes them still
present to the mind. And only when imagination abandons this uncertain state
of inadequate knowledge of things and becomes productive of an adequate
knowledge, do we say that it reaches an affirmative status. There it becomes a
common notion, the certain knowledge of what is common to my body and to
others. We will see how this common element will determine the body's power
of action – the Spinozan theory of affects.

The same happens with Marx's notion of the fetish character of the commodity and with the notion of phantasmagoria in Benjamin, who takes it from
Marx and develops it. Both are expressions of the relations between things and
men; the main character of these *relations* is abstraction, and their form is an
abstraction-form.[5]

---

5   According to Marx, the fetish character of the commodity is that 'transcendent aspect' given
     to the commodity by the equivalent-form, once the commodity appears on the market.
     The phantasmagoria is the aspect assumed by the relation between men when it becomes,
     'to their eyes', a relation *as if between things*. It is, in other words, the fetish character of
     the relations between men. Both the fetish character of the commodity and the phant-
     asmagoria belong, therefore, to the first category, that of the abstraction-form. At the same
     time, however, the material from which they abstract (the relation between men or things)
     has been intoxicated with this same form: in the case of the fetish character, the form of equi-
     valence shows that it can operate *only if it abstracts from* the material, physical reality of the
     commodity; in the case of the phantasmagoria, the experience of the relations between men
     as relations between things shows that such relations are possible because things themselves

The relation experienced is a *relation of equivalence*, it is the process which makes things commensurable, that process of reciprocal belonging that comes by way of a definition reliant on a common, *other*, element. This element is an 'external' element in the case of value (Marx):[6] if A = B, and B = C, then A = C. To make A equivalent to C we need to introduce a virtual B, even if this does not appear in the last equivalence. In other terms, an element (A = C) comes to be, thanks to the expropriation and through the exploitation of a third element (B in A = B, B = C, A = C).[7] In the case of common notions, this element is an 'internal' one (Spinoza): it belongs to all and comes to be, not through an expropriation or destruction of an element in the chain of relation, of identity, but thanks to a commonality among all the elements (in this case, the bodies).

The *knowledge of this experience of relation is a common notion*, in the Spinozan sense; and this 'external' element is exactly the common which *belongs to all*.

The example of phantasmagoria can help, here. It in fact establishes a *relation of equivalence* between four terms: two men embark upon some experience, involving both themselves and other things, of the relation of equivalence between two things (in this case, between two commodities). They have an experience, as we have seen, of the *relation* of equivalence, that is of the process of making things commensurable, of putting them into relation, thanks to a common element.

If, in fact, A and B are two men and C and D two things; if the relation between A and B is equal to the one between C and D, it derives from this that it is possible to have the same relation between A and C as between B and D (the common notion in Euclid). Thus what occurs in phantasmagoria can be read according to the common notion in Euclid. But this is still an abstract

---

have been humanised. A relation is possible only if the terms are commensurable, if they have something in common. In the case of phantasmagoria, the terms have become commensurable, they have something in common. This 'something in common' between two men in relation and two things in relation is the *relation itself*; and the experience of this relation is what the phantasmagoria expresses. The phantasmagoria thus expresses something not in its abstract form (the relation of equivalence) but in its concreteness (the experience of 'intoxication' of a man with a thing, of a thing with a man).

6   See the concept of '*hétéronomie de la politique*' in Balibar, 'Le politique, la politique: De Rousseau à Marx, de Marx à Spinoza', *Studia Spinozana*, n. 9, 1993, p. 205.

7   This third element is labour-power. This is the same principle which we find between commodities in a relation of value: the body of B is the form of A; the concrete labour becomes the expression of abstract labour. A first analysis of this mechanism can be found in Marx's dissertation.

knowledge: it does not help us to understand what really happens between two men who experience a relation as a relation between things. Just as the common notions in Euclid do not exhaust the definition of the common notion in Spinoza, the definition of common notion in Spinoza can give us the tools for concretely understanding what happens in a relation of phantasmagoria, where men embark upon an experience of themselves as things.

For Spinoza, a common notion is what is common to all bodies. If we want to understand the fetish character of the commodity or the phantasmagorical relation between two men in a concrete way, we should find a common element which is not their abstraction-form. If we follow the Spinozan concept of common notion, this element is what is *common to all bodies*; that which, *being common, allows us to form an adequate idea.*

In other terms, the common element – between two bodies, for example – is what allows for the knowledge, not only of the relation itself but *of the constitution of the two elements in relation.* In my relation with A, I understand what is common to me and A because I and A, or rather, our constitution, agree in something (we both embody the concept of the attribute-extension and of the attribute-thought; we are both made of many bodies and the traces that these bodies leave in us (affects) become parts of our constitution as well as becoming degrees of composition with other bodies, and so on.)

The common element of the Aristotelian commensurability, which is postulated for exchange and which produces virtual identities through equivalences, becomes in Spinoza the 'agreeing in something'; it becomes the index of the composition of one body in another.

We will see how the index of this composition is the affect as active cause. When, in fact, we have a passion instead of an affect, we become passive and the relation is no longer a relation of composition but becomes a relation of decomposition. For now, what is important is to see how it is possible to know the commodity as a common notion: this is what happens in phantasmagoria, what happens in contemporaneity with immaterial labour, what happens in today's poverty.[8] In all these cases the zones of indiscernibility between the abstraction-form and the concrete material, whose place the form-abstraction occupies, could solve the mystery of commodity through knowledge. Money, their form-abstraction, is made knowable and known, embodied in human beings (a common notion): it is the 'dismeasure' in the concept of value; the affect in immaterial labour; the actuality of the poor; the struggle for liberation of the oppressed people.

---

8   This constitutes the object of analysis of the last part of this book.

1.2   The Definition of Value and of the Character of Form-Equivalent

> it has the name 'money' (*nomisma*) – because it exists not by nature but
> by law (*nomos*) and it is in our power to change it and make it useless.
>
> ARISTOTLE, *Nicomachean Ethics*, v, 8

Before defining what is the value of a commodity in Marx, let us briefly go over
the definition which Marx gives of the commodity in its simple form.

The commodity is 'an object outside us, a thing that by its properties satisfies
human wants'.[9] We may look at the commodity 'from the point of view of quality (a) or of quantity (b)' (Marx 1975a, I, p. 35).[10] When we consider it from the
point of view of quality (a) we have a commodity as use value; when we consider it from the point of view of quantity (b) the commodity is an exchange
value (ibid., I, p. 36). The use value is the utility of a thing; it is limited to physical properties of commodities; it does not have existence beyond them. The
exchange value is a quantitative relation, the proportion in which values of a
certain kind are exchanged for those of another kind (ibid., I, p. 36).

Human labour is what is embodied in commodities. Commodities are crys-
tals of a social substance; the social substance is human labour.[11] It is in this
sense that it is said that they are value: **value is the expression of a relation
between commodities and the labour embodied in the time of their production**. Value is the expression of a **pure social reality** (ibid., I, p. 38). Both
the physical properties of commodities – use value – and their 'quantities', *the
proportion for which they can be exchanged and made equivalent to something
else*[12] – exchange value – define the 'body' of commodities. Value is thus the

---

9   With the definition of the commodity as 'a thing that by its properties satisfies human
        wants' right at the beginning of *Capital*, Marx explains that the measure-unit of his dis-
        course is 'need' as the value at play in production. If we look back to Aristotle, in the same
        passage of the *Nicomachean Ethics* which Marx took as an example for his explanation
        of value, *chreia*, need, is the real measure of all commodities. For a detailed analysis of
        this, see Micheal DeGolyer, 'The Greek Accent of the Marxian Matrix', in McCarthy 1992.
        In this current study we show how *chreia*, the need *qua* measure of all commodities, is
        human labour liberated from all dominion imposed on it and connected to the totality of
        all labours according to its potency (*'dunameī'*).
10   Marx 1975a.
11   If we think, in Spinozan terms, of substance ('that which is in itself and is conceived
        through itself' [*Ethics*, I, Def. 3]) as *causa sui* ('that whose essence involves existence; or
        that whose nature can be conceived only as existing' [*Ethics* I, Definition 1]), we can see
        how labour is the social substance: the continuous production of a creative relation.
12   The first dimension leaves the commodity somehow in its identity; the second transforms
        it, or is able to make it change place and form.

measure of the proportion for which commodities are exchanged; and, exactly because of this aspect, value is also the expression of a relation, the expression of a 'pure social reality'. Value is the *definition of a social relation in its quantity*.

This social relation – labour – is measured by time. Indeed, value is also defined as the 'definite mass of congealed labour-time' (ibid., p. 40), crystallised as commodity.

The bodily mass of the commodity, in terms of the time and of the activity that it embodies, can be defined as a *congealed mass of labour-time, the power of human labour in its congealed state*. The power of human labour creates value, it becomes value in a 'congealed' state when it is embodied in the form of an object (I, p. 40).[13]

The body of the commodity is thus an activity – human labour – and its congealment in definite masses of time – value. Its corporeality, what 'satisfies human need' is the power of labour expressed in the terms of a relation – a social relation. This relation plays out in commensurable terms, in crystallisations: it is value as measure of the proportionality of the commodity with and in the common.

The proportionality of the commodity to the common is measured as crystallised time.[14]

The explanation for these definitions is contained in a single page of *Capital*, volume I (pp. 59–60), where Marx defines value,[15] the form of 'equivalent', and the passage from use value to exchange value, as the expression of the form of equivalent (pp. 55–6):

> We have seen that commodity A (the linen) by expressing its value in the use-value of a commodity differing in kind (the coat), at the same

---

13   Also of a service. We will go on to discuss this later.

14   To summarise: a commodity is an object outside us, whose properties satisfy human need. This object can be considered as a quantity and as a quality. As a quantity it is the expression of a proportionality, of a purely social relation (value; value of exchange). As quality it is the expression of the utility of the thing (use value). The body of the commodity can be defined as: an object, an object defined by a quantity (exchange) and a quality (use), an object which is the embodiment of human labour, an object which, being the embodiment of human labour, that is of an activity – since the measure of human labour is time – becomes the 'keeper', the reserve of the time used to produce it. The relation between this object and the human labour embodied in it as time is called value. Commodity is thus defined as the 'state of congealed human labour embodied in the form of an object'. We can **know** this object as: an object – *form* of the congealed state of human labour stored, embodied in it, an object as *crystal* of the social substance which produces it (human labour), an object whose form is *time* (in its particular crystallised state), an object whose *time-form* is the *crystal of a social relation*.

15   In this definition of value we can already see the feature which makes Capital function: value as the active motor *in process*, with the quality of being able to add value to itself.

time **impresses upon the latter a specific form of value, namely that of the equivalent.** The commodity linen manifests its quality of having a value by the fact that the coat, without having assumed a value-form different from its bodily form, is **equated** to the linen. The fact that the latter therefore has a value is expressed by saying that the coat is directly exchangeable with it. Therefore when we say that a commodity is in the equivalent form, we express the fact that it is *directly exchangeable with other commodities.* ... The first peculiarity that strikes us, in considering the form of the equivalent, is this: **use-value becomes the form of manifestation, the phenomenal form of its opposite, value. The bodily form of the commodity becomes its value-form.** But, mark well, that this *quid pro quo* exists in the case of any commodity B, only when some other commodity A enters into a value-relation with it, and then only within the limits of this relation. Since no commodity can stand in the relation of equivalent to itself, and thus turn its own bodily shape into the expression of its own value, **every commodity is compelled to choose some other commodity for its equivalent, and to accept the use-value, that is to say, the bodily shape of that other commodity as the form of its own value.**

MARX 1975a, pp. 55–6, my emphasis

The body of the commodity that serves as the equivalent, figures as the materialisation of human labour in the abstract, and is at the same time the product of some specifically useful concrete labour. *This concrete labour becomes, therefore, the medium for expressing abstract human labour.* If, on the one hand, the coat ranks as nothing but the embodiment of abstract human labour, so, on the other hand, the tailoring which is actually embodied in it, counts as nothing but the form under which that abstract labour is realised. In the expression of value of the linen, the utility of the tailoring consists, not in making clothes, but in making an object, which we at once recognize to be Value, and therefore to be a congelation of labour, but of labour indistinguishable from that realised in the value of the linen. In order to act as such a mirror of value, the labour of tailoring must reflect nothing besides its own abstract quality of being human labour generally ... the second peculiarity of the equivalent form is, that *concrete labour becomes the form under which its opposite, abstract human labour, manifests itself* .... We have then a third peculiarity of the equivalent form, namely, that *the labour of private individuals takes the form of its opposite, labour directly social in its form.*

ibid., pp. 58–9

We know that the explanation that Marx gives of value derives from a passage of Aristotle's *Nicomachean Ethics* (book v, chapter on Justice):

> The two latter peculiarities of the equivalent form will become more intel-
> ligible if we go back to the great thinker who was the first to analyse so
> many forms, whether of thought, society, or Nature, and amongst them
> also the form of value. I mean Aristotle. In the first place, he clearly enun-
> ciates that the money-form of commodities is only the further develop-
> ment of the simple form of value – i.e., **of the expression of the value of
> one commodity in some other commodity taken at random.**[16]
> 'Exchange' he says, 'cannot take place without equality, and equality
> not without commensurability' (*out'isotes me ouses summetrias*). Here,
> however, he comes to a stop, and gives up the further analysis of the
> form of value. 'It is, however, in reality, impossible (*te men oun aleteia
> adunaton*), that such unlike things can be commensurable', – that is *qual-
> itatively equal*. Such an equalisation can only be something foreign to
> their real nature, consequently only 'a makeshift for practical purposes'.
>
>   ibid., my emphasis

According to Marx, the difficulty that brought Aristotle's analysis to a halt was
the lack of a *concept of value qua* the **form of labour of equal quality**. The
common substance,[17] that allows the value of a thing to be expressed through
another, by way of equivalence, is *human labour*.

> What is that equal something, that common substance, which admits of
> the value of the beds being expressed by a house? Such a thing, in truth,
> cannot exist, says Aristotle. And why not? Compared with the beds, the

---

16   'for he says: "5 beds = 1 house" (*klinai pente anti oikias*) is not to be distinguished from
     5 beds = so much money (*klinai pente anti ... osou ai pente klinai*). He further sees that
     the *value-relation* which gives rise to this *expression* makes it necessary that the house
     should *qualitatively be made the equal* of the bed, and that, without such an equalisation,
     these two clearly different things *could not be compared with each other as commensurable
     quantities*' (Marx 1975a, p. 59.)
17   That the substance is the common was made clear already by Spinoza. The importance of
     the Spinozan concept of immanence and of his entire system lies here. In value – in the
     Western world, since the seventh century BCE coined as money – this common has been
     produced as an abstraction-form and given the commodity its 'transcendent character'.
     The heart of Spinozan ethics and politics is the affirmation, not only that this common is
     already given, in as much as *we are the common*, but that it can rightly be known only as
     concrete form and as praxis.

house does represent something equal to them, in so far as it represents
what is really equal, both in the beds and the house. And that is – human
labour

ibid.

Because of the structure of Greek society, which was based on slavery and
had 'for its natural basis, the inequality of men and of their labour powers'
(ibid., p. 60), Aristotle could not see that 'to attribute value to commodities
is merely a mode of expressing all labour as equal human labour, and consequently as labour of equal quality' (ibid., pp. 59–60). But 'the brilliancy of
Aristotle's genius is shown by this alone, that he discovered, in the **expression
of the value of commodities**, a *relation of equality*' (ibid.).[18]

This relation of equality is the expression of something which has been
made comparable; it is the expression of the need of being made equal. It shows
the formation of the 'common' (*koinonia*), which constitutes society.

The means to this formation is money – as the 'only universal standard of
measurability':

> It follows that such things, as the subjects of exchange, should be in a cer-
> tain sense comparable ... the necessity of a single, universal, standard of
> measure ... This standard is in truth the necessity [*chreia*] of mutual ser-
> vices which keeps together the society.[19]
>
> ARISTOTLE, *Nicomachean Ethics*, v, 5

---

18   For this passage, see also DeGolyer 1992, p. 112.

19   'For it is not two doctors that associate for exchange, but a doctor and a farmer, or in gen-
     eral people who are different and unequal; but these must be equated. This is why all
     things that are exchanged must be somehow comparable. It is for this end that money has
     been introduced, and it becomes in a sense an intermediate; for it measures all things, and
     therefore the excess and the defect – how many shoes are equal to a house or to a given
     amount of food. The number of shoes exchanged for a house (or for a given amount of
     food) must therefore correspond to the ratio of builder to shoemaker. For it this be not
     so, there will be no exchange and no intercourse. And this proportion will not be effected
     unless the goods are somehow equal. All goods must therefore be measured by some one
     thing, as we said before. Now this unit is in truth demand [*chreia*], which holds all things
     together (for if men did not need one another's goods at all, or did not need them equally,
     there would be either no exchange or not the same exchange)' (Aristotle, *Nicomachean
     Ethics*, v, 5). This chapter on justice is important for our discourse. See, for example, the
     section on distributive justice, where Aristotle explains how 'what is just or equal' is a
     middle between two extremes [v, 3] – it is a *relation*. 'And since the equal is intermediate,
     the just will be an intermediate. Now equality implies at least two things. The just, then,
     must be both intermediate and equal and relative (that is for certain persons)'. 'The just,
     then, is a species of the proportionate (proportion being not a property only of the kind

Money (*nomisma*) has become by convention a sort of representative of demand; and this is why it has the name 'money' (*nomisma*) because it exists not by nature but by law (*nomos*), and it is in our power to change it and make it useless
>   ibid.

Money, then, acting as a measure, makes goods commensurate and equates them; for neither would there have been association, if there were not exchange, nor exchange if there were not equality, nor equality if there were not commensurability[20]
>   ibid.

The law of value, the form of equivalent, is to be found entirely in that '*to*' (A is *to* B as B is *to* C, etc.), expression of a relation which makes two things comparable, thus exchangeable.

We have seen that commodity A (the linen) by expressing its value in the use-value of a commodity differing in kind (the coat), at the same time **impresses upon the latter a specific form of value, namely that of the equivalent.** ... He [Aristotle] sees that the value-relation which gives rise

---

of number which consists of abstract units, but of number in general). For proportion is equality of ratios, and involves four terms at least' (ibid.). In the discussion Aristotle highlights: 'Thus, if people are equal, things will be equal, because what is a thing to the other thing, is a person to the other person' (ibid.). In the concept of *phantasmagoria*, where Marx speaks with regard to the fetish character of commodity, and which was also taken up by Benjamin in his analysis of the commodity as a poetical object, this is what occurs. Phantasmagoria is the comprehension – and before it is perception through images – of this relation of proportion as 'equality of more ratios' at the basis of the law of value. 'This, then, is what the just is – the proportional; the unjust is what violates the proportion' (Aristotle, op. cit., v, 3). The dimensions and implications that the discourse on justice thus takes on here are immense; our analysis is limited to those passages to which Marx refers.

20   'Now in truth it is impossible that things differing so much should become commensurate, but with reference to demand they may become so sufficiently. There must, then, be a unit, and that fixed by agreement (for which reason it is called money); for it is this that makes all things commensurate, since all things are measured by money. Let us A be a house, B ten minae, C a bed. A is half of B, if the house is worth five minae or equal to them; the bed, C, is a tenth of B; it is plain, then, how many beds are equal to a house, that is to say, five. That exchange took place thus before there was money is plain; for it makes no difference whether it is five beds that exchange for a house, or the money value of five beds' (Aristotle, *Nicomachean Ethics*, v, 5). For a detailed analysis of this, see Alliez 1991; and E. Alliez–I. Stengers 1988. On *chreia* as the principle of unity which unites society, see further, *Nicomachean Ethics*, v, 5.

to this expression makes it necessary that the house **should qualitatively be made the equal of the bed,** and that, without such an equalisation, these two clearly different things could not be compared with each other as commensurable quantities.

MARX 1975a, p. 55, p. 59

This 'to' which defines the relation between two commodities, introduces an ontological affirmation: by expressing the value of a commodity in the use value of another, a *commodity comes to be defined through another.*[21] The act which produces the definition is the impression of a form of equivalence: if a commodity expresses its value in the use value of another, the commodity A establishes a relation between itself and the commodity B which has the stamp of the equivalent-form. It is a *double movement*: the definition of itself through another *and* the production of an equivalence; the definition of itself *in the* production of an equivalence.

This is one of the basic concepts of this study: the concept of the commodity being conceived through an other (the conception of the commodity form through the equivalence-form). This 'being conceived through another' is a concept which we find in Spinoza, as a main characteristic of mode: where the substance (God, nature) is *causa sui*, which is to say conceived through itself, the mode is what is conceived through an other.[22]

In combining the concept of value (hence the commodity form) and the concept of common notion (hence the possibility of knowing the commodity form as common notion), we arrive at this point of convergence: the concept of 'being conceived through another' is common to the Marxian commodity and to the Spinozan mode. And, precisely in the definition of the commodity as common notion, we have the possibility of making, of being conceived through an other, a *causa sui.*[23]

Knowledge is the element which *virtually* connects the commodity and the common notion. In Spinoza, we find a concept of the 'common' as relation of composition[24] between things, the knowledge of which is later defined as the

---

21   Labour, inasmuch as it is the activity which produces the commodity, is the *affirmative* productive repository of this cause-through-another. In this, it is like love (see Negri's introduction here).

22   We can ask whether labour may not be the possibility given to man of producing things in their conceivability.

23   See Yovel 1993: man-in-nature is a *causa sui.*

24   This commensurability should be understood in the sense of the degree of composition or decomposition of one body with another.

'common notion': 'Those things that are common to all things and are equally in the part as in the whole, can be conceived only adequately' (*Ethics*, II, P 38).[25] The Corollary to this: 'Hence it follows that there are certain ideas or notions common to all men. For (by Lemma 2) all bodies agree in certain respects, which must be (preceding Pr.) conceived by all adequately, or clearly and distinctly'. 'Of that which is common and proper to the human body and to some external bodies by which the human body is customarily affected, and which is equally in the part as well as in the whole of any of those bodies, the idea, also in the mind, will be adequate' (*Ethics*, II, P 39).

The aim of making the commodity a common notion is to try to take the commodity away from its abstraction-form and to transform it into a concrete knowledge. The attempt is that of moving the axis of the relation, of changing the constitution of the relation of equivalence, of proportionality, of commensurability in a relation of composition. The aim is to arrive at a knowledge of the true structure of the 'common', and, before that, the structure of the commensurable: the common is what all bodies agree in; what defines them as a composition of knowable relations.

The common, the association which is at the basis of society, which Plato and Aristotle called *koinonia*, is this composition, a composing unit. It is not the suspension of a third term of the relation, for the equivalence of the other two terms; it is not a process of expropriation of properties from the common; it is a composition, the multitude of bodies which constitute the single, and the knowledge of the properties of their being common.

Let us dwell briefly – we will come back to all this in the next part – on this factor common to the bodies, which can be known as the common notion, and on the materiality of its knowledge; that is, on the point of encounter of the common notions (koinai ennoiai) *and the social relation expressed through value* (koinonia).

The common factor to the bodies is that they each involve the concept of an identical attribute, an expression of the substance.

In Proposition 37 of the book II of the Ethics, *Spinoza writes: 'That which is common to all things (see Lemma 2 above) and is equally in the part as in the whole, does not constitute the essence of any one particular thing'.*[26] Lemma 2: 'All bod-

---

25   The demonstration to this Proposition explains how this 'common' could be conceived only adequately. See the Proof to *Ethics*, II, P 38 and 39.

26   This common which 'does not constitute the essence of any one particular thing', constitutes, we could say, the *existence of the individual thing and the essence of the whole*. Between essence and existence is a distinction of reason, of knowledge.

ies agree in certain respects. Proof. All bodies agree in this, that they involve the conception of one and the same attribute (Def. 1, 11) (...)' (Ethics 11, Lemma 2).[27]

This common factor to the bodies can be known as common notion.

For the same reason for which the factor common to the bodies, their constitution, their composition in relations is the agreeing in the expression of the same attribute, this common between bodies can be known only adequately, that is, it can be known only as common notion.

The materiality of this knowledge consists in the fact that the elements in relation – a relation of composition – are bodies.

The basic structure of common notions – that is, their embodying knowledge in materiality – can be known in the structure of the Spinozan imagination. Here, the knowledge of the general is embodied in human beings in an assemblage weaker than that of common notions,[28] but still made of material traces.

The imagination is the expression of a knowledge, even if it is not yet clear and is expressed in a confused state. To track down the knowing role of the imagination is important because in virtue of its being made of images (which are nothing other than traces which other bodies or events leave in us), the imagination has the capacity to capture things, and work through them, treating them even in their condition of abstract forms. To build a knowledge of commodities as common notions, we cannot neglect the alienation that they run into; that is, that process of abstraction to which they are subject in their becoming 'materially immaterial things' once they make their appearance on the market.

Once the knowledge of commodities as common notions has been explained, along with how common notions and the imagination are linked in the Spinozan

---

27   We know that the Spinozan system is composed, at its base, by three figures: the substance [God or Nature], the attributes [of which we know two, extension and thought] which are its expressions, and modes, its affects. To say that *'All bodies agree in this, that they involve the conception of one and the same attribute'* – the attribute of motion and rest, for example – means that, in virtue of the unity of the substance, the bodies have a commonality, a common factor: they are expressions of an attribute, which, in its turn, is the expression of the only substance. In knowledge, they represent the *general idea* of that attribute.

28   The common notions are the middle term between a less clear knowledge, but which is still made of material traces – imagination – and a clearer knowledge, the beatitude, or intuitive intellect. It is important to highlight that all three forms (imagination, common notions and intuitive knowledge) are different forms of the same knowledge, of which they are degrees of clarity.

system of knowledge, it is easier to move forth once more from the imagination –
in itself an abstraction-form – to proceed toward a material knowledge of com-
modities.

The point of encounter of common notions and the social relation expressed
by the value of commodity is human labour.

'What is common to all bodies' is, for Spinoza, the object of knowledge of com-
mon notions. The 'body' of a commodity can also be known as common notion,
that is, as the embodiment of a general idea [that of association, koinonia*] whose*
abstraction [value] is the equivalent-form of that of which the commodity [as
thing] is the material embodiment [human labour].

In order to be able to know the commodity as a common notion, we need to find
that element which defines the relation of commonality among commodities. We
have seen that as concerns exchange this element is value; but value is a common
element in abstracto; *it comes out of abstraction. The common notion, however, is*
the knowledge of a material element common among two or more bodies, among
two or more things. To know the commodity as a common notion thus means to
find a common material element of their relation. This common material element
is human labour, its being independent in virtue of a social relation from the 'lev-
elling' for the exchange.

Human labour as a force, as labour-power, is the common factor between bod-
ies, that which 'they all agree in' and which can be known as a common notion.

The link between common notions and the value of the commodity is that
aspect of 'commensurability, proportionality', which, thanks to human labour, can
become the composing aspect, with the capacity of expressing the 'general in the
common': 'koinai ennoiai', *common notions, and* 'koinonia', *the social relation*
expressed by value.

1.3   Common Notions as *'koinai ennoiai'*

The advantage that we get from things external to us, apart from the
experience and knowledge we gain from observing them and changing
them from one form to another, is especially the preservation of the body,
and in this respect those things above all are advantageous which can so
feed and nourish the body that all its parts can efficiently perform their
function. For as the body is more capable of being affected in many ways
and of affecting external bodies in many ways, so the mind is more capable of thinking (see Props. 38 and 39, IV). But there appear to be few
things of this kind in Nature; wherefore to nourish the body as it should
be one must use many foods of different kinds. For the human body is

composed of numerous parts of different natures, which need a continual supply of food of various sorts so that the whole body is equally capable of all that can follow from its nature, and consequently that the mind too is equally capable of conceiving many things

SPINOZA, *Ethics*, IV, Appendix, 27

Now to provide all this the strength of each single person would scarcely suffice if men did not lend mutual aid to one another. However, money has supplied a token for all things, with the result that its image is wont to obsess the minds of the populace, because they can scarcely think of any kind of pleasure that is not accompanied by the idea of money as its cause.

ibid., 28

Common notions in Spinoza define the second level of knowledge:[29] they are ideas common to all men, conceived in a clear and distinct way. Spinoza defines the knowledge of common notions in the second book of the *Ethics* and their formation at the beginning of book four.[30] 'Things that are common to all things and are equally in the part as in the whole, can be conceived only adequately' (*Ethics*, II, P 38).[31] They are called common notions 'not because they are common to all minds, but because they represent something common to the bodies, to all bodies (extension, movement, rest) or to some body (at least two, mine and another)'. 'In this sense common notions are not at all *abstract* ideas but *general* ideas (they do not constitute the essence of any singular thing, II, 37 (...)) (Spinoza, *Theological-Political Treatise*, chap. 7)' (Gilles Deleuze, *Spinoza. Practical philosophy*, p. 54).

In the following propositions and scholia[32] Spinoza explains how common notions are different from the Universals (*Ethics*, II, 40), and how they form the second kind of knowledge, the knowledge of Reason:

... we perceive many things and form universal notions: 1. Firstly, from individual objects presented to us through the sense in a fragmentary

---

29   The first is imagination, the third the intuitive intellect.

30   Respectively, 'The nature and the origin of the Mind', from Prop. 37 to Prop. 40 and 'On human bondage'.

31   The demonstration to this Proposition explains how this 'common' could be conceived only adequately. See the Proof to *Ethics*, II, P 38 and P 39.

32   See *Ethics*, II P 39 and P 40 for a more detailed explanation of the formation of the common notions and the adequate ideas.

(mutilate) and confused manner without any intellectual order (see Cor. Pr. 29, II) ... ; 2. Secondly, from symbols. For example, from having heard or read certain words we call things to mind and we form certain ideas of them similar to those through which we imagine things (Sch. Pr. 18, II). Both these ways of regarding things I shall in future refer to as 'knowledge of the first kind', 'opinion' or 'imagination'. 3. Thirdly, from the fact that we have common notions and adequate ideas of the properties of things (see Cor. Pr. 38 and 39 with its Cor., and Pr. 40, II). I shall refer to this as 'reason' and 'knowledge of the second kind'. Apart from these two kinds of knowledge there is, as I shall later show, a third kind of knowledge, which I shall refer to as 'intuitive'. This kind of knowledge proceeds from an adequate idea of the formal essence of certain attributes of God to an adequate knowledge of the essence of things. I shall illustrate all these kinds of knowledge by one single example. Three numbers are given; it is required to find a fourth which is related to the third as the second to the first. Tradesmen have no hesitation in multiplying the second by the third and dividing the product by the first, either because they have not yet forgotten the rule they learnt without proof from their teachers, or because they have in fact found this correct in the case of very simple numbers, or else from the force of the proof of Proposition 19 of the Seventh Book of Euclid, to wit, *the common property of proportionals*. But in the case of very simple numbers, none of this is necessary. For example, in the case of the given numbers 1, 2, 3, everybody can see that the fourth proportional is 6, and all the more clearly because we infer in one single intuition the fourth number from the ratio we see the first number bears to the second.

Ethics, II, Schol. 2, P 40, my emphasis.

Thus, given A, B, C, and D = x, we should establish an 'equal ratio' relation so that D:C = A:B.[33] What is 'equal' is the *relation of proportion* of two or more mag-

---

33   'A ratio is a sort of relation in respect to the measure between two magnitudes of the same kind' (Euclid, v. Def. 3). On 'ratio' or 'logos' as relative magnitude; on magnitude as quantuplicity; on the incommensurable, see the comment of Heath to the English edition of the *Elements*, Euclid 2002, pp. 116–19. For a detailed analysis of the Euclidean definition of common notions in relation to Aristotle and Plato, in Proclus' commentary (who, like Aristotle, talks of 'axioms' referring to the common notions), see Euclid 2002, vol. 1, pp. 221–32. Spinoza combines the definition of common notions as we find them in Euclid, *Elements*, book I, Common Notions and the proposition 19 in *Elements*, book VII. In the first book of the *Elements* Euclid defines five common notions [*koinai ennoiai*]: the term of the relation which comes to be expressed through these definitions is given by an 'equality'; if A and B are equal to C, then A is equal to B, etc. ... Equality is the 'ratio', the principle of

nitudes, which are the terms of the relation.[34] Combining the definition of the common notion and proposition 19 of book VII we can maybe better understand the Spinozan concept of common notion: the common notion is the knowledge of what is common to all bodies, of what they agree in. This 'common' is, in Euclidean terms, the 'equal' of his definition of common notions. But, in Proposition 19 of the *Elements*, quoted as example by Spinoza, the 'equal' basis of the relation between elements becomes, as we saw, the same *relation of proportion* in which the elements find themselves. In Spinozan terms, in fact, the knowledge of the 'common' can occur only if we understand 'the common property of all proportionals' [*Ethics*, II, 40], that is the 'relation of proportion' of book VII Prop. 19.

The 'relation of proportion' is, for Spinoza, a degree of composition between bodies; what constitutes the common in which the bodies agree and which, by virtue of being a common element, can be known [common notion].

This 'common' which is 'equal', and which arises in relations of equivalence or of proportionality, is the same principle of the form of equivalent which we saw in Aristotle and which, in turn, constitutes the basis of the structure of the law of value in Marx.

The adequate ideas of the 'properties of things' – which properties are expressed in terms of proportional relations – are the common notions. But, whereas, in geometry, they are ideas *in abstract*, as common notions they are embodied in human beings – the bodies in Spinoza: 'Whereas geometry only captured relations *in abstracto*, the common notions enable us to apprehend them as they are, that is, as they are necessarily embodied in living beings'.[35]

We saw that the Spinozan common notions derive from Aristotle. Aristotle, in the *Posterior Analytics* defines them – '*ta koina*'; '*koinai doxai*' – as

---

'congruence' (see Euclid 2002, p. 225, p. 228 and pp. 327–8). Spinoza, we just saw, in the Proposition where he defines the common notions, in order to explain the passage from common notions to the intuitive knowledge, refers to book VII of the *Elements*, Pr. 19: 'If four numbers are proportional, the number produced by the first and the fourth will be equal to the number produced by the second and the third; and, if the number produced by the first and the fourth is equal to that produced by the second and the third, the four numbers will be proportional' (op.cit., vol. 2, p. 318). What interests our study is simply that **the terms of the relation of equality** are now **figures in proportion.** Euclid explains that two magnitudes which have the same 'ratio' can be called proportional; and that the 'ratio' is a 'sort of relation, in respect to the measure, between two magnitudes of the same kind' (*Elements*, book v, def. 6, def. 3).

34   To venture a parallel, we could say that whereas the Euclidean definition of common notions reminds us of the concept of value, in as much as its 'ratio' is equality, the theory of proportion reminds us of the concept of phantasmagoria, its 'ratio' being a relation.

35   Deleuze 2001, p. 57.

axioms, *axiomata*.[36] Their object is that demonstrative reasoning which, as it is
expressed in every syllogism, 'must start with premises which are true, primary,
immediate, more known than, prior to, and the causes of, the conclusion'.[37]
Wolfson explains the origin of the common notions in Spinoza as a combination of the Aristotelic definition of 'axiom' and of Euclidean common notions:
'These premises which are the immediate propositions (*protaseis amesoi*) of a
syllogism are called by him [Aristotle] axioms, with which are correlated definitions and hypothesis, corresponding roughly to the first principle enumerated
by Euclid at the beginning of his *Elements*. In Euclid, however, the axioms are
designated by such terms as "first notions" and "known notions"'.[38]

Thus, common notions, as a second kind of knowledge, can be defined as
axioms, *axiomata* (Aristotle, *Posterior Analytics*, I, 2, 71b 21–2) or *koinai ennoiai*
(Euclid, I, Common Notions; Prop. VII, 19), that is 'common property of proportional numbers'.[39] In the terms of the Spinozan theory of knowledge, this
occurs when reason knows the *general ideas* embodied in the thing.[40] *This*

---

36   Aristotle, *Posterior Analytics*, book I chap. 2 (71a 21–2 e 72a, 20–2). For the non-technical
      use that Aristotle makes of common notions, and other places where he mentions them,
      see Euclid 2002, vol. 1, pp. 221–2.
37   Wolfson 1934, II, p. 118, fl. These premises form the *koinai doxai*. See Aristotle, *Post. An.* I, 2,
      72 a, 14–22; *Post. An.* I, 11, 77a 30; and *Metaphysics* 996b 26–30. See also Euclid 2002, vol. 1,
      pp. 120–1.
38   Wolfson 1934, II, p. 118, fl.
39   We saw this from a geometrical point of view. For the discourse on proportion and equal-
      ity in ontology; for the proportion as measure of equality ['*aequalitas proportionum cum
      scilicet aequalem proportionem habet hoc ad hoc & illud ad illud*' (Di Vona)] so import-
      ant for the Scholastic, and which here it is not possible to go deeper into, especially as
      concerns the analysis of the traces of the Scholastic discourse on analogy and proportion-
      ality in Spinoza and for the relation between Spinoza and Suarez, see Di Vona 1960; 1969.
      According to Di Vona, Spinoza abandons the concept of *trascendentia entis* to maintain
      the concept of analogy between *res* and *ens*. See also Wolfson 1934. Differently from Di
      Vona, we think that Spinoza does not provide for the possibility of an analogy between *res*
      and *ens*. The Spinozan concept of immanence sets itself totally free of the even residual
      possibility of the analogy. We can rather think, along with Deleuze, of a system of expres-
      sion. See the explanation of this system in Deleuze 1969 (in English, Deleuze 1992).
40   Deleuze explains: 'Consider two bodies that agree entirely, two bodies, that is to say, all
      of whose relations can be combined: they are like parts of a whole, the whole exercising
      a general function in relation to these parts, and the parts having a common property as
      belonging to the whole. Thus two bodies that agree entirely have an identical structure.
      Because all their relations may be combined, they have an analogy, similarity or com-
      munity of composition. Now consider bodies agreeing less and less, or bodies opposed to
      one another: their constitutive relations can no longer be directly combined, but present
      such differences that any resemblance between the bodies appears to be excluded. There
      is still however a similarity or community of composition, but this from a more and more

'common property of proportional numbers', which defines the basic structure of the common notions in Spinoza and which can be detected also in the principle of Euclidean common notions [koinai ennoiai], *shares with the Aristotelian discussion of money* [to nomisma] *as "measure of all things"* (Nicomachean Ethics, book v), *that principle of commensurability which, first in Aristotle then in Marx, is value. The common property of proportionality of things, without which these same things (numbers, bodies) cannot be put in relation one with another, and therefore cannot be exchanged; and without which, mainly, they cannot constitute that social relation which is the basis of the association* [koinonia] *is shared by the Aristotelian value and the Spinozan common notion. If the* koinonia *is the aim of commensurability, of exchange and of equality, as the 'just relation' of things, the common notions* [koinai ennoiai] *are the elements for its knowledge.* Because this commensurability is also the source of the explanation that Marx gives of his concept of value, it turns out that commodities, as things in which this commensurability is embodied, can be *known* as common notions: they are the general ideas which *that embodiment* consists of.[41]

How can the *common notions* be defined in relation to the concept of value? To know a commodity as a *common notion* means to know it as 'body' (*Verkörperung*) of a general idea. This general idea is that of the association (*koinonia*). The abstraction (value) of this idea is the equivalent form of something whose material body (*Verkörperung der menschlichen Arbeit*) is the commodity

---

general viewpoint which, in the limit, brings Nature as a whole into play. One must in fact take account of the 'whole' formed by the two bodies, not with one another directly, but together with all the intermediary terms that allow us to pass from one to the other. As all relations are combined in Nature as a whole, Nature presents a similarity of composition that may be seen in all bodies from the most general viewpoint. One may pass from one body to another, however different, simply by changing the relation between its ultimate parts. For it is only relations that change in the universe as a whole, whose parts remain the same. We thus arrive at what Spinoza calls a "common notion". A common notion is always an idea of a similarity of composition in existing modes' (Deleuze 1969, p. 254; in English, Deleuze 1992, p. 275).

41   The commodity in Marx is what value *embodies* in a thing. It is the 'expression of labour as labour of *same equality*'. Value is the common factor *qua* element of proportionality, through which commodities can be compared and exchanged. This unity of proportionality expressed through the 'same equality' of labour, can be known in the Spinozan definition of the *common, in which all bodies agree and through which they can be known*: 'what is common to all and is equal in the part and in the whole'. The difference, though, is an essential one: whereas, in the concept of value, the common factor consists in a process of abstraction, in the concept of that common 'in which my body and the other agree' this common factor is material. In the first, the common factor is produced as an external act, whereas in the second it is known as the essential constitution of the body and of the common (*koinonia*).

(*as* thing). In order to know the commodity as a common notion, we should find a common element, which could define this relation of commonality between commodities. We have seen that as concerns exchange this common element is value; but value is a common element *in abstract*, it occurs as act of abstraction. The common notion, instead, is the knowledge of a common material element between two or more bodies, two or more things. To know a commodity as a *common notion* means to find a *common material element* of its relationship with other commodities. This common material element is human labour, which defines the social aspect of the commodity, its existence based on a social relation, independently from its setting itself in relations of equivalence with the aim of the exchange.

Human labour as force, as *potentia* we could already say, is the common factor between bodies,[42] 'that in which they all agree' and which can be known as the *common notion*.

1.4   How are Common Notions Linked to Affects?

Two aspects have been highlighted until now: 1. the commodity and the mode are both 'conceived through other'; 2. the commodity can be known as common notion, that is as general idea of the activity of which it is composed, that is of human labour as social relation. These two points will be extremely important for what we want to arrive at later, that is the concept of *potentia* as social relation and the definition of poverty as *potentia*, which will be understood exactly from the knowledge of commodity as common notion.

There is another aspect of the principle of 'commensurability' which the link between '*koinonia*' – *qua* association in virtue of commensurability – and the 'common' among all things – as known in common notions – expresses. It is the fact that the *body* is composed, in Spinoza, by many other bodies. At the beginning of our reflection, the body was a simple unit of commensurability: 'All bodies agree in something'. To see how far the parallel between 1) the composition of the body with other bodies and 2) the commensurability at the basis of both the value-form and common notions can take us, we should first analyse the relation between common notions and affects in Spinoza.

Affects are those 'affections of the body by which the body's power of activity is increased or diminished, assisted or checked, together with the ideas of

---

42   By 'human labour as *potentia*' we refer to the *expression* of all labours organised *dunamei*, as Marx defined it.

these affections'.[43] We will see that by virtue of the formation of the common notions, there can be an increase in this power of the body to act – that is, its capacity to produce affections and be affected.

We saw that to have a common notion of something means to have an adequate idea of that same thing. To have an adequate idea of something means to know it in a clear and distinct way. We understand that the functioning of the affects fundamentally relies on a knowledge of their causes. At the same time, these causes can be adequate or inadequate. Hence the knowledge which derives from them can be adequate (common notions) or inadequate (the imagination).

The first definition in book III of the *Ethics* is that of an 'adequate cause': 'I call that an adequate cause whose effect can be clearly and distinctly perceived through the said cause. I call that an inadequate or partial cause whose effect cannot be understood through the said cause alone'.

Let us try to explain the mechanism on which this principle of commensurability turns – as the 'being in relation' of one thing with another – in the terms of the Spinozan body. This, in order to see to what extent this 'principle of commensurability' can work for the utility or the harming of the relation itself.

Gilles Deleuze[44] gives a wonderful explanation of how the common notions are representations of agreement or disagreement, composition or decomposition between two or more bodies, and the origin of the affects:

> Each existing body is characterised by a certain relation of motion and rest. When the relations corresponding to two bodies adapt themselves to one another, the two bodies form a composite body having a greater power, a whole present in its parts.[45]
>
> 1. We were asking how we might attain adequate ideas. Everything about existence condemned us to having only inadequate ideas: we had ideas neither of ourselves, nor of external bodies, but only ideas of affections, indicating the effect of some external body on us. But precisely from such an effect, we can form the idea of what is common to some external body and our own. Given the conditions of our existence this is for us the only possible way of reaching an adequate idea. The *first adequate idea we have* is a common notion, the idea of 'something common': 2. This idea is explained by our power of understanding or thinking. But the power of

---

43   Spinoza, *Ethics*, III, 'Concerning the origin and nature of the affects', Def. III.
44   The way in which Deleuze explains common notions interacts perfectly with the paradigm that we want to outline here in relation to Marx and the knowledge of commodities.
45   Deleuze 2001, p. 54.

understanding is the soul's power of action. We are therefore active insofar as we form common notions. The forming of a common notion marks
the point at which we enter into full possession of our power of action. It
thereby constitutes the second stage of reason. Reason in its initial development is the effort to organize encounters on the basis of perceived
agreements and disagreements. The very activity of reason is the effort
to conceive common notions, and so to intellectually understand agreements and disagreements themselves. When we form a common notion
our soul is said 'to use reason': we come into the possession of our power
of action or of understanding, we become reasonable beings. 3. A common notion is our first adequate idea. But whatever it be, it leads us directly to another adequate idea. An adequate idea is expressive, and what
it expresses is the essence of God. Any common notion gives us direct
knowledge of God's eternal infinite essence. Any adequate, that is to say,
expressive idea, gives us knowledge of what it expresses, that is, adequate
knowledge of God's essence itself.[46]

The common notion is the representation of this 'unity of composition', of the
integration of the singular into the whole; a unity of composition necessary to
the body to be happy, whose knowledge is the product of an activity.[47]

---

46   Deleuze 1992, pp. 279–80.

47   In Balibar and Althusser's *Reading Capital*, we find the necessity of the unity of compos-
     ition for the happy life of the body and the definition of this knowledge as the product
     of an activity: in the immanence of the concept of *'Darstellung'* [representation] (Louis
     Althusser) and in the concept of *'combinaison comme mode de production'* [combination
     as mode of production] (Étienne Balibar). Althusser speaks of a relation between struc-
     ture and effect, where the structure is not only visible in its effects, but is present there
     inasmuch as it has *a mode of presence in its effects*. This mode of presence is nothing else
     than a specific *combination of its proper elements:* 'It can be entirely summed up in the
     concept of "Darstellung", the key epistemological concept of the whole Marxist theory
     of value, the concept whose object is precisely to designate the mode of presence of the
     structure in its effects, and therefore to designate structural causality itself … on the con-
     trary, it implies that the structure is immanent in its effects, a cause immanent in its effects
     in the Spinozist sense of the term, that the whole existence of the structure consists of its
     effects, in short that the structure, which is merely a specific combination of its peculiar
     elements, is nothing outside its effects' (Althusser and Balibar 1970, pp. 188–9 [*Lire le Cap-
     ital*, pp. 64–5], my emphasis). And Balibar: 'We can define this analysis as a differential
     determination of forms, and define a "mode" as a system of forms which represents one
     state of the variation of the set of elements which necessarily enter into the process con-
     sidered' (Althusser and Balibar 1970, II, p. 211 [*Lire le Capital*, II, p. 94]). 'Whatever the social
     form of production, labourers and means of production always remain factors (*Faktoren*)
     of it. But in a state of separation from each other either of these factors can be such only

This definition of the common notion as 'unity of composition' takes us back to that 'unity of commensurability' of the commodities which composes the common of which, according to Aristotle and Marx, the concept of value is made.

> All bodies, even those that do not agree with one another (for example, a poison and the body that is poisoned) have something in common: extension, motion and rest. This is because they all compound one another from the viewpoint of the mediate infinite mode. But it is never *through* what they have in common that they disagree (IV, 30). In any case, by considering the most general common notions, one sees from within where an agreement ends and a disagreement begins, one sees the level at which 'differences and oppositions' (II, 29, school.) are formed.[48]

Because the common notions represent a unity of composition, being equally in the part and in the whole, they are necessarily adequate ideas, that is, clear and distinct for knowledge. The problem, writes Deleuze, is to know how *to form them*. It is here that, for our discourse, the figure of *potentia* comes in. In this formation of the common notions as a 'process of becoming adequate', Deleuze underlines the passage from passivity to the becoming actual of the *potentia* through the particular role that joyful passions have in the formation of the common notions.[49]

---

potentially (*der Möglichkeit nach*). For production to go on at all they must combine (*Verbindung*). The specific manner in which this combination is accomplished distinguishes the different epochs of the structure of society one from another (Marx 1976, Vol. II, p. 34: modified)' (ibid., p. 212, my emphasis).

48 Deleuze 2001, p. 55.

49 See Deleuze 1992: 'When we encounter a body that agrees with our own, when we experience a joyful passive affection, we are induced to form the idea of what is common to that body and our own. Thus Spinoza is led, in Part Five of the *Ethics*, to recognize the special part played by joyful passions in the formation of common notions: "*So long as we are not torn by feelings contrary to our nature* [feelings of sadness, provoked by contrary objects that do not agree with us], the power of the mind by which it strives to understand things is not hindered. So long, then, the mind has the power of forming clear and distinct ideas". It is enough, in fact, for the hindrance to be lifted for the power of action to become actual, and for us to come into possession of what is innate in us. One can see why it was not enough just to accumulate joyful passions, in order to become active. The passion of love is linked to the passion of joy, and other feelings and desires are linked to love. All increase our power of action, but never to the point that we become active. These feelings must first become 'secure'; we must first of all avoid sad passions which diminish our power of action; this is reason's initial endeavour. But we must then break out of the mere concatenation of passions, even joyful ones. For these still do not give us posses-

Deleuze asks: why do we become active when we form a common notion or we have an adequate idea?

> Common notions are necessarily adequate ideas; indeed, representing a unity of composition, they are in the part and the whole alike, and can only be conceived adequately (II, 38 and 39).
> DELEUZE 2001, p. 55

> Adequate ideas are formally explained by our power of understanding or action. ... A mind that forms an adequate *idea* is the adequate *cause* of the ideas that follow from it: this is the sense in which it is active
> DELEUZE 1992, pp. 282–3

'Inadequate ideas imply a concatenation of ideas which follow from them'. The same happens for adequate ideas. The more ideas we have, the more we become the adequate cause of the ideas that derive from them, thus becoming more active. To become active means to increase our capacity of acting. Active affects are those which increase our power of acting, our *potentia*; passions, instead, leave us in a passive state, by diminishing our *potentia*. From joyful passions, which are a sort of middle term in between passions and affects, we can form an idea of what is common to other bodies and ours. The idea which we form is the common notion. Deleuze explains to us how, in the formation of common notions, we proceed from the less general to the more general, from 'those which represent something in common between my body and another which affects me with joy-passion', to 'those which represent what there is in common *even* between our body and bodies that do not agree with ours, that are contrary to it, or affect it with sadness'.[50]

'For when we encounter a body that agrees with ours, we experience an affect or feeling of joy-passion, although we do not yet adequately know what it has in common with us. Sadness, which arises from our encounter with

---

sion of our power of action; we have no adequate idea of objects that agree in nature with us; joyful passions are themselves born of inadequate ideas, which only indicate a body's effect on us. We must then, *by the aid of joyful passions*, form the idea of what is common to some external body and our own. For this idea alone, this common notion, is adequate. This is the second stage of reason; then, and then only, do we understand and act, and we are reasonable: this not through the accumulation of joyful passions as passions, but by a genuine "leap," which puts us in possession of an adequate idea, by the aid of such accumulation' (Deleuze 1992, pp. 282–3 [French original, Deleuze 1969, pp. 261–2]).

50   Deleuze 2001, p. 56.

a body that does not agree with ours, never induces us to form a common notion; but joy-passion, as an increase of the power of acting and of comprehending, does bring this about: it is an *occasional* cause of the common notion'.[51]

These are the less general common notions, the first to be formed which represent something in common between my body and another which causes an affect of joyful passion within me. From the formation of the first common notions, affect and joy follow in their turn: the active joy, by virtue of the comprehension of that 'something in common', takes the place of the passion. The joyful passion is substituted by the affect of joy.

More general common notions are thus formed, which represent what there is in common between our body and *even those* bodies that do not agree with us, which are contrary to our body, or which are the cause of our sadness. From the formation of these *even* more general common notions, 'new affects of active joy follow, which overcome sadness and replace the passions born from sadness'.[52] These new affects derive from a wider and general comprehension of our relations with others; from the conception, that is, of a more expansive index of commonality – those relations which represent what is in common *even* between our body and the bodies that do not agree with ours. They leave us more active, more powerful.

Thus, by knowing and comprehending the nature of an encounter – that is, if a body agrees with ours or not, and to what extent – we become able to recognise what increases our power of action and comprehension (the case of a joyful encounter) or what diminishes this same power (the case of a sad encounter). In the case of a joyful encounter, we experience an affect of joy (increase of our power of action and comprehension); in the case of a sad encounter, we make experience of sadness, a decrease of that power of comprehending and acting. Common notions, as general ideas which express reason's capacity to comprehend our relations, define a sort of human geography of the common, which can be inserted into the geography set out by commodities in the concept of Aristotelian association (*'koinonia'*) and in the Marxian market. Reason, by perceiving and comprehending the relations of composition or decomposition of the bodies, becomes a sort of index of our capacity of moving in the common as active figures, with joyful affects, empowered to increase our power of comprehension and the production of life.

---

51   Ibid., p. 55.
52   Ibid., p. 56.

Indeed, reason is

> 1. an effort to select and organize good encounters, that is, encounters of
> modes that enter into composition with ours and inspire us with joyful
> passions (feelings that *agree* with reason); 2. the perception and compre-
> hension of the common notions, that is, of the relations that enter into
> this composition, from which one deduces other relations (reasoning)
> and on the basis of which one experiences new feelings, active ones this
> time (feelings that *are born* of reason).[53]

Common notions, instruments of reason, are the building blocks of that material knowledge of the real, which is the object of this study. The importance
of the common notions resides, in fact, 'together with the redefinition of the
entire Spinozan conception of reason and knowledge', in this: they 'form a
mathematics of the real or the concrete which rids the geometric method of
the fictions and abstractions that limited its exercise':

> But they are not at all fictitious or abstract; they represent the composi-
> tion of real relations between existing modes or individuals. Whereas geo-
> metry only captured relations *in abstracto*, the common notions enable us
> to apprehend them as they are, that is, as they are necessarily embodied in
> living beings, with the variable and concrete terms between which they
> are established. In this sense, the common notions are more biological
> than mathematical, forming a natural geometry that allows us to compre-
> hend the unity of composition of all of Nature and the modes of variation
> of that unity.[54]

Thus common notions as general ideas, embodied in living beings that allow us
to apprehend and comprehend them as they are, can, in fact, be defined as the
first element of which we have provided the material knowledge. At the same
time, as we have seen, they share a common basis with the concept of value.

To summarise what we have seen thus far: 1) the concept of value and
that of the common notion have a similar origin ('equality', the relation of
proportionality or composition); 2) the concept of *being conceived through
another* is shared by the Marxian commodity and the Spinozan mode [onto-
logical consequence]; 3) the commodity can be known as a 'common notion'.

---

53   Ibid., pp. 55–6.
54   Ibid., p. 57.

The commodity-form is the abstract aspect of knowledge, whose material aspect is the common notion. What is known is the relation between things (commodity-form, value) or between bodies (common notion). To know the commodity as idea or common notion means to know this relation in an adequate way. To know the relation in an *adequate* way means to give its elements the capacity to become their own adequate cause [gnoseological, ethical consequence]; 4) the capacity of becoming the adequate cause of ourselves is our *potentia*. We discover that the *common element* from which we moved is *potentia as relation*: potentia as mode of the common or *common mode* [political consequence].

To understand that the 'being conceived through other' is a '*causa sui*' and that the *common element between bodies is the same potentia as common mode*, that is that potentia is a relation, we should refer to the Spinozan concept of imagination, in which the similar origin of the common notions and of the concept of value shows its ambivalent character.

It is in the Spinozan concept of imagination that the common basis of the common notions and of the concept of value as equivalent-form shows its ambivalence. It can function as an abstraction-form, by making equivalents out of things that are not in proportion (as in the case of imagination and of exchange value) and by constituting an abstract knowledge of things and events. Or it can instead be conjugated according to its materiality and become an instrument of the selection and organisation of relations, such as to serve the formation of a 'happy' body. This second case is what we call practical knowledge.[55]

---

55   It is important to emphasise that in his working material on Spinoza, the *Heft Spinoza*, Marx annotated those passages of the letters which deal with the imagination-essence relation. This is the theme analysed in Chapter 2.

Marx's Notebook on Spinoza: Imagination and Revolutionary Praxis

Berlin 1841 – Marx reads Spinoza and extracts some passages from the *Theological-Political Treatise* and from the *Letters*.

2.1   *Theological-Political Treatise*

Marx notes down the quotations from the *Treatise* in the following order: the first five chapters come at the end of the notebook, the chapters from VII to XIII are in the middle, while those from the XXV to XX (in inverse sequence) come after the XIV and the XV.[1] These in turn follow chapter VI, which comes first. In the structure of these notes we can detect a line of approach followed by Marx, which it is useful for us to delve into here.

For each chapter we have thought of some concepts that constitute a possible index, allowing their articulation into a connected reading.[2] Hence for chapter VI (On miracles)[3] we have imagination; for chapter XIV (What is faith), faith, history and language, its difference from philosophy and common no-

---

1   Rubel 1977, p. 13. For Maximilien Rubel, there is no document which explains Marx's decision for the order in which he writes down the quotations. But we can note that: *'Les extraits du Tractatus sont notés dans l'ordre suivant: chapitre VI (sur le miracle); chapitre XIV (sur la foi); chapitre XV (sur la raison et la théologie) chapitre XX (sur la liberté d'enseigner); chapitre XIX (sur le droit dans le domaine sacré); chapitre XVIII (sur quelques enseignements politiques dérivés de l'organisation de l'Etat des Hébreux); chapitre XVII (sur l'Etat des Hébreux); chapitre XVI (sur le fondements de l'Etat); chapitre VII (sur l'interprétation de l'Ecriture); chapitre VIII (sur les auteurs du pentateuque); chapitre IX (sur le travail d'Esdra et la leçon des notes marginales); chapitre X (sur les autres livres de l'A.T.); chapitre XI (sur le role des apotres dans les épîtres); chapitre XII (sur l'Ecriture sacrée et la parole de Dieu); chapitre XIII (sur la simplicité des enseignements de l'Ecriture et leur nature pratique); chapitre I (sur la prophétie); chapitre II (sur les prophètes); chapitre III (sur la vocation prophétique des Hébreux); chapitre IV (sur la Loi divine); chapitre V (sur les cérémonies religieuses et la foi dans les récits)'* (Rubel 1977, I, p. 13). Differently for Alexandre Matheron (Matheron 1977) and Bruno Bongiovanni (Bongiovanni 1987), to which we refer for a deepened reading of the composition of the Notebook from the point of view of the *Treatise* (Matheron) and of its historical-theoretical contextualisation (Bongiovanni).

2   The conceptualisation that introduces each assemblage of quotes is thus mine.

3   In the original edition of *La potenza della povertà* the quotations were taken from the Italian

tions, on God;[4] for chapter XVII (On the Jewish republic), nature; for chapter XVI (The foundations of the State), nature, law of nature; for chapter VII (On the interpretation of the Scripture), language, scripture, history; for chapter VIII (On the authors of the Pentateuch), knowledge of the scripture, sincerity of history; for chapter XII (On Holy Scripture and the word of God), sacred and use; for chapter XIII (On the simplicity of the teachings of the Scripture and their practical nature), wisdom and existence; for chapter I (On prophecy), our mind contains God; for chapter II (On the prophets), imagination; for chapter III (On the prophetic vocation of the Jews), potentia of natural things and God's potentia; for chapter IV (On the divine law), to consider things as possible under a kind of eternity [*sub specie aeterni res ut possibile considerare*].

Chapter VI talks about miracles, and how it is through our imagination that we can somehow compensate for our ignorance, a defect in our knowledge, the impotence of our intelligence. People call 'miracles' those 'extraordinary phenomena' that they are unable to grasp. The only way in which the common people ['*vulgus*'] can adore God is to refer everything to his sovereign will and to suppress natural causes by overturning the order of the world through the imagination. When we name an event – what happens – a 'miracle', this simply indicates our ignorance.

> [7] Now it has been established that nothing happens in nature which does not come from its laws, that these laws embrace all that the divine intellect itself is able to conceive ... the word 'miracle' cannot be understood except in regard to men's opinions, and does not mean anything else than an event of which we cannot ... explain the natural cause by analogy with other causes which we frequently observe.[5]

The passage transcribed after this concerns the existence of God. This latter should be deduced from certain notions with such firm and solid truth that no force can exist or be conceived that could change them. Other subsequent passages highlight the capacity of our intellect and a clear and distinct knowledge:

> [9] a miracle, that is something which surpasses our intelligence, cannot make us comprehend either the essence or the existence of God, noth-

---

edition of the *Heft Spinoza* – Karl Marx, *Quaderno Spinoza* (see Bongiovanni 1987). Here, we refer to the aforementioned Rubel 1977, I, and to the English translation of Spinoza (Spinoza 2007). The German edition is Marx 1976.

4 The following chapters are not analysed here: XV, XX, XIX, XVIII, IX, X, XI, V.

5 Rubel 1977, I, p. 35, my translation. These passages [from 7 to 69] have been added in this edition and do not appear in the original Italian version.

ing ... either on God or on nature: on the contrary, when we know that all things are determined and regulated by God, that the operations of nature result from the essence of God, that the laws of the universe are the eternal decrees and wills of God, we know; [10]

When one ignores a thing ... to recur to God's will; one confesses through that, most ridiculously, his own ignorance.[6]

It is not from miracles that we can deduce the evidence for God. We can simply conclude that 'a cause exists, the force of which is bigger than that of the effect produced' [11].[7] If men do not hold a true knowledge and an honest love of God, miracles can make them adore false gods as easily as the true God. 'When I say', Spinoza writes, 'that the Scripture teaches these things ..., I mean simply that the prophets considered miracles as we do' [16].[8]

Chapter XIV. Spinoza here separates faith from philosophy (the principal object, he writes, of the entire work). The main aim of the Scripture is to teach obedience: 'faith consists in thinking about God, what cannot be ignored without losing every feeling of obedience to its decrees ...' [21] (ibid.). Faith was handed down to us in a language adapted to the capacities and opinions of the prophets and their contemporaries – and today, likewise, each of us should adapt it to his own opinions.

'What is God, that is this model of truthful life? Is it fire, spirit, light, thought? This does not concern faith' [24].[9]

Our task is to make known that between theology and philosophy there is 'neither commerce nor any affinity', because 'philosophy does not have as aim nothing but truth, whereas faith ... does not have in sight nothing but obedience and devotion. Philosophy, on the other end, has at its foundation the common notions and they should be drawn only from nature; faith, it has as foundation history and language, and should be drawn only from the Scripture and the revelation' [25].[10]

Chapter XVII is about the republic of the Jews. It wonderfully prepares the way for the following chapter on the foundations of the state. 'What makes someone a subject, are not the motifs he obeys, but the fact itself of obeying' [52].[11]

---

6   Ibid.
7   Ibid., p. 37.
8   Ibid., p. 39.
9   Ibid., p. 41.
10   Ibid.
11   Ibid. p. 53.

[55] To organise the State so that all citizens, whatever their character or spirit, prefer the common law before their interests is the work and the difficult mission of power. ... We could never prevent that the dangers for the State came from within more than from outside and that the governments should fear their citizens more than the enemies.[12]

[57] There are no men, unless they are entirely barbarians, who let themselves be fooled or agree to become slaves and renounce themselves. Others ... are made believe that their royal Majesty was sacred because of representing God on earth, that their authority came from God and not from men ...[13]

[58] This is why, in this state, civil law and religion – consisting ... in simple obedience to God's will – were the one and only thing.[14]

They were obeying the commandments dictated by God to Moses [59] and if the people believe that what the sovereign commands is an order revealed by God, the people will be even more subjected [60].[15] [63] 'From this reprobation, expressed daily, an eternal hatred is born ... which originates from devotion and piety and which, by being considered a religious act, does not have an equal for violence and obstinacy'.[16]

Their path was like a perpetual sacrifice to obedience. But nature, Spinoza continues, 'creates individuals, not nations, and individuals are sorted out into nationalities only by differences of language, laws and accepted customs'. [67] 'The divine or religious right is based on a pact, by the lack of which only the natural right would exist; it is for this reason that the Jews were not obliged by religion to any duty towards the other nations that did not take part in this pact, but only to the duties toward their citizens'.[17]

Chapter XVI is on the foundations of the state. Here, together with the concept of nature, we can find the concepts of collective and utility; the concept of freedom and self-cause. Chapter XVI begins with a firm statement on the

---

12   Ibid.

13   Ibid., p. 55.

14   Spinoza continues: 'that is, the dogma of the religion for the Jews were not teachings but laws and prescriptions' (ibid.).

15   It continues: 'when the interpretation of the laws depends exclusively on the administrators of the State or the sovereigns, whatever will be their action, they strive to clothe it with the colours of justice' (ibid.)

16   Ibid., p. 57.

17   Ibid.

relation between natural right, nature and each individual's striving to exist:
[68] 'by natural right and institution of nature, we mean nothing else than
the natural laws according to which we conceive each individual as determined to exist and act in a certain way' [69].[18] 'And since it is the supreme law
of nature that each thing strives to persist in its own state so far as it can ...
it follows that each individual has the absolute right to live and act according to what he is naturally determined'.[19] It is not some reason to determine
natural right, but the 'orientation of man's desires and his degree of potentia'
[70].[20]

Here we find the concepts of utility and the collective:

> [71] We shall realize very clearly that it was necessary for people to com-
> bine together in order to live in security and prosperity. Accordingly, they
> had to ensure that they would *collectively have the right to all things that
> each individual had from nature and that this right would no longer be
> determined by the force and appetite of each individual but by the power*
> [potentia] *and will of all of them together.*[21]

From this we conclude, Spinoza writes, that a pact can oblige only by virtue of
its utility: 'if the utility disappears, the pact evaporates with it and it remains
without juridical effect' [72].[22]

> [73] only if every person transfers all the power they possess to society,
> and society alone retains the supreme natural right over all things, that
> is, supreme power, which all must obey, either of their own free will or
> through fear of the ultimate punishment. The right of such a society is
> called democracy. Democracy therefore is properly defined as a united
> gathering of people which collectively has the sovereign right to do all
> that it has the power to do.[23]

---

18   Ibid. p. 57.
19   Ibid., p. 59.
20   Ibid.
21   Ibid. [71] '... *ut jus, quod unusquisque ex natura ad omnia habebat, collective haberent,
      necque amplius ex vi et appetitu uniuscujusque, sed ex omnium simul potentia et volunt-
      ate determinaretur*'. For the English translation, see Spinoza 2007, p. 197.
22   Ibid.
23   [73] '... *Talis vero societatis jus Democratia vocatur, quae proinde definitur coetus universus
      hominum, qui collegialiter summum jus ad omnia quae potest habet*' [Engl. tr., Spinoza
      2007, p. 200.]

We find further the explanation of the concept of freedom, of self-cause (*causa sui*):

> [75] Perhaps someone will think that in this way we are turning subjects into slaves, supposing a slave to be someone who acts on command, and a free person to be one who behaves as he pleases. But this is not true at all. In fact, anyone who is guided by their own pleasure in this way and cannot see or do what is good for them, is him or herself very much a slave. The only [genuinely] free person is one who lives with his entire mind guided solely by reason ...[24]

The freest state, therefore, is that whose laws are founded on sound reason; for there each man can be free whenever he wishes, that is, he can live under the guidance of reason with his whole mind. ... With this, I think, the fundamentals of the democratic republic are made sufficiently clear, this being the form of state I chose to discuss first, because it seems to be the most natural and to be that which approaches most closely to the freedom nature bestows on every person.[25]

> [76] Besides, if we take piety and religion into account, we shall also see that it is criminal for anyone who holds power to keep their promises if this involves loss of their power. For they cannot fulfil any promise which they see will result in loss of their power, without betraying the pledge that they gave to their subjects. This pledge is their highest obligation, and sovereigns normally swear the most solemn oaths to uphold it.[26]

---

24   This is an important part which I cannot quote in the body of the text, on account of its length, but want to reproduce here: 'Acting on command, that is, from obedience, does take away liberty in some sense, but it is not acting on command in itself that makes someone a slave, but rather the reason for so acting. If the purpose of the action is not his own advantage but that of the ruler, then the agent is indeed a slave and useless to himself. But in a state and government where the safety of the whole people, not that of the ruler, is the supreme law, he who obeys the sovereign in all things should not be called a slave useless to himself but rather a subject' [Ibid., p. 201].

25   Ibid., p. 61 [75] '*et solus ille liber, qui integro animo ex solo ductu rationis vivit* (...) *ibi enim unusquisque, ubi velit, liber esse potest, h.e. integro animo ex ductu rationis agere* (*4*) ... *maxime naturale videbatur* (*sc. imperium democraticum*) (*5*) *et maxime ad libertatem, quam natura unicuique concedit, accedere*'. Rubel notes that at point 4, Marx writes '*agere*', Gebhardt: '*vivere*'; number 5 is added by Marx. [For English translation, Spinoza 2007, pp. 201–2.]

26   Ibid., pp. 203–4.

[77] The state of nature is not to be confused with the state of religion, but must be conceived apart from religion and law, and consequently apart from all sin and wrongdoing.[27]

[78] For no one would be obligated by the law if he considered it to be directed against his faith and superstition, and on this pretext everyone would be able to claim licence to do anything.[28]

In chapter VII, the concepts of interest to us are the use of language, scripture and history:

[79] The universal rule then for interpreting Scripture is to claim nothing as a biblical doctrine that we have not derived, by the closest possible scrutiny, from its own [the Bible's] history.[29]

[80] In order not to confuse the genuine sense of a passage with the truth of things, we must investigate a passage's sense only from its use of the language or from reasoning which accepts no other foundation than Scripture itself.[30]

Chapter VIII indicates the knowledge of the scripture and the sincerity of history:

[81] In the previous chapter we dealt with the foundations and principles of knowledge of Scripture, and proved that these amount to nothing more than *assembling an accurate history of it*.[31]

Important in chapter XII are the sacred and its customary use:

[107] Something intended to promote the practice of piety and religion is called sacred and divine and is sacred only so long as people use it reli-

---

27   Ibid., p. 205.
28   Ibid., p. 206.
29   Ibid. [79] '*Regula igitur universalis interpretandi Scripturam est, nihil Scripturae tamquam ejus documentum tribuere, quod ex ipsius historia quam maxime perspectum non habeamus*'. [Engl. tr., Spinoza 2007, pp. 99–100].
30   Ibid. [80] '*ex solo linguae usu erit investigandus, vel ex ratiocinio, quod nullum aliud fundamentum agnoscit, quam Scripturam*'. [Engl. ed., Spinoza 2007, p. xii, and chap. 7, par. 2.]
31   [81] '*In praecedenti Capite de fundamentis et principiis cognitionis Scripturarum egimus, eaque nulla alia esse ostendimus, **quam harum sinceram historiam***' [Engl. ed., Spinoza 2007, p. 118]

giously. If they cease to be pious, the thing in question likewise, at the same time, ceases to be sacred.[32]

and

> [108] From this it follows that nothing is sacred, profane, or impure, absolutely and independently of the mind but only in relation to the mind.[33]

In chapter XIII we read that 'no one can be wise by command any more than he can live or exist by command' [110].[34]

Chapter I is about prophecy (*de prophetia*). We learn that our mind objectively contains the nature of God and, by consequence, participates in potentia:[35]

> [114] Since therefore our mind possesses the power to form such notions from this alone – that it objectively contains within itself the nature of God and participates in it – as explain the nature of things and teach us how to live, we may rightly affirm that it is the nature of the mind, in so far as it is thus conceived, that is the primary source of divine revelation. For everything that we understand clearly and distinctly is dictated to us (as we have just pointed out) by the idea of God and by nature, not in words, but in a much more excellent manner which agrees very well with the nature of the mind, as every man who has experienced intellectual certainty has undoubtedly felt within himself.[36]

This same first chapter is concerned with voice:

---

32   Ibid., p. 73. [107] *'Id sacrum et divinum vocatur, quod pietate et religioni exercendae destinatum est, et tamdiu tantum sacrum erit, quamdiu homines eo religiose utuntur; quod si pii esse definant, et id etiam simul sacrum esse definet'* [Engl. ed., Spinoza 2007, p. 165].

33   Ibid. [110] *'Ex quo sequitur nihil extra mentem absolute, sed tantum respective ad ipsam, sacrum aut profanum aut impurum esse'* [ibid.]

34   Ibid., p. 75. [110] *'neminem posse ex mandato sapientem esse, non magis, quam vivere, et esse'* [Engl. ed., Spinoza 2007, p. 175]

35   [114] *'Cum itaque mens nostra ex hoc solo, quod Dei Naturam objective in se continet, et de eadem participat, potentiam habeat ad formandas quasdam notiones rerum naturam explicantes, et vitae usum docentes, merito mentis naturam, quatenus talis concipitur, primam divinae revelationis causam statuere possumus; ea enim omnia, quae clare et distincte intelligimus, Dei idea ... et natura nobis dictat, non quidem **verbis**, sed modo longe excellentiore et qui cum natura mentis optime convenit, ut unusquisque, qui certitudinem intellectus gustavit, apud se, sine dubio expertus est'.*

36   Ibid. p. 75.

[117] It was with a real voice that God revealed to Moses the Laws which he wished to be given to the Hebrews;[37]

[120] ... and that is why God revealed himself to the Apostles through the mind of Christ, as he did, formerly, to Moses by means of a heavenly voice. Therefore the voice of Christ may be called the voice of God, like the voice which Moses heard. In this sense we may also say that the wisdom of God, that is, the wisdom which is above human wisdom, took on human nature in Christ, and that Christ was the way of salvation.[38]

On imagination: [122] 'and therefore prophecy does not require a more perfect mind but a more vivid imagination'.[39]

On comprehending potentia:

[126] it is certain that we fail to understand the power of God to the extent that we are ignorant of natural causes. Therefore it is foolish to have recourse to this same power of God when we are ignorant of the natural cause of some thing, which is, precisely, the power of God.[40]

and of perceiving, seizing imagination:

[127] Since therefore the prophets perceived the things revealed by God through their imaginations, there is no doubt that they may have grasped much beyond the limits of the intellect. For far many more ideas can be formed from words and images than from the principles and concepts alone on which all our natural knowledge is built.[41]

---

37   Ibid., p. 77. [117] 'haec sola, qua scilicet lex (sc. Mosi) (1) prolata fuit, vera fuit vox (sc. Dei) (2) ut mox ostendam'. [Engl. ed., Spinoza 2007, p. 15]. Numbers 1 and 2, writes Rubel, are added by Marx.

38   Ibid., p. 79. [120] '... adeo ut Deus per mentem Christi sese Apostolis manifestaverit, ut olim Mosi mediante voce aerea. Et ideo vox Christi, sicut illa, quam Moses audiebat, vox Dei vocari potest. Et hoc sensu etiam dicere possumus, sapientiam Dei, hoc est, Sapientiam, quae supra humanam est, naturam humanam in Christo assumpsisse, et Christum viam salutis fuisse' [Engl. ed., Spinoza 2007, p. 19]

39   Ibid. [122] 'ad prophetizandum non esse opus perfectiore mente, sed vividiore imaginatione' [Engl. ed., Spinoza 2007, p. 20].

40   Ibid., p. 81. [126] 'certum est nos eatenus Dei potentiam non intelligere, quatenus causas naturales ignoramus; adeoque stulte ad eandem Dei potentiam recurritur, quando rei alicujus causam naturalem, hoc est, ipsam Dei potentiam ignoramus' [Engl. ed., Spinoza 2007, p. 25]

41   [127] 'Cum itaque Prophetae imaginationis ope Dei revelata perceperint, non dubium est, eos multa extra intellectus limites percipere potuisse; nam ex verbis et imaginibus longe plures

The following quotation introduces a *chiasm*, an inner reversal of the terms of the discourse: namely, in that it is thanks to the imagination that the spiritual truth is materially expressed. Prophets, the bearers of the most vivid imagination, are those that can materially express the spiritual truth. The material expression of a spiritual thing is what mostly suits imagination:

[128] It also becomes clear why the prophets understood and taught almost everything in parables and allegorically, expressing all spiritual matters in corporeal language; for the latter are well suited to the nature of our imagination.[42]

[129] we are now compelled to ask what could be the source of the prophets' *assuredness or certainty about things* which they perceived only via the imagination and not from clear reasoning of the mind.[43]

In chapter II, on prophets, we have the explanation of the notion of imagination in respect to the history and nature of knowledge, which, for its nature implies certainty: history is knowledge according to potentia [and virtuality, I would add].[44] Knowledge does not need any sign, because it contains, for its nature, certainty:

[132] Plain imagination does not of its own nature provide certainty, as every clear and distinct idea does. In order that we may be certain of what we imagine, imagination must necessarily be assisted by something, and that something is reason;[45]

---

ideae componi possunt, quam ex solis iis principiis, et notionibus quibus tota nostra naturalis cognitio superstruitur' [Engl. ed., Spinoza 2007, p. 26].

42   Ibid. [128] *'Patet deinde, cur Prophetae omnia fere parabolice et aenigmatice perceperint ut docuerint et **omnia spiritualia corporaliter expresserint: haec enim omnia natura imaginationis magis conveniunt'** [Engl. ed., Spinoza 2007, ibid.]*

43   Ibid. [129] *'(...) Cum hoc ita sit, cogimur jam inquirere, unde Prophetis oriri potuit **certitudo eorum**, quae tantum per imaginationem, et non ex certis mentis principiis percipiebant'* [Engl. ed., Spinoza 2007, ibid.]

44   In the original Italian edition, the conceptualisation which I envisioned, in order to give visibility to a possible order of Marx's quotations, was left in parentheses in Latin. Here, together with potentia, I had referred to 'the virtual'. This generated a misreading, to the effect that 'virtual' had been in Spinoza's text (which Marx had noted) – yet this was only my own conceptualisation, which I accidentally left in Latin. This was discussed by some critics who underlined that in Spinoza there is no concept of the virtual. However, this fortunate accident gave me the possibility of deepening the 'virtual' discourse of the virtual in Spinoza in *Causa sui*.

45   Ibid., p. 83. [132] *'Cum simplex imaginatio non involvat ex sua natura certitudinem, sicuti*

[133] prophecy is inferior to natural knowledge since it has no need of any sign but provides certainty by its very nature. For this prophetic certainty was not mathematical certainty but only moral certainty.[46]

Chapter III, *On the prophetic vocation of the Jews, and whether the prophetic gift was peculiar to them*, is concerned with the potentia of natural things and the potentia of God:

[139] By 'God's direction', I mean the fixed and unalterable order of nature or the interconnectedness of [all] natural things;[47]

[140] as the power of all natural things together is nothing other than the very power of God by which alone all things happen, it follows that whatever a man, who is also part of nature, does for himself in order to preserve his being, or whatever nature offers him without any action on his part, is all given to him by divine power alone, acting either through human nature or through things external to human nature. Whatever, therefore, human nature can supply from its own resources to preserve man's own being, we may rightly call the 'internal assistance of God', and whatever proves useful to man from the power of external causes, that we may properly term the 'external assistance of God'.[48]

[141] For given that nobody does anything except by the predetermined order of nature, that is, by the eternal decree and direction of God ...

---

omnis clara et distincta idea, sed imaginationi, ut de rebus, quas imaginamur, certi pos-
simus esse, aliquid necessario accedere debeat, nempe ratiocinium ...' [Engl. ed., Spinoza
2007, p. 28].

46   Ibid. [133]: 'Prophetia igitur hac in re naturali cedit cognitioni, quae nullo (3) indiget signo,
sed ex sua natura certitudinem involvit. Etenim haec certitudo Prophetica mathematica
quidem non erat, sed tantum moralis'. Marx underlined several more times the word 'nullo'.
[Engl. ed., Spinoza 2007].

47   Ibid., p. 87. [139] 'Per Dei directionem intelligo fixum illum et immutabilem naturae ordinem,
sive rerum naturalium concatenationem' [Engl. ed., Spinoza 2007, p. 44].

48   Ibid. [140] 'quia rerum omnium naturalium potentia nihil est nisi ipsa Dei potentia, per
quam solam omnia fiunt et determinantur, hinc sequitur, quicquid homo, qui etiam pars
est naturae, sibi in auxilium, ad suum esse conservandum parat, vel quicquid natura ipso
nihil operante, ipsi offert, id omne sibi a sola divina potentia oblatum esse, vel quatenus
per humanam naturam agit, vel per res extra humanam naturam. Quicquid itaque natura
humana ex sola **sua** potentia praestare potest ad suum esse conservandum, id Dei auxilium
internum et quicquid praeterea ex potentia causarum externarum in ipsius utile cedit, id Dei
auxilium externum merito vocare possumus' [Engl. ed., Spinoza 2007, p. 45].

Finally, by 'fortune' I understand nothing other than the direction of God inasmuch as he governs human affairs through external and unforeseen causes.[49]

Chapter IV has to do with the divine Law: we, as part of the potentia of nature, establish the law in pursuit of a better life and, so long as necessary, consider things to be possible:

[153] Firstly, in so far as man is a part of nature, he is also a part of nature's power. Hence whatever follows from the necessity of human nature (that is, from nature itself in so far as we understand it to be expressly determined by human nature) results also, albeit necessarily, from the capacity of men. Hence the decreeing of these laws may quite correctly be said to follow from human will, because this depends especially on the power of the human mind in the sense that our mind, so far as it perceives what is true or false, can very clearly be conceived without these decrees, but not without the necessary law of nature as we have just defined it.[50]

Law – and here, indeed, it has to do with knowledge, the supreme good – 'has to be divided into human and divine ... By divine law I mean the law which looks only to the supreme good, that is, to the true knowledge and love of God' [157].

This is linked to the perfection of the intellect, since understanding is the best part of us – 'our highest good should consist in its perfection' [158].[51]

---

49   Ibid. [141] '... Deique per fortunam nihil aliud intelligo, quam Dei directionem quatenus per causas externas et inopinatas res humanas dirigit'; and [148] 'omnes aeque Judeos scilicet et gentes sub peccato fuisse; peccatum autem sine mandato et lege non dari' [Engl. ed., Spinoza 2007, ibid.]

50   Ibid., p. 91. [153] 'Quia homo, quatenus pars est naturae, eatenus partem potentiae naturae constituit; quae igitur ex necessitate naturae humanae sequuntur, hoc est, ex natura ipsa, quatenus eam per naturam humanam determinatam concipimus, ea, etiamsi necessario sequuntur tamen ad humana potentia quare sanctionem istarum legum ex hominum placito pendere optime dici potest, quia praecipue a potentia humanae mentis ita pendet, ut nihilominus humana mens, quatenus res sub ratione veri, et falsi percipit, sine hisce legibus clarissime concipi possit, at non sine lege necessaria, ut modo ipsam definivimus' [Engl. ed., Spinoza 2007, pp. 57–8].

51   Ibid. p. 95. [157] 'Lex distinguenda viedetur in humanam et divinam, et ... per divinam (sc. intelligo) (1) autem, quae solum summum bonum, h.e. (2), Dei veram cognitionem et amorem spectat' [Engl. ed., Spinoza 2007, p. 59]. Rubel notes that no. 1 is added by Marx, and that at number 2 Marx has written h.e., for 'hoc est'. [Engl. ed., Spinoza 2007, p. 58] 'in ejus (sc. intellectus) (3) enim perfectione summum nostrum bonum consistere debet'. No. 3 is added by Marx. [Engl. ed., Spinoza 2007, p. 59].

The Decalogue was interpreted as law on account of a deficiency of knowledge:

> [165] It is for the same reason too, namely deficiency of knowledge, that
> the Ten Commandments were law only for the Hebrews;

> [166] imagined God as ruler, legislator, king, merciful, just, despite the fact
> that all the latter are merely attributes of human nature and far removed
> from the divine nature[52]

> Christ understood things in an adequate way: 'of Christ … he [on the con-
> trary] understood things truly and adequately. Christ was not so much a
> prophet as the mouth-piece of God' [167].[53]

*We have, in sequence: the concept of nature, for which each thing strives to per-
severe as much as it can, in its own proper state, and the concepts of utility and
collective, indicating the collective possession of the right that each has by nature
(democracy). Then follows the definition of who is free: free is the one who lives
entirely according to reason – the democratic form of government is the most
natural and the most consistent with the freedom that nature gives each of us. To
interpret the Scripture as it results from its own history, on the basis of the use of
language. The foundation of the knowledge of the Scripture is that it is the genuine history of the Scripture itself. Sacred is what is useful to the mind: we are wise
inasmuch as we live and exist. The mind objectively contains the nature of God
and participates in his potentia. Imagination is knowledge without certainty; in
order to be certain of the things we imagine, we should add reason. The concatenation of natural things is divine direction. The concept of freedom and necessity
comes into outline: freedom is necessity. We are part of the potentia of nature, we
can conceive things as possible. Within this consideration of things as possible, we
have to know that freedom is necessity, that contingency does not exist – otherwise
we lack true knowledge, that is, we lack the knowledge of the free necessity of God's
nature, and we conceive the divine law as a law instead of an indication for life. If*

---

52   [165] '*ob defectum cognitionis, Decalogus, respectu Hebraeorum tantum, lex fuit*'; [166] '*hinc
      factum est, ut Deum rectorem, legislatorem, regem, misericordem, justum etc. imaginetur;
      cum tamen haec omnia solius humanae naturae sint attributa*' [Engl. ed., Spinoza 2007,
      p. 63].
53   [167]: '*de Christo … sentiendum … eum res vere et adequate percepisse; nam Christus non
      tam Propheta quam os Dei fuit*' [Engl. ed., Spinoza 2007, p. 63].

we go through the quotations following the concepts that inhabit them, a system of knowledge emerges in outline, leading from imagination to true knowledge, the clear and adequate knowledge.

2.2   Imagination

Let us thus start with imagination (*imaginatio, potentia, intellectus*), a means of knowledge, but in this text a measure of the miracle. Spinoza explains that miracles are to be found where there is a lack of knowledge. Prophets are those who, through imagination, can see the space between true and untrue knowledge. The content of belief is the degree to which *Nature* refers to real history. There are two ways to arrive at true knowledge (the beatitude, intellectual knowledge of God): the intellect, the mind, and imagination (*intellectus/mens* and *imaginatio*). In the *Ethics*, imagination is the first kind of process of knowledge. True knowledge (*beatitudo*) is the third kind.

In this text, quoting from the *Theological-political Treatise*, imagination is the prophets' means of arriving at knowledge. This is already defined and Marx quotes it once again in the middle of his notebook, when he quotes from chapter I, on prophecy: [122] 'prophecy does not require a more perfect mind but a more vivid imagination'.[54] Chapter I's position and its content make it the very peak of this discourse. Also to be found in this same position is the quote on the **nature** of our mind: our mind objectively contains God's nature (*mens nostra Dei Naturam objective continet*).

The discourse on '*nature*' develops further as it proceeds – this time, in its political sense. In chapter XVI, which concerns the foundations of the state, it seems to us that the key concepts are: nature, law of nature, collective, utility (*natura, ius naturae – collective, utilitas*). As we have seen, Spinoza writes on nature and the law of nature: 'And since it is the supreme law of nature that each thing strives to persist in its own state so far as it can' [69]; and further, on collectivity and utility: 'that they would *collectively have the right to all things that each individual had from nature and that this right would no longer be determined by the force and appetite of each individual but by the power and will of all of them together*' [71].

On the definition of democracy, he writes: 'The right of such a society is called democracy. Democracy therefore is properly defined as a united gath-

---

54   [122] '*ad prophetizandum non esse opus perfectiore mente, sed vividiore imaginatione*' [Engl. ed., Spinoza 2007, p. 20]

ering of people which collectively has the sovereign right to do all that it has the power to do' [73].

The next concept which concerns us, henceforth, is freedom; freedom and causality; freedom in relation to causality – and for Spinoza, the one who is free is the one who is the adequate cause of himself.

In chapter VII, *On the interpretation of Scripture*, Marx's quotations turn back to the relation between language, history and scripture, as if to affirm that the knowledge of the scripture should imply and entail a relation with that history which is sincere.[55] The following quotation seems to identify the sacred as what people 'use religiously'.[56] This affirmation is fundamental to understanding chapter I, which is the central point of the discourse, the climax of the sequence: it explains the nature of our mind, which objectively contains God's nature. Our mind is full of God's nature: man is part of nature and, in this, also part of God's nature. The structure of the quotations then becomes clear: from a given situation – a point in history, its intelligibility and conceivability, as in the example of the scripture and of God's nature – which presents itself in the miracle, we can understand the nature of the mind. Through imagination, the knowledge combined with history, nature and their signs, we arrive at the knowledge of God, which is knowledge of our nature. The content of our mind is God, as potentia, whose essence, whose mode, is existence.

The prophets' imagination 'expresses' the potentia of the mind,[57] not only because imagination perceives,[58] but also because it produces a chiasm:[59] '*omnia spiritualia corporaliter expresserint*: *haec enim omnia natura imaginationis magis convenient*' – '**expressing all spiritual matters in corporeal language**; for the latter are well suited to the nature of our imagination' – everything which is *spiritual*, comes to be *bodily expressed*: all that is spiritual is adequate to the nature of our imagination [128]. Imagination can express it corporeally. What does this mean?

The materiality of the imagination consists in the perception of a trace, in the comprehension of an encounter, of a relation. Imagination is, materially, a fold and the expression of the potentia of the mind. Chapter II highlights this: the imagination belongs to the **nature of knowledge** and understands thanks

---

55   Chapter VIII is about the authors of the Pentateuch, the knowledge of the Scripture and the 'sincere history'.

56   Chapter XII is concerned, as we saw, with the sacred and the useful: see above [107].

57   See [122] and [126].

58   See [127].

59   Which we could call '*Umwälzung*', revolution.

to the certainty of this nature. Or rather, as part of the knowing structure, it is still uncertain but able to achieve clarity.

This certainty is the moment where history as content and its truth meet in knowledge. A further moment is indicated here: history is knowledge according to a caesura of potentia, which we could call 'virtuality' and which is here figured as imagination.

Potentia is, as we have seen, nature collected in God. The caesura, which we can call 'virtuality', is our participation in it. This caesura is a trembling knowledge – it also consists of our mistaken comprehension of the Commandments, of the Decalogue as rules, whereas they intend only to show direction for life; it is a lack of clear knowledge of which imagination bears the signs.

There is a reason, I believe, why chapter IV, which has to do with the divine law, is at the end of the notebook: if the law is linked to knowledge, which is concerned with the 'supreme good' (*summum bonum*), with the just, happy life, then our failure to understand the Commandments as an indication for life expresses our lack of knowledge.

The aim is to become capable of conceiving things, within a necessary and free nature, as possible for a better life. The capacity to consider things as possible is an important indicator for us: the plane of this conceivability becomes reality when we can achieve our own actualisation.

We should see how this conception of history as caesura – of which the Spinozan imagination is the cipher and both the liberation and the ransom – conjugates with the disclosure of the secret mechanism of Capital, the production of surplus value.

In order to comprehend surplus value, we must analyse the *time* of the function of capital. The time of surplus value begins in Marx's analysis of time in Epicurus, the object of his doctoral thesis. The beginning of his reflection was in the years 1839–41, when Marx was writing his dissertation and noting down the above-cited passages from Spinoza.

We have seen how the figure of imagination takes up a vast space in Marx as a reader of Spinoza. Let us now delve deeper into the place and the role that time has in Marx. We will analyse the notes that Marx takes from Spinoza's correspondence, and read them in parallel with his doctoral thesis. The procedure is the same: for each letter we introduce a concept which textures it.

2.3   Berlin 1841: Letters: *umwälzende Praxis* [Revolutionary Praxis]

The letters from which Marx copies some excerpts are the following: XIX, I, II, IV, V, VII, XI, XIII, XIV, XVI, XXVI, XXXI, XXXII, XXXIII, LXI, LXII, LXVIII, LXXIII, LXXV, LXXVIII, VIII, IX, X, XII, XVII, and LXXVI. Here, I analyse only the excerpts from letters XIX, I, II, IV, XXXII, LXXIII, LXXV, LXXVIII, IX, X, XII, and XVII.

Letter XIX (Spinoza to Blyenbergh, 1644) concerns perfection, the essence of the thing and privation: the perfection and essence of the thing belong to one another.

'[W]e know that whatever is, when considered in itself without regard to anything else, possesses a perfection co-extensive in every case with the thing's essence, for essence is the same as perfection' [174];[60] 'imperfection ... [conceived] in regard to other things possessing more reality';[61] 'for since his [God] will is identical with his intellect'; 'privation is ... so termed in respect of our intellect, not God's intellect'.[62]

In letters I and II – respectively, from Oldenburg to Spinoza and from Spinoza to Oldenburg (1661) – their concern is the concept (*conceptus*). Spinoza defines God in terms of the concept, its being composed of an infinity of attributes:

> I shall therefore begin with a discussion of God, whom I define as a Being consisting of infinite attributes, each of which is infinite or supremely perfect in its own kind. ... – first, that in the universe there cannot exist two substances without their differing entirely in essence; secondly, a substance cannot be produced, since to exist is of its essence; thirdly, every substance must be infinite, or supremely perfect in its kind.[63]

Bacon and Descartes erred, writes Spinoza, because they remained far from the knowledge of the first cause and origin of all things; they did not recognise the true nature of the human mind and, therefore, did not recognise the true cause of the error: 'only those who are completely destitute of all learning and scholarship can fail to see the critical importance of true knowledge of these three points'. Already in these first letters the most important point for us is defined:

---

60   Rubel 1977, p. 101. For the English translation, we use here Spinoza 1992, pp. 272–3.
61   Spinoza 1992, p. 273.
62   The letter is quoted by Marx extensively. I refer, for this, to Rubel's French edition: Rubel 1977, I, pp. 99–103.
63   Ibid., pp. 103–5. Spinoza 1992, pp. 263–4.

that is, being and conceivability belong to one another and express themselves through one another.

They intertwine and co-implicate, therefore, the political and the ethical plane: we must comprehend and know in order to be free and able to change; in order to have that capacity which becomes potentia and allows the construction of our own perseverance in being, our own happiness. Let us read the order of Marx's quotations as a comment on the letters: it is an index of the ethical aspect of his philosophy, an Ethics. We can thus affirm that Spinoza's system is a composition of the Political (the *Political Treatise* was in fact Spinoza's last work).[64]

If, for example, we represent both these systems in a plane, we can identify what from Spinoza 'came to compose' Marx's theory (which I define as 'Ethics'); and what Marx 'read' in Spinoza (which I define as 'Political').[65]

Plane of Ethics

Spinoza	Marx
ordo rerum//ordo idearum	materialism (to summarise in
order of ideas//order of things	a figure: history as *dunamei*)[66]

[*Grundrisse*], Virtuality
umwälzende Praxis, revolutionary praxis

Plane of the Political

Spinoza	Marx
Ethics-/-Political Treatise	Surplus value as the secret of Capital

We could summarise both these planes in two *concepts*: history must be known as *virtuality*; the surplus of surplus value is *surplus of being* anticipated, to

---

64   If we think of the incomplete *Compendium Hebraice Linguae*, we can find in it the conjugation, the 'grammar' of this composition: the ethical-theological-political.

65   This composition is of course entirely my own, and lies outside the reading of Marx's notebook on Spinoza. What we previously analysed constitutes the path identified, whose traces we follow in order to deepen our reflection.

66   *Dunamei* means 'in potency'. Marx takes it from Aristotle, for whom it is a core concept, in relation to *energeia* (see *Metaphysics*, book Theta). It should be made clear that Aristotle's concept of *dynamis* is not Spinoza's concept of potentia: the following chapters will explain it. At the same time, in the concept of '*dunamis*' as we think Marx was using it, and as we conceive it here, is contained the virtual, inasmuch as it contains that caesura, and threshold, between what is and what is not, or not yet, or no longer.

which, because it is being anticipated, lacks potentia [duration].[67] In order to understand the concept at the centre of this second affirmation, we must think of the Spinozan concept of potentia as an intensive mode: the extension of the potentia (of each one) is the extension of its mode (mode-essence) and of its existence. This is why we have the series necessity-freedom-*causa sui*: this series outlines the magnitude of the extension of potentia/nature and the magnitude, the extension of essence (mode-essence) and of existence. What is necessary is also free – or, conversely, freedom is necessity, that is, its own cause of existence.

Letter IV, from Spinoza to Oldenburg, deals with the definition (*definitio*):

> I don't say that from the definition of any thing the thing's existence follows; it follows only ... from the definition or idea of some attribute, that is, of a thing that is conceived through itself and in itself. (I explained this clearly in relation to the definition of God.) [184].[68]

And with priority (*prioritas*): 'From this it is clear that ... substance is by nature prior to its accidents, for without it they can't be or be conceived' [186].[69]

The relation of the substance to its accidents can be expressed through conceivability.[70] This relation has a temporal character: it has the character of 'prioritas', of anticipation. The substance is *prior* to its accidents, originally it is the Whole, in it essence is the same as existence, which is the same as potentia; whereas we, its modes, express of it only the existence. This natural 'priority' of the substance, which is to say, its precedence to its accidents, means simply that they can neither be known, nor exist without it.

Having itself in itself or through itself – conceivability as a founding element of *causa sui* – expresses this priority. The being-'before' of the substance implies the capacity to embrace, to comprehend things, as a virtuality of the occurring, in that system of necessary freedom which is nature. Its conceivability is a productive capacity, which allows what happens to become life. Priority thus means to express and to experience the *virtuality* of the mind,

---

67   And, I would now add, the self-causation.
68   Rubel 1977, p. 107. [184] For the English translation of those letters which are not included in the previous quoted edition, I use here Spinoza, *Correspondence*, Early Modern Text, 2014–2020, Peter Millican, p. 4, http://www.earlymoderntexts.com/assets/pdfs/spinoza16 61.pdf, [access November 2016]
69   [186] Ibid., p. 5.
70   Deleuze has called it expressionism.

its capacity to create and to act. It is the index of a conceivability: 'being' and 'being conceived' are here essentially, that is from the temporal point of view, linked.

What is created, here, is the plane of immanence.

Virtuality is, in this sense, the pulsating heart of the content of history. It is not yet, but becomes.[71] Between actuality and virtuality there is a plus of being, time. Time, that is, as the production of the new.[72] To actualise thus means to be produced from that plus of being which is time. To read history according to its virtuality, along the virtual points that compose it, means to comprehend that freedom is necessity.

And it means to experience the fact that priority means conceivability. What has occurred itself entails an opportunity: *to become comprehended*. Here, its existence, which had forever seemed lost, finds a new beginning, another name, a new life.

Within the meaning of the concept as expression of the substance, the principle of virtuality explains the disclosure of the secret of Capital in Marx's system.

Let us take the concept of time, priority, as a first route in:

the substance	precedes by nature	its accidents
substantia	*sit prior natura*	*suis accidentibus*

Capital as a Whole	precedes	each single worker/ each single commodity

What capital does is an anticipation. First it defines, in agreement with what is conceived in itself and through itself, the plane of the being-commodity, the process of exchange and the definition of one thing through another. We find the secret of capital in value in general, mainly in exchange value: something is produced from a surplus – and this surplus is not a product, *qua* expression of free labour, but an exploitation of the relation of expression which exists between things.

For example: if we add, to the Spinozan definition of self-conception through oneself or through another, that taking A and B as commodities, self-conception through oneself corresponds to the use-value of A and self-conception through the other corresponds to the exchange-value of A defined

---

71   Here is understood the force and importance of economy, when it serves life (the economy of joy).

72   On time as ontology, as production of further being, see Negri 2013.

by its relation with B, we understand that the anticipation that the capitalist produces is a switch of the temporal relation of 'being-being conceived' to
'being conceived-being'.

A, which conceives itself through itself, is produced through the relation of
identity established between A and B – that is, in the market it comes to be
conceived through another (A = B). A has value in the market only inasmuch
as it can be made equivalent, that is, exchanged, with B.

We see, as earlier in Aristotle, that to get the causality of one thing through
another there needs to be something in common. This common matter is
value – as *concept*.

This is why it is so important to 'revolutionise' value in common notions.

> 'If two things have nothing in common with one another, one cannot be
> the cause of the other'
> ['*Quarto denique, quod rerum quae nihil commune habent inter se, una
> alterius causa esse non potest*']
> Letter IV, Spinoza to Oldenburg

In letter XXXII, Spinoza explains to Oldenburg – after a series of questions
Oldenburg had asked on this same topic in other letters – how the mind and the
body are parts of nature; how in nature there is the infinite potentia of thought
which contains everything objectively; how the mind is potentia:[73]

> So you see how and why I hold that the human body is a part of Nature.
> As regards the human mind, I maintain that it also is a part of Nature,
> for I hold that in Nature there also exists an infinite power of thinking
> which, in so far as it is infinite, contains within itself the whole of Nature
> as an object of thought, and whose thoughts proceed in the same manner
> as does Nature, which is clearly its object of thought. Further, I maintain
> that the human mind is that same power of thinking, not in so far as that
> power is infinite and apprehends the whole of Nature, but in so far as it is
> finite, apprehending the human body only. The human mind, I maintain,
> is in this way part of an infinite intellect ...[74]

---

73   '*Cum de natura substantia sit esse infinitam, sequi ad natura substantiae corporeae unam-
     quamque partem pertinere, nec sine ea esse, at concipi posse*'; '*Dari etiam in natura poten-
     tiam infinitam cogitandi, quae, quatenus infinita, in se continet totam naturam objective et
     cujus cogitationes procedunt eodem modo, ac natura, ejus nimirum ideatum*'.
74   Rubel 1977, p. 121. Engl. ed., Spinoza 1992, p. 282.

Within the discourse on ignorance and wisdom,[75] which follows that on the mind as potentia, in letter LXXIII Spinoza tells Oldenburg that for the salvation of each man it is not necessary to know Christ according to the flesh, but rather according to God's wisdom, which is in the human mind.[76]

To know Christ according to wisdom means to understand that nature itself is the matter that constitutes the human mind.

> I conceive that all things follow with inevitable necessity from the nature of God. Everyone thinks that it follows necessarily from God's nature that God understands himself, but no-one thinks that God is compelled by some fate. Rather they think he understands himself completely freely, even if necessarily.[77]
>
> Letter LXXV, Spinoza to Oldenburg

The relation freedom-necessity is deployed in the 'conceiving oneself' (*libere – necessario – se ipsum intelligere*). 'But do you think that we puny men have so much knowledge of Nature that we can determine how far its force and power extend themselves, and what surpasses its force?'[78]

'Nothing belongs to a thing's nature except what follows necessarily from its given cause' (letter LXXVIII, Spinoza to Oldenburg).[79]

Thus far we have understood that the perfection and essence of the thing belong to one another and that in God the will coincides with the intellect. What is the concept, here? It is a composition of attributes; the attribute is conceivability, an expression of the being. Being and conceivability belong to one another and express themselves through one another. History should be known as virtuality, as conceivability (ethics). Surplus value is an anticipated surplus of being, from which has been taken the potentia of becoming (politics), the time of potentia and its causa sui, that is, where the expressive relation of being-conceivability has been manipulated. Freedom is necessity. What is the defini-

---

75 *'Deum enim rerum omnium causam immanentem, ut a ajunt, non vero transeuntem statuo ... divinae revelationis certitudinem sola doctrinae sapientia'*

76 '*in Christum secundum carnem noscere, sed de aeterno illo filio Dei, hoc est, Dei aeterna sapientia, quae sese in omnibus rebus, et maxime in Mente humana, et omnium maxime in Christo Jesu manifestavit, longer aliter sentiendum*' [Engl. ed., Spinoza 2014–2020, p. 105]

77 Rubel 1977, p. 127. Engl. ed., Spinoza 2014–2020, p. 106.

78 Rubel 1977, pp. 129. Engl. ed., Spinoza 2014–2020, p. 107.

79 Marx notes down, from this same letter: 'I accept Christ's passion, death, and burial literally, as you do, but I understand his resurrection allegorically' ('*Caeterum Christi passionem, mortem, et sepulturam tecum literaliter accipio, ejus autem resurrectionem allegorice*') [Rubel 1977, pp. 129–131. Engl. ed., Spinoza 2014–2020, p. 111].

tion, here? The existence of the thing derives from the definition or idea of an attribute, that is, of what is conceived in itself and through itself. Mind and body are parts of nature. The mind is potentia. Nature is the matter that constitutes the human mind. The relation freedom-necessity is explained in conceiving one-self.

Let us try to put these annotations in some order. The theoretical framework in which they must be inserted is the experience of the human mind, *qua* expression of the idea of God. This last letter, LXXVIII, is composed of two parts: 1 – nothing belongs to the nature of a thing if not that which follows necessarily from its cause; and 2 – 'I understand literally Christ's passion, death, and burial, but I understand his resurrection allegorically [*allegorice*]'.

Letters LXXVIII and LXXIII must be read and understood together: 'I intend resurrection as Paul knew Christ, not according to the flesh but according to the spirit'. 'To understand resurrection allegorically' means to understand that what belongs to the nature of a thing, comes and develops from its cause. That is, by 'that which belongs to a nature of a thing' we should understand the essence of God, which is equal to his existence; for '*allegorice*', the virtuality of the infinite mode – the virtuality of the expression of the cause; the virtuality of the distance, that is, of the differential and productive time which exists between the nature of a thing and its cause. Politically, this distance is a) given by singularity (the singularity manipulated in solitude); and b) by historical time (the comprehension, or not, of things under a kind of eternity).

To 'understand the resurrection allegorically' tells us: to know Christ according to the spirit – that is, to know the human mind as an idea of God – explains what it means to comprehend an 'infinite mode'. The human mind is the expression of the idea of God – not temporally, but only allegorically (under a kind of eternity).

The order with which Marx transcribes the quotations – their sequence – is, in this sense, clear: letter VIII, which now appears in the notes, has to do with attributes and their conceivability: 'it is of the nature of a substance that all of its attributes (I mean each of them) should be conceived through themselves, since they have always been in it together'.[80]

In letter IX common notions start to be outlined. Explained within them is the nature of the mind: 'the intellect, although infinite, belongs to Natura naturata, not to Natura naturans'; 'By substance I understand that which is in itself

---

80   Engl. ed., Spinoza 2014–2020, p. 11.

and is conceived through itself; that is, that whose conception does not involve the conception of another thing'.[81]

We have, on one side the (infinite) intellect, expression of the idea of God; on the other, the substance which is conceived in itself. Common notions are the common element to the substance (concept) and the intellect (knowledge of the concept); they are the bridge element between the two.

If we think of the Marxian concept *general intellect*,[82] it seems to be a blooming of the common notions. In other words: commonality, which is necessary in order for a thing to be defined through another, is defined by the knowledge of the concept. This same knowledge of the concept, before its being, is at the basis of Capital's mechanism for producing surplus value. Common notions say: all bodies are similar in some thing which is common to them. This common thing is the attribute, which is knowable. In Marx something more is said: the 'general intellect' is the commonality of the mind, we could say, the collective substance of the mind, whose nature is to know, to produce the knowable, to conceive, within the necessary freedom, that plus of being that we here identify as 'virtual'.

We thus have two indicators of the character of the commonality of being, or of the union, of the composition of existence and essence: value and the common notions. Both are summarised in the concept of 'general intellect'.

Letter IX ends with the creation of the plane of immanence and with the clear explanation of the conceivability-existence relation.

The heart of this relation is the composition of the concept. The mind – even the infinite mind – belongs to the created, produced nature (*natura naturata*) and not to the nature which creates (*natura naturante*).

The relation between created nature (*natura naturata*) and nature which creates (*natura naturante*) is explained in the definition of the concept. The *concept ('una eademque res duobus nominibus insigniri possit')* is defined as a

---

81   Engl. ed., Spinoza 1992, pp. 266–7.

82   'The development of fixed capital indicates to what degree general social knowledge has become a direct force of production and to what degree, hence, the conditions of the process of social life itself have come under the control of the general intellect and been transformed in accordance with it; to what degree the powers of social production have been produced, not only in the form of knowledge, but also as immediate organs of social practice, of the real life process'. *The Grundrisse, Notebook VII, Fixed capital and circulating capital* as two particular kinds of capital. Fixed capital and continuity of the production process. – Machinery and living labour. (Business of inventing). On the general intellect, see Virno 2001 [English translation Virno 2007], and C. Vercellone, 'L'originalità dei Grundrisse: il general intellect come superamento della sussunzione reale del lavoro al capitale', in Vercellone (ed.) 2006; Vercellone 2007; see also Smith 2013.

cipher:[83] a thing which can carry two names (the noun A is defined through its relation with the noun B).

Spinoza gives as an example of the composition of the concept – a thing carrying two names – the definition of the 'plane', by which he means a flat surface 'that reflects all rays of light without any change. I mean the same by "white surface", except that it is called "white" in respect to a man looking at it'.[84] The plane is specified and defined in respect to the man who looks at it; at the same time, it is its own feature to reflect everything without changing it. It is a regulator of modulation.

If the substance can be conceived only through itself, the concept as cipher is the constitution of a plane of definition of things, where they are conceived through one another.

Letter X is about experience and its field of action:

> We don't need experience for things whose existence is not distinguished from their essence, and therefore is inferred from their definition. Indeed, experience *can't* come in here, because experience doesn't teach any essences of things; the most it can do is to affect *which* essences of things our minds think about.[85]

Experience cannot tell us anything about the essence, but it can determine that our mind will think of some of the modes of the essence of things. The concept is the 'substance' of the modes, it is our mind, whose content is the idea of God; the plane is the life of the substance, the movement of its existence; and the experience is the time of its deployment, of its movement. 'You ask, next, whether even things or their affections are eternal truths. I say certainly'.[86]

At this point, Marx notes down a part of letter XII[87] on the 'affections (*affectiones*)'. It is an important passage, because through this we arrive at the defi-

---

83   We should think of the definition that Deleuze and Guattari give of the concept in *Qu'est-ce que la philosophie*.

84   In Italian the word used is *'piano'* [plane] meaning the same as surface. I prefer to translate what in the English translation appears as 'surface' with the English 'plane'.

85   Rubel 1977, p. 135. Engl. ed., Spinoza 2014–2020, op. cit., p. 13.

86   Engl. ed., ibid.

87   Letter XII is about the infinite, its nature and the force of its definitions. The problem of the infinite has always seemed the most difficult, because one cannot distinguish between what is infinite for its nature or force of its definition, and what has no limits because of its cause. We should distinguish between what is infinite, because it has no limits, and what we cannot represent, even when we know the maximum and minimum of the infinite. The same thing happens between conception and representation: we cannot distinguish between what we conceive, without being able to represent it, and that which we con-

nition of virtuality. Indeed, this latter is essential for any comprehension of materialism, mainly as a feature of the relation affections-substance; or even as relation eternity-duration:

> The affections of Substance I call Modes. The definition of Modes, in so far as it is not a definition of Substance, cannot involve existence. Therefore, even when they exist, we can conceive them as not existing. It therefore follows that when we have regard only to the essence of Modes and not to the order of Nature as a whole, we cannot deduce from their present existence that they will or will not exist in the future, or that they did or did not exist in the past. Hence it is clear that we conceive the existence of Substance as of an entirely different kind from the existence of Modes. This is the source of the difference between Eternity and Duration. It is to the existence of Modes only that we can apply the term Duration; the corresponding term for the existence of Substance is Eternity, that is, the infinite enjoyment of existence or – pardon the Latin – of being (*essendi*).[88]

The existence of the substance is defined through eternity: it is the infinite enjoyment of existing, the infinite enjoyment of being. The modes' existence can be defined only through duration: the definition of the modes does not imply existence, they can even be thought of as non-existent. But what mainly counts for us as an indicator is the difference between our thought on the existence of the substance and on the existence of the mode: 'Hence it is clear that we conceive the existence of Substance as of an entirely different kind from the existence of Modes'. The difference between the two is exemplified in the two figures of the eternity and of the duration: through the duration we can explain only the existence of the modes, but the existence of the substance can be explained only through eternity, through, that is, the infinite enjoyment of existing, the infinite joy of being.

We can propose a further reading: we could say that in the substance, production and consumption are the same thing.[89] The consumption is the realisation, the completion of production. What should be underlined, here, is

---

ceive and can represent. If we could comprehend this difference, we could then clearly understand which infinite is divisible and which is not.

88   Rubel 1977, p. 137. Engl. ed., Spinoza 1992, p. 268.

89   See also Bongiovanni 1987, p. 58. Following the thesis of Enzo Rullani, knowledge is the good which is used but not consumed (see, for example, 'The Industrial District (ID) as a cognitive system', Rullani 2003). In this sense, we could dare to venture a parallelism

that the modes, in the production process which Marx cast light on, become substance as the Spinozan '*conatus*', the persevering of each one in his being, becomes a fruition of being, a fulfilment of one's own essence. With Marx the substance finds its realisation, or the realisation of its essence, in us, in the production of the modes. We, the modes, are the realisation of the essence of the substance, of its productive, expressive capacity.

The infinite enjoyment of being, the infinite joy of existing [*infinitam existendi, essendi fruitionem*] find in the equivalence of production and consumption in the substance their expression in life. The territory of this equivalence is the political task of the modes. Neither a comparison nor a reduction, but the infinite definition of one thing through another: it is the birth of the concept as commonality of being.

In order to see how all this relates to Capital, we should advance further through Marx's reading of Spinoza. Why, Spinoza asks, do we tend to divide the substance? Because we conceive it in two ways: in an abstract way, of surface, as the imagination and the senses give it to us; or as substance, which can proceed only from the mind.

In the first case (imagination) we think of it as quantity. It is because of this that we find it divisible, composed of parts. But when we consider it as it is given to us in the mind, we find it as infinite, indivisible and one alone. The first mechanism 'says' what the capitalist does: he captures, divides, equalises, thanks to the anticipation of which he is capable: he uses a priori time and can thus direct the movements of the economic. Spinoza gives us a key to understanding this anticipatory movement. He writes that we can define the duration [time as duration and its quantity (mass)] when we conceive it outside of the substance. To conceive the duration outside of the substance helps us to represent it. But it is here that the capitalist plays with the possibility of dividing the substance from its modes, that is, with the division of the essence from the existence – a division which occurs in the exchange of commodities – in order to manipulate time as duration, to dispose of the character of existence without essence, to produce time itself as surplus value.

To think of the modes as separate from the substance is the origin of both the mistake and the confusion of the imagination.

> To say that Duration is made up of moments is the same as to say that Number is made up by adding noughts together. Further (...) Hence one

---

between substance and knowledge: in them, production and consumption are the same thing, inasmuch as potentia and essence coincide. For more on this, see Chapter 4.

can easily see why many people, confusing these three concepts with reality because of their ignorance of the true nature of reality, have denied the actual existence of the Infinite.[90]

Spinoza suggests to us here that conceivability is a causality, but a causality which should be understood as expressivity (being conceived through itself – *causa sui*).

The caused exists thanks to the force of nature of another thing. But, Spinoza writes,

> the force of the argument lies not in the impossibility of an actual infinite, or an infinite series of causes, but in the assumption that things which by their own nature do not necessarily exist are not determined by a thing that necessarily exists by its own nature[91]

Given their nature, things and modes do not *necessarily* exist; they can also not exist. Their existence is, we could say, virtual. And, furthermore, they are not determined to exist by a thing which necessarily exists by its nature (the substance).

Spinoza seems here to say that the modes, which according to their own nature do not exist necessarily, because they are not defined to exist by something which necessarily exists through its nature, can thus – and should – be defined by other modes.

But if the modes can conceive and define other modes, by virtue of the principle that the mode can only be and be conceived *through an other* – and this *other* can be only what is on the same plane of *non-necessary existence* – then the passage substance-modes is a question of reason, and temporal; whereas the passage causal-expressive – attributes, affections – is a question of modal being, a question of production. Yet this latter occurs through the concept and through time.

The modes produce (conceive) the modes, the substance expresses this productive capacity of the relation between modes.

Thus, from a cause through other [*causa ab alio*] (modes) we have a self-cause [*causa sui*] (substance); or rather, it seems to become outlined that the self-cause [*causa sui*] is the expression of the relation of cause-through-other [*causa ab alio*]. From the attributes, the affections, we have the plane of the

---

90   Rubel 1977, p. 141. The entire context of letter XII of Spinoza's *Correspondence* (On the nature of the Infinite) is of fundamental importance. [Engl. ed., Spinoza 1992, p. 270]

91   Rubel 1977, p. 145. Engl. ed., Spinoza 1992 p. 271.

conceivability of things: the plane of the becoming, where A and B blend into, and found, one another.

What divides the essence from the existence is, thus, that the essence is the index of the 'cause of itself' [*causa sui*]; whereas the existence is the index of the 'being conceived through other' [*causa ab alio*].

Here, we find the force of imagination and its ambiguity. The plane where the capitalist catches the events, the plane where the concept becomes composition, still made of pieces and multiplicity, this plane of the creative imagination is also the plane where the 'self-cause' [*causa sui*] and the 'cause through other' [*causa ab alio*] realise their union.

The next letter which Marx annotated is in fact about imagination. This is letter xvii, where Spinoza writes to Balling: 'so that we can hardly understand anything unless the imagination picks up its traces and forms an image from them'.[92]

The drawing that we find in letter xii is the same that Spinoza uses in the *Ethics* to explain Euclid. Of Euclid and Aristotle, and their presence in Spinoza, we know already from the first chapter. What is at stake, we have seen, is the *commonality* of the character of the definition of common notions and the commodity. In letters xii and xvii we see that imagination is at stake. From the *Ethics* we know that imagination is the first degree of the system of knowledge whose second degree is the common notions. If in the first chapter, the commonality of the common notions and of the commodity implied the true knowability of both, we see now that *also the modes are knowledge*. Modes can include, thanks to their nature, also the non-existing. And for this, because they are 'things' that can also be considered as non-existent, the cause of their knowing, of their being knowledge, is to be conceived *ab alio* – *one through the other*. Or, vice-versa: because the modes are what is 'conceived through other', and this 'other' cannot but be their same plane, of all modes, of expression of the substance, to know through them, that is in their modality, means to be able to comprehend that absence of which imagination is accused, but which is only creative force.

And this is because the mode can be and not be. And from the moment in which the mode is, i.e. exists, since it is conceived through an other, there is inscribed in the relation between the mode and this other the possibility of its being, or of its not being.

We saw that in the structure of the Spinozan knowledge it is imagination which can conceive being and not being: imagination makes things present

---

92   Engl. ed., Spinoza 2014–2020, p. 24.

even when they are not, or are no longer. This is the source of its mistake, but also its force.

If imagination knew that what it imagines is no longer present, it would not be in error, but it would become an instrument of knowledge, of knowledge of the passage of things in being, from the absence. To read this play of presence-absence, where imagination 'falls', but of which it is also the expression, on the plane of the conceivability of the modes, allows us to comprehend that the production of presence[93] at the place of the absence, which imagination does, is the expression of the conceivability through an other, a common element to the commodity, the common notions and the modes. Imagination is a powerful knowing instrument – of exactly what is conceived through an other.

The secret centre of all this is *virtuality*, the heart of the mind. Imagination can be the first knowing instrument (of common notions, of commodity, of the modes) thanks to the virtuality of which it is composed, that *dunamis* which is at once nature, the property of things, the productive capacity of becoming and the expression of the substance.[94] This *dunamis* is the pulsating heart of the mind, of the mind as function in movement and of the mind as the action of the capacity of comprehending, of the mind as knowledge, as known and as knowability, of the mind as cipher of the composition into being.

To know virtuality means to follow its trace where necessity and freedom are but one movement, where we understand, in matter, the heart of the mind itself.[95] *Virtuality means that what is past becomes the content of thought – not to be enclosed in it, but to produce therein infinity, the infinity of the mode. The infinity of the mode is the encounter of production and consumption in the substance; the realisation of its essence in existence. The substance is where production and con-sumption are only the rhythm of* conatus, *the rhythm of the becoming actuated.*

93   'A time which is presence inasmuch as action constitutive of eternity ... Eternity is a formal dimension of the presence' (Negri, *Spinoza e noi*, op. cit., my tr., pp. 50–1)

94   This force for which I use here the term '*dunamis*' should not be resolved in the Aristotelian *dunamis*. It is something more, and different. It should be understood as the virtual which here is only hinted at but of which we talk extensively in *Causa sui*.

95   And since the 'object of the idea constituting the human mind is the body' (E, II, P 13), this heart which is our understanding, by increasing, by living, makes us more eternal, that is full of that time, production of further presence, which is the intensity of being gathered in the folds of our body. It is the fulfilment of desire, the becoming actuated which opens to new virtualities.

CHAPTER 3

The potentia of Poverty: *For an Economy of Joy*

From the path travelled thus far, we can see that both the commodity and common notions are 'conceived through another' and that imagination is the knowledge of this 'being conceived through another'. This owes to the fact that the imagination is a knowledge of abstract things and occurs by way of anticipation. It shares this quality with capital. Thanks to imagination's basic element – virtuality – inasmuch as it is knowledge per anticipation it can help us in understanding capital's mechanism in relation to poverty.

We have to redefine the relation between capital and poverty, and the relation between poverty and *potentia*, at the level of an adequate (or inadequate) knowledge of relations. But in order to do that, we first have to read capital's mechanism according to two features that allow us to understand its conceptual relation to poverty: the possible/anticipatory abstraction and the establishment of 'aconceptual' relations (relations 'without any concept', that is, ones deprived of the possibility of being known).

Both these features have virtuality at their core.

3.1 Atom of Virtuality and the Anticipatory Abstraction

In order to understand the place that virtuality – or *dunamis*, as we find written in Marx – has in the Marxian system, we have to read in parallel the *Notebook Spinoza* with Marx's doctoral thesis, *On the difference of nature in Democritus and Epicurus*.[1]

The structure of the deviation of the atom, as analysed by Marx, is linked to the concept of 'being conceived through an other' that we have seen thus far. We can see this by introducing a further concept which was already outlined, even if not explicitly, in the previous chapters, namely the concept of the *potentia* as 'common mode'. But how is the deviation of the atom linked to the concept of 'being conceived through an other'?

Whereas Democritus's system is built on necessity, Epicurus's system is based on chance, a 'reality that has only the value of possibility' (Marx 1975b,

---

1 It is interesting to notice how Deleuze, in the Appendix to *Logic of Sense*, analyses the Lucretian *clinamen* with theoretical traits similar to Marx's analysis.

pp. 25–30). In opposition to this real possibility, we have an 'abstract possibility'[2] which consists of 'being free from contradiction'. 'Since all the possible is
allowed as possible, *that which corresponds to the character of abstract possibility is openly translated from the chance of being (only) to the chance of thinking*'.
The abstract possibility is the vehicle of translation from the chance of being
to the chance of thinking.

> The abstract possibility does not concern the object which is explained
> but the subject which explains. The object should only be possible, think-
> able. What is 'possible abstract', what can be thought, is not an obstacle
> to the subject, it is not a limitation for it ... It is the same if this possibility
> be also real, because the interest is not in the object as object.[3]

This foresees and explains the basic mechanism of Capital:[4] it is this abstract
possibility, given in thought – the abstract use of time, for example – that
the capitalist elaborates as chance. The matter's chance of being becomes an
abstract possibility of thought which, in turn, produces other matter.

What does this abstract possibility – the passage from the chance of being
to that of thinking – 'technically' mean? The atom falls in a straight line. This
fall in a straight line is a special way of being, following which the atom gives
up its individuality. The atom is pure form, the 'negation of all relative modes
of being, of each relation to another mode of being'.[5] In order to give reality
to this form, Epicurus introduces deviation from the straight line (*parenklesis*,
which Lucretius would later call *clinamen*): in deviating, the atom obtains its
autonomy, its individuality. It does so through abstracting from its relative
mode of being – that is, from the straight line.

Marx's conceptual move is the following: in abstracting from its relative
mode of being – which is represented by the straight line – the atom takes on
its individuality. In this act, the atom expresses its material definition. It is a
chiasm: a material definition occurs through an abstraction; the definition of
an individual autonomy occurs through the deviation from a relative mode of
being. It is here that we can recognise the two figures of the 'being conceived
through an other' and of the 'cause of itself' (*causa sui*).[6]

---

2 'The abstract possibility is the antipode of the real'.
3 Marx 1975b.
4 We refer to Capital not only as Marx's *Capital* but also as general conceptual persona.
5 In a certain sense it is an idea: 'nothing else than itself'.
6 The deviation, the *clinamen*, corresponds to the Spinozan infinite mediate mode, that uncertain space and uncertain time where the *causa sui* [cause of itself] (the substance, the atom)
   becomes a 'being conceived through an other'.

The self-determination of the atom, the fulfilment or attainment of the *causa sui*, is achieved by abstracting from the straight line, by abstracting from the atom's relative mode of being. This act of abstracting from the atom's relative mode of being, which is at the same time the material definition of itself, is explained thusly:

> And in reality: **the existent immediate individuality realizes itself first according to its concept,** in as much as it refers to the other which is itself, even if the other in the form of immediate existence opposes it (...) Because man as man could become its only real object, he should have crashed within itself its relative mode of being.
>
> MARX 1975b, pp. 39–42, my translation and emphasis

This shattering of the relative mode of being explains the movement of that which, in order to become *cause of itself*, should be conceived through an other. Such movement produces, from an abstractive process which we could call cognitive ('according to its concept'), something material: 'When I relate to myself as an immediate other, this relating is material' (Marx 1975b, pp. 10–11.)

The 'being conceived through an other' becomes *causa sui* – or rather, the need for the '*causa sui*' to 'be conceived through other' is acted out according to potency (*dunamei*), according to the concept. In relating to myself through another, or in my relating to myself as if I were another, my relating is material.

Atoms should give up all aspects of their relative mode of being, they should give up every aspect of their mode which relates to the other, in order to be able to meet: they should abstract from their opposites and establish themselves, define themselves as nothing other than themselves (idea = concept). In this passage, they produce an abstract possibility, they allow the flow of being into concepts and of concepts into being: they are able to compose themselves, to unite. Each individual particularity lays its own foundations in the other. The difference between the concept and the being is here overcome: it has been transformed into a flow.[7]

---

7   What is to be overcome, here, is the same difference between existence and essence that we have seen earlier in Spinoza. In the concept of 'being conceived through other/*causa sui*' the difference between existence and essence is 'synthetically united': existence passes into essence and essence into existence. This occurs thanks to the potentia as common mode, to potentia as relation. This is nothing other than the Spinozan concept of body constituted by many bodies, thus the founding of a political praxis.

Thus already in Marx's dissertation on Democritus and Epicurus we have two foundation theses: the cause of itself (*causa sui*) derives from the 'being conceived through an other' (*causa ab alio*); this is a process of abstraction which defines a material relating.

3.2 The Establishment of a-Conceptual Relations

The second feature of capital important for us, here, is that capital establishes 'a-conceptual' relations. There is a passage, in the second book of *Capital*, where Marx, in explaining the metamorphosis of capital in circulation and production, declares that money is indefinite value and differentiates itself, or defines itself, only from a conceptual point of view, as **function**:

> M became capital by virtue of its relation to the other part of M', which it has brought about, which has been effected by it as the cause, which is the consequence of it as the ground. Thus M' appears as the sum of values differentiated within itself, functionally (conceptually) distinguished within itself, expressing the capital-relation.[8]
>
> MARX 1975C, p. 51

That Marx refers, here, to the concept and exposes it as function, is fundamentally important. Where the difference, the definition is taken away – as in the case of Capital, when at the end of its process it expresses itself in money – where it is no longer possible to distinguish among the 'various modes of existence' of Capital,[9] the conceptual definition fails. What remains is an 'a-conceptual expression' of relations which capital produces. 'A-conceptual' means not only that we are no longer able to understand the different, basic parts which compose Capital, but also that in its function we can no longer see the anticipation and the dismeasure.

Its function – which Marx explains as 'definable from a conceptual point of view', and through which Capital defines and distinguishes itself, for which it can be known – is neither cognisable nor conceivable.

---

8 '*Da in dem einfachen Dasein dieser Geldsumme die Vermittlung ihrer Herkunft ausgelöscht und von der spezifischen Differenz, welche die verschiednen Kapitalbestandteile im Produktionsprozeß besitzen, jede Spur verschwunden ist, so existiert der Unterschied nur noch* in der begrifflichen Form einer Hauptsumme' (*Das Kapital, Buch II, erste section, dritte Stage*).

9 *Das Kapital*, II, pp. 50–5.

The money-function escapes the plane of the concept, the plane of conceivability of things. The function that expresses the relation devoid of its concept, which capital produces, is the plane of the escape from the conceivability of the relation; the plane, we could say, of the escape from its *potentia*.[10]

The definition of the money-capital function[11] is similar and parallel to another fundamental feature of Capital: namely, its self-valorisation. Self-valorisation is another mode of self-realisation, a product of the anticipation.

We have thus different features of Capital, which are linked one to another: self-valorisation, anticipation, and the a-conceptual expression of a relation. What unites them is time. In the processes of self-valorisation and anticipation, the central mechanism is represented in the figure of virtuality (*'dunamis'*).[12]

---

10   See MEW p. 24, p. 50 (*'also begriffliche Unterscheidslosigkeit*, (...). *Es ist daher begriff-sloser Ausdruck des Kapitalverhältnisses, worin hier am Schluß seines Prozesses das realisierte Kapital in seinem Geldausdruck erscheint'*) and pp. 51–5 (*'Der begriffslose Unterschied'*).

11   This function finds its expression also in the figure of immaterial labour. See Lazzarato 1997, and Chapter 4 here. For a wider context, see my doctoral thesis, Pascucci 2003.

12   The role of the figure of *dunamis* in the work of Marx is an important theme; here it is enough to know that this figure of virtuality [*] materialises the knowledge of history. At the beginning of the *Grundrisse*, Marx defines the materialistic comprehension of history according to potency (*dunamei*) as capacity, through the self-critique, of looking at the movement of history from two sides: to know the course of things according to potency inasmuch as it is 'differential' among states, among events. 'The so-called historical presentation of development is founded, as a rule, on the fact that the latest form regards the previous ones as steps leading up to itself, and, since it is only rarely and only under quite specific conditions able to criticise itself – leaving aside, of course, the historical periods which appear to themselves as times of decadence – it always conceives them one-sidedly. The Christian religion was able to be of assistance in reaching an objective understanding of earlier mythologies only when its own self-criticism had been accomplished to a certain degree, so to speak, *dunamei*.' (Introduction, Notebook M, *Method of political economy*. See also other passages where *dunamis* is used, for instance the one where it is a mediation between production and consumption, a movement of the respective position of the one and of the other.) The same figure of the *dunamis* embodies, I believe, the structure of the *umwälzenden Praxis*, being its motif and motive power. To change a situation we have to conceive things according to *potency* (*dunamei*). And to conceive things 'according to potency' means to unite the present with the past in a way that this union could become the organisation of the experience in accord with potency [**], in accord with the presence of time of life. Both, past and future, open their relation to the present: they are virtual inasmuch as they are capable of molding themselves into a composition – life – or bringing themselves to decomposition – death. The force of the materialistic comprehension of history, which produces the *'Umwälzung'*, consists in comprehending this arrow of time, which is what history is about. [*] On the role of virtuality in Marx and its stemming from an initial complicity with 'dunamis,' I refer the

Also, in the a-conceptual expression of the relation, is hidden the figure of the *dunamis*, as conceivability of things.

The time of *dunamis*, which is potentia and virtuality together, is a contracted present and a moving assemblage of being and becoming. In it, too, time is anticipation – but only inasmuch as it is a differential involved in the capacity of being, in the capacity of producing other being, pure *prolepsis*.[13] It is a 'differential of thought" and of the thought-body. It is a continuous becoming and is known as a distinction of reason, not as a distinction of being. With a short-circuit, we could say that this difference of knowledge is also what passes, as a temporal arrow, through the actual distinction between local and global, between the internal and external of the production processes, between the existence and essence of things. In order to be able to constitute a composition of existence and essence, of local and global, of internal and external, in accord with virtuality, we have to acknowledge and know this difference of reason.[14]

> The formula M–C ... P ... C'–M', with its result M' = M + m, is deceptive in form, is illusory in character, owing to **the existence of the advanced and self-expanded value in its equivalent form, money.** (...) The so-called monetary system is merely an expression of the irrational form M–C–M', a movement which takes place exclusively in circulation and therefore can explain the two acts M–C and C–M' in no other way than as a sale of C above its value in the second act and therefore as C drawing more money out of the circulation than was put into it by its purchase.
>
> MARX 1975C, p. 68

The self-valorisation, the anticipation, the a-conceptuality of the relation are moments of the same mechanism: the creation of the plane of abstract possibility (C in the second act is sold above its value) as prerequisite of production.

---

reader to Pascucci 2009. [**] Here I maintain a distinction between the Aristotelian *dunamis* (potency) and the Spinozian *potentia*.

13   In the Aristotelian sense of the *Poetics*. The *prolepsis* is quoted also by Marx in his notes on Epicurus; by Kant, in the *Kritik der reinen Vernunft, Antizipation der Wahrnehmung*; and by Deleuze in the Appendix to *Logique du sens*.

14   I have analysed these theoretical passages, in more detail, and within a reading of history according to virtuality (to which I partly refer in the next section), in Pascucci 2003a.

3.3   The Virtuality of History

This is the frame at which we have arrived: we are on that plane of immanence where the commodity, common notions and mode are conceived 'through
an other'. The conception through an other is made possible by the nature of
commodities and common notions, constituted by virtuality. This is, at once,
productive capacity and force of expression, nature and composition.

In the introduction to the *Grundrisse*, Marx talks about the comprehension
of history *dunamei*, that is according to potency, according to virtuality.[15] The
movement of this virtuality, its metamorphosis, can be outlined for the theor-
etical path that reads poverty as potentia, as follows:
- Pre-Socratic dunamis
- Platonic dunamis
- Aristotelian dunamis
- Spinozan potentia
- Virtuality in Deleuze
- Critique of value in Negri and concept of 'dismeasure'
- contemporary poverty

We saw how the centre of this movement can be read in Marx – and how
this has been developed by the most recent philosophy. The 'dunamis' in the
Aristotelian sense is quoted by Marx both in the *Grundrisse* and in *Capital*; he
studied Spinoza and we have his annotations on both the *Theological-Political
Treatise* and on the *Letters*. Already in his doctoral thesis, Marx had outlined
the concept of anticipation *qua* mechanism of Capital – of this we also find
traces in Deleuze's later analysis of the *clinamen* (Appendix to *Logic of Sense*)
and in his concept of virtuality. Ultimately, to comprehend the act of anticipation as the heart of capital's mechanism means to understand the essential
reason of value and its secret as production of dismeasure (Negri). This is the
place of actual poverty.

---

15   It is important to notice that the Aristotelian potency (*dunamis*) is not immediately the
       Spinozan *potentia*. I am grateful to Antonio Negri for making this clear to me. The aim of
       this book is to show the possible theoretical path that would connect the pre-Socratic
       dunamis to contemporary poverty, including the transformation Aristotelian *dunamis*-
       Spinozan *potentia* as well as the possibility of reading the Spinozan *potentia* as the pro-
       ductive process of virtue, which is what I mean here by 'virtuality'. In the history of
       thought, this virtue/virtuality has been differently used and exploited. I dedicated a book
       (Pascucci 2009) to explaining this shadow of meaning. Besides my text – on the possibility
       of reading the Spinozan *potentia* as imbued by virtuality, of reading it as the productive
       process of *causa sui* known and textured, moved by desire, and in that liberating the value
       of the *wahre Reichtum* – see Negri 2012, pp. 42–3.

This is also the reason why to comprehend virtuality, or rather to comprehend and produce history as virtuality, means to produce new political praxis and new coordinates for the reality of each singular development of the force of life.

Capital teaches us that it can be conceived and comprehended through imagination, through the force of knowledge, from its weakest state to the most effective one. It also tells us that it creates a-conceptual relations, that its main mechanism is based on anticipation, on the abstract possibility given in thought. Anticipation, the abstract possibility given in thought, produces by taking away at the same time the comprehension of that production, of the elements of production – the knowing mechanism of Capital continues to produce the illusion of presence, as the imagination when it does not realise that what it imagines is no longer present.

To think of poverty as potentia takes the problem back to the plane of *knowledge* of these a-conceptual relations established by Capital.

It is from the point of view of knowledge that we can now engage with the two concepts important to us: the concept of potentia – that is Marx's 'interpretation' of the Spinozan potentia – and the concept of poverty.[16] From the intertwining of the two comes a further concept of political Ethics.[17]

Thus far we have seen how, in Marx's annotations on Spinoza, potentia takes form as mind, as the capacity of conceiving things *in* and *through* an other. And we saw that 'to be conceived through an other' is the common element in both the commodity and common notions – and that it occurs thanks to virtuality, the nature of things and their expressive capacity.

Now we need to see how poverty is connected to all this. How, that is, we could think of poverty as potentia.

---

16   A theme worthy of further investigation is if – and where – the 'virtualiter pauper' of the *Grundrisse* finds its causality in Spinoza.

17   The importance of a reading of Spinoza in Marx has already been addressed in fundamental works such as those by Emilia Giancotti, Étienne Balibar, Pierre Macherey, Alexandre Matheron, Pierre François Moreau, Maximilian Rubel, Antonio Negri, Gilles Deleuze and others. Without these, much of Spinozan thought and of the relation Marx-Spinoza would have remained misunderstood.

3.4   Excursus on the potentia (Ontological) and How This Defines
        Poverty

In Joseph Souilhé's study on the concept of *dunamis* in the Platonic dialogues
(*Etudes sur le terme dunamis dans les dialogues de Platon*, 1919), *dunamis* is
defined as the constitutive property of the being in relation. Before this definition, the history of its concept swung between various different meanings: it is
value, to be equivalent-to;[18] it is 'to mean'[19] and the 'fertility of the earth';[20] it is
force,[21] nature,[22] and productive power;[23] it is virtue.[24]

In Pythagorean mathematics, *dunamis* expresses the potentia of becoming:[25] to call the tetrad the dunamis of the decade is to affirm its potentia of
becoming; the *dunamis* is the fundamental property of numbers, which also
explains their graphic representation.

In Parmenides, the *dunameis* are opposed qualities; before him, Alcmaeon
of Croton, disciple of Pythagoras and the first Italian physiologist, affirmed that
health is an equilibrium of *dunameis* that alone can ensure the body's proper
functioning; whereas for Ecphantus of Syracuse, a contemporary of Plato's,
dunamis moves the indivisibles – it is the intelligence, the soul. Still for Parmenides, ideas and things should have certain determinations (*dunameis*) in
order to become objects of knowledge.[26]

Of all definitions that the *dunamis* takes on, it has two further aspects
besides the fundamental aspect of nature and force (hence, the productive
aspect). One is the aspect of value, the basis for the commensurability of things.
The other aspect is the fundamental property of the elements which, as such,

---

18   For example, Herodotus, *Discourse of Alexander to the Athenians* II, 142 in Souilhé, p. 5;
      Thucydides, *Pericles' Funeral Oration*, II, 97; VI, 40; VII, 58, in Souilhé, pp. 5–6, 8.
19   Herodotus, *Discourse of Alexander to the Athenians*, II, 30; IV, 110; I, 194; VI, 86.3.
20   Thucydides, *Pericles' Funeral Oration*, I, 2; Xenophon, *Oeconomicus*, VII, 14; XVI, 4.
21   Aristophanes, *Pluto*, 748, 449, 842.
22   Xenophon, *Memorabilia*, vedi Souilhé, pp. 8–16.
23   Xenophon, *De Vectigalibus*, IV, 1; IV, 47, in Souilhé, p. 16.
24   See Souilhé, pp. 34, 36, 69, 73, 79, 87–89, 94, 97, etc.
25   '*Appeler la tétrade dunamis de la décade, c'est affirmer la puissance de développement que
      renferment les quatre premiers entiers groupés et additionnés, la propriété constitutive du
      nombre 10 (...) La tétrade est dunamis de la décade parce qu'elle la constitue, parce qu'elle la
      réalise et l'exprime, ainsi qu'on peut le constater dans le triangle équilatéral, parce qu'elle est
      en définitive sa propriété distinctive, son élément primitif (...) C'est pourquoi les idées de pro-
      priété fondamentale ou distinctive ne paraissent assez exactes pour traduire cette dunamis
      dont le mathématiciens Grecs faisaient le principe, la source de développement des nombres
      ...*' Souilhé, p. 25. See also pp. 27–8.
26   See Souilhé pp. 148–9; 158; 190.

can be known. We can already see a definition of potentia taking shape, as being conceived through an other.

The *dunameis* are entities that constitute the externalisation of the substance; but they cannot be known if not *in actu*. Action is like their *raison d'être*, that which characterises them and individuates them.

The term of *dunamis* thus designates their essence and their way of manifesting themselves, their expression.[27] It is the expression of the substance, as being and nature.[28]

The *dunamis* is defined also as virtue, the active principle and organiser of life; or as the property of things, a property of being related.[29]

3.4.1 *The* dunamis *as Mode of Being Related – the Essence of the Idea*

The *dunamis* is, therefore, *property* qua *mode of being related*. This property is the heart of one of the hidden roles that *dunamis* has in Plato: that is, to be the nature, the essence of the idea.

In the *Phaedo* (70 b) the *dunamis* is a property, an active reality, a sign of existence. In the *Republic* (346a–b) 'the *dunamis* of the arts is a property that distinguishes them and specializes them, that manifests their nature hidden from its active reality. In fact this *dunamis* is essentially the source of action: it produces advantages, as Plato says, or rather, results, an *ergon*, and this is its immediate consequence'.[30]

It is potentia and justice; it is *dunamis* that gives the other the power of existing and that preserves them in as much as it resides in them.[31]

Knowledge (*episteme*) is the more powerful among the arts – it is the one which has more *dunamis*.[32]

'What I mean by the second division of the intelligible is that reason comprehends thanks to the faculty of the dialectics'; 'everybody has the faculty of apprehending': this faculty is the *dunamis* (ibid., p. 99; *Republic* VII, 517

27   Souilhé, p. 36.

28   '*Generaliser la conclusion que suggérait déjà le dépouillement du* Peri arkaies ietrikes. *Dans les Traités de la collection hippocratique, dans ceux surtout où l'influence des idées cosmologiques des premiers physiciens est particulièrement manifeste, le terme dunamis désigne la propriété caractéristique des corps, leur coté extérieur et sensible, celui qui permet de les déterminer et de les spécifier. Grâce à la* dunamis, *la* fusis *mystérieuse, l'*eidos *substantiel, ou élément primordial se fait connaître, et se fait connaître par action*' (Souilhé, 61–62).

29   Souilhé 1919, pp. 69–70; 74–75; 77.

30   Ibid., p. 91.

31   Ibid., pp. 91, 94.

32   Ibid., p. 96.

b), the 'capacity of conceiving and reaching the real' (ibid., p. 166; *Republic*, v 477 b and fll.; 478 a, 479 d).

It is also the capacity of looking at the Sun, of reaching the knowledge of being;[33] 'potency proportioned to the ideas, that allows for the man to rise toward the sphere of immutable truths ... this potentia resides in the soul with its organ and deflects the whole soul from the obscure world of the appearances to plunge it in the light of being that the shadows do not obfuscate'.[34]

It is producer of *poietiké*, which consists of bringing the non-being to existence (*Sophist*, 219 b; ibid., p. 151). It is the knowledge of the object through its properties, through that on which the essence acts and by which it can be affected; the beings will be known, thanks to their mutual relations (*Phaedrus*, 270 d; ibid., p. 153).

Of all the Platonic passages analyzed by Souilhé,[35] the most important ones for our analysis of the *dunamis* are the *Sophist* and the *Parmenides*. We should not confuse the two spheres of *dunamis* and *ousia* or *fusis* – spheres that Plato keeps well separated (ibid. and fl.).[36] But it is fundamental for us to see the places where the two draw so close as to almost converge: the definition (*Sophist*) and the ontological-gnoseological parallelism (*Parmenides*).

3.4.2   Definition
In the *Sophist*, a hint is made which Plato never comes back to regarding the **definition of being through *dunamis*** (247 e):[37]

> everything which possesses any power [*dunamin*] of any kind, either to produce a change in anything of any nature or to be affected even in the least degree by the slightest cause ... has real being. For I set up as a definition [*horon*] which defines the things that are [*ta onta*], that it is nothing else than power.
>
> 247d–e

---

33   Ibid., pp. 99–100.
34   Ibid., pp. 166.
35   Souilhé gives a detailed scheme of each place in the dialogues where the term *dunamis* is used, as well as of its different meanings (Souilhé 1919, pp. 150–2).
36   'It is thanks to the *dunamis* that the being will be defined', even if this does not mean that it is confused with the being [*ens*], 'the being will not be grasped and therefore known if not through its external manifestations, because its intimate nature remains hidden' (Souilhé, p. 157). *Dunamis* and *ousia* are bound as the expression and the substance, 'the property derives immediately from being, it participates to its evolution, to its vicissitudes, and it is thus that every change of nature corresponds to a change of *dunamis*' (ibid.).
37   Ibid., p. 155.

Here the *dunamis* expresses 'the physical real movement of *poiein* [to do and produce], and a modification also real, consequently a change and another movement of *paskein* (to be acted, "suffer") ...'[38] 'The *koinonia* which links together the ideas will represent nothing but this possibility of relations (relations of *poiein* and of *paskein*) explaining the link of the intelligibles'.[39] The possibility of the definition proper to the *dunamis* is thus a commonality, a *koinonia*, of the ideas: it is the possibility of knowable relationships of relation.

3.4.3 *Ontological-Gnoseological Parallelism*

In the *Parmenides* (133d–e; 134 d) the *dunamis* is in parallel with the *ousia* and it seems to have, step by step, the same meaning. It is after all the only case of such a combination of these two terms in the Dialogues. And furthermore the *dunamis* here designates the essence relative to the beings in the act of relation. Every act of relation supposes a certain external manifestation which makes the relation knowable. The *dunamis* expresses the essence of these beings and their manifestation outside of their properties.[40]

Souilhé had previously analysed how, in *Parmenides*, it is stated that there is no relation between us and ideas

> none of the *essences* which exist in themselves, *autén tina kat'autén ekàstou ousian*, exist in us ... the ideas related one to the other also have their mutually relative *essence*, *autai pròs autàs ten ousian ekousin*, but are not related to the similarities that are in us, similarities which owe to participation in these ideas and which allow us to affirm their existence ... these participations are related to each other, not to the ideas in themselves. For example, if someone is a slave or master, one is not the slave of the master in himself or the master of the slave in himself, but these relations do exist between the two men. Despotism is despotism relative to slavery and slavery relative to despotism. But the despotism or the slavery that are in us do not have their *essence* in relation to the essence of despotism or of servitude in themselves: these ideas are relative to each other and so are their mutual imitations [... *all'ou ta en emin pros eeina ten dunamin ekein oudè ekeina pros emas*].[41]

---

38   Ibid., p. 154.
39   Ibid., pp. 154–5, my translation.
40   Ibid, p. 158.
41   Ibid.

Souilhé notes that whereas in the first example, the essence of the ideas in themselves is defined as *ousia*, in the second example, talking of the relative essence of beings (the slavery or despotism that are in us), he defines it as *dunamis*. *Ousia* is for the things in themselves and *dunamis* for what is defined 'in other'.

The parallelism could end here – if it were not that in Plato, as we have seen, the *dunamis* is that property of expression of beings that reveals their mode of being relative. In this case, we could say that it is thanks to the *dunamis*, to the essence of slavery or despotism in us, that *we know* their relative mode of being: I am not the slave of the master in himself, I am the slave of that master; the master is not the master of the abstract slave, of the slave in himself, but he is master of that slave.

The *dunamis* is the principle of *episteme*, of true knowledge. It is also the principle of difference, of differentiation, and through this, an inner critique of the Idea – or, rather, exactly because of this, its principle of expressive multiplicity?

Thus in Plato the *dunamis* is a property of things that expresses their mode of being relative. It is a sign of existence and a source of action, it is a producer of results and of capacities of existing.

It is, furthermore, a faculty of comprehending – that property of things which allows for their knowability. It is 'the property or quality revealing of being ... it reveals the intimate and hidden nature of beings; more than that, it distinguishes the essences among them ... it is at the same time, a principle of knowledge and principle of diversity'.[42] It is the 'active property, that resides in different natures, as an expansive force, which shows these natures, giving to each of them a potency of particular exercise'.[43]

It can be read as an 'embryonic theory of the faculties'.[44] But in any case, *dunamis* is 'linked to a new idea, to a kind of particular beings, *genos ti ton onton*, the conception of these beings (*onta*) as potencies or capacities of action different and respectively proportioned to a special object, to a determinate mode of operation'.[45]

This Platonic *dunamis* seems to touch on the most profound nature of things, the *fusis* and the *ousia* of the Idea, because it allows for the knowledge of the shadows at the bottom of the cave – it allows for looking at the Sun. And since the Sun is the motor, the very essence of the idea, there springs from

---

42   Ibid., p. 149.
43   Ibid.
44   Ibid., p. 168.
45   Ibid.

it the idea as expression of a relative mode of being, of the being conceived through an other.[46] The idea is nothing other, at this point, than the general, undetermined expression, we could say using Spinoza *sub specie aeterni*, of the *dunamis*.

The definition, proper to the *dunamis*, is the *koinonia* of ideas, the possibility (according to *dunamis*) of their binding themselves in knowable relations.

The idea in itself, then, is something that has not yet reached the direction of being, of reality; which has not yet been conceived through an other; but which, thanks to its commonality with other ideas – thanks to the definitional capacity of the *dunamis* which constitutes this same commonality – can bind itself to a knowable relation and become an expression. This is what would happen in Aristotle.

Aristotle resumes and widens the multiple notion of *dunamis* elaborated by Plato.

His first, and major, conceptual change resides in his definition of it as the 'principle of change in another being, or in the same in as much as it is in an other'.[47] In Aristotle *dunamis* is not only the 'power of modifying, of acting; it can consist of the being itself, in the property of being moved by another in as much as it is other'.[48] Thus the active and passive sense of the *dunamis* live together within it.

This meaning of the term *dunamis* in Aristotle carries on the Platonic idea of property:[49] the *dunamis* defines the characteristic property of being, the principle source of action, of modification, of resistance. At the heart of the definition of this *dunamis*, which seems bivalent, we find the further step that Aristotle takes with respect to Plato: 'he comprises the idea of relation within his notion of *dunamis*, by giving it a definition: the principle of movement or change situated in another being, or in the same being but in as much as it is other' (ibid., pp. 173–174).[50] 'The *dunamis* is a being oriented by nature *pros allos* (towards, to the others)' (ibid., p. 175).

Aristotle not only defines the *dunamis* as 'change in an other' – thus widening the Platonic notion – but clarifies how this change in an other could

---

46   This seems to show a different Plato, new, in as much as it is the contrary of the definition
      of idea as expression of nothing but itself that is found in the classic Plato.

47   Ibid., p. 170; Aristotle, *Metaphysics*, Delta 12 and Theta 1; Delta 12, 1019 a 15.

48   Ibid., p. 171; Aristotle, *Metaphysics*, Delta 12, 1019 a 20.

49   Soilhé 1919, p. 172.

50   'Aristotle explains that this relative is said of the double and of the half, of the triple and
      of the third and, in a general sense, of the multiple and the multiplied, of what surpasses
      and what is surpassed' (Souilhé 1919, p. 174).

not occur but as a relation between act and potency, between *dunamis* and *energeia*, where the *dunamis* expresses a sort of direction of being, of realisation:

> the act will not take place if it has not the potency of realizing itself, nor will the potency produce the act if it remains undefined and does not prepare, with its direction, the appearing of such a distinct being. We can thus define the *dunamis* as the possibility of being in a determinate way ...[51]

Within the Platonic division between being and idea, between noumenon and phenomenon, there is a bridge-principle: 'an external and relative side that makes them appear, the phenomenon which expresses the noumenon: this is the *dunamis*'.[52] This happens by virtue of the mutual relation that beings, and their ideas, have among themselves. It seems that the ontological parallelism (ideas with ideas; beings with beings) through the gnoseological parallelism (the *dunamis* as property of relation and knowability inasmuch as in other) could draw the *dunamis* near to the cause, the conceiving in an other to the conceiving in itself.

Whereas in Plato this remains a hint, in Aristotle it is delved into: 'both are the principle of movement and transformation: the active potency is nothing but an attitude to donate, a possibility of cause inherent to this or that fundamental property of beings; the passive potency [is] an attitude to being acted upon, to receive, a possibility of effect'.[53]

3.5   How the *dunamis*-Virtue is the Spinozan potentia

The *dunamis* is a constituent virtue. Virtue is defined as a power of procuring the good for oneself.[54]

This is the Spinozan definition of potentia, as a capacity of persevering in one's own being.

---

51   Ibid., p. 185; Aristotle, *Metaphysics*, Theta, 1047–48.
52   Soilhé 1919, p. 188.
53   Ibid., p. 189. This reading is my own. Souilhé clarifies (p. 190) that the cases in which the *dunamis* is applied to ideas are very rare (out of 468, two of the *Parmenides*, 134 d, 150 c–d, one of the *Timaeus*, 28 a, and some passages from the *Sophist*, 252 e, 254 c, where it is talked about power, and the property of ideas to communicate between them).
54   Souilhé 1919, p. 82. See also p. 78, 'the force of multitude'.

The Spinozan definition of potentia[55] is heir to the Aristotelian *dunamis*-virtue, as a capacity of producing oneself in life *qua cause of itself* – exactly that which is stolen from the slave. But, I find, the Spinozan potentia also composes itself with these other meanings of a pre-Aristotelian *dunamis*, where its simultaneously economic – so to speak – and ontological nature is clear.

That is, something else is synthesised within the ontological-gnoseological parallelism: the Aristotelian *dunamis* as [the active potency] 'possibility of cause inherent to this or that fundamental property of being', [the passive potency] 'an attitude to being acted upon',[56] is transformed into potentia. This is, then, no longer an abstract possibility of cause but the inner mechanism of the cause, the essence of the principle of individuation. In the pre-Aristotelian meanings of *dunamis*, it seems that the capacity of producing oneself in life, of becoming cause of itself, depends on the relative mode of being of each, from its defining itself in relation to an other, from its conceiving itself, and being capable of conceiving itself, through an other. In my further reading of the Marxian terms set out above, the abstract possibility [Aristotle's *dunamis*] is divested of its 'possibility'-dialectic and becomes the material, necessary production of oneself [Spinoza's *causa sui*].[57]

---

55   The Spinozan potentia is not the simple translation of the Aristotelian *dunamis*. It is, further, the sign of the absence of the subject, of having gotten rid of contingency forever. It is the definition of being as free and necessary.

56   Ibid.

57   In order to explain how we come to read potentia as the inner mechanism of the cause, the essence of the principle of individuation, let me refer briefly to the following schema. From Souilhé we see that in the pre-Socratic philosophy of nature *dunamis* is meant as value, as being equivalent-to, as meaning, as Earth's fertility, force of production, nature, virtue ... In Plato there is an essence of ideas (*ousia*) and an essence of beings (*dunamis*): the *dunamis* is the property of being in relation. Aristotle widens the notion of *dunamis* (not only the principle of inner faculties which we started to see in Plato): it expresses a relation, it is change in as much as it is relation: the change/transformation is 'in other'. In Spinoza, *dunamis* loses its 'possibility' side and becomes potentia as constituent virtue, the force of self-production (*causa sui*), as substance's necessity of being. We can then perhaps understand Marx's reading of the *clinamen* as that abstract possibility (conceiving oneself according to *dunamis*, as transformation in an other) which becomes real: there the transformation becomes material. The further step we try to make here is the following: it is no longer an abstract possibility (the realm where Capital has the lion's share and inserts its power in between the abstract possibility and the real) but the subjectivity of the worker/the potential/force of living labour itself that shows how the principle of transformation lies intrinsically in a relation of production; the *causa sui* has its constituency in the subject, that is, the production lies in the *causa sui* which is substantially and intrinsically a relation (formal = objective). Thus, in my further reading of the Marxian terms seen above, the abstract possibility [Aristotle's *dunamis* and its transformations] becomes material production of oneself [Spinoza's *causa sui*].

To conjugate this excursus on the *dunamis* to the discourse on poverty, we take as our example Deleuze on Spinoza and take the inverse path, from the formation of passions (joyful) to the formation of the affect. We find in Deleuze's and Negri's reading of Spinoza an alphabet of a political ethics of love, which indicates the path for the composition of that 'adequate' life which gives happiness. By adequate life, I mean that life which is full deployment of its potentia, its virtue. And I consider the object of politics the enabling of this achievement, the means given by the collective to the full deployment of each one's life. This is the reason why I try to read together the path of liberation from the passions to the formation of the affect with a dynamic which takes us from poverty to the 'true wealth', the compositional process of that adequate and happy life. Poverty today is the place where our own potentia is alone, and kept captive – captive of a superstructure which dominates it, which directs it, which encroaches upon it so deeply with its deployment as to touch potentia's very core of productive force: the self. It is here that the main nature of our singularity, the force of life, our causa sui, the self-production, is encroached upon by that stealing and appropriative mechanism of Capital which makes our singular life force its own productive principle, masking it as a collective task/ownership (economic field). We try a parallelism of these two paths: in Spinoza's *Ethics* the path of the liberation of the affect from passions, and in our world the path of liberation of what is unalienable, and yet abused, the poor's potentia, from the encroachment of power upon it, to investigate where one path can serve the other.

In Spinoza's system of knowledge, we pass from imagination to knowing the good or sad encounters (common notions) to choosing, organising the joyful encounters and avoiding the sad ones (reason). In the hypothesis of an economy of joy, an economy whose political aim is to collectively organise the means for the full development of each singular life – which we are here just hinting at – the path runs from the commodity as abstract thing and known only confusedly (phantasmagoria), to its knowledge. That is, given A and B as commodities, we know that A is determined by its relation with B; we thus know the value of A, that is its being related to B. That the value of A is defined by its being related to B recalls what we previously saw of the dynamics of *dunamis*. {If we can read this relation defining value as *dunamis* – and its later transformations – we can understand the productive force at the core of each singularity: what produces value is the relation, it is the definition through an other. Moreover, when we understand that *causa sui* is the *potentia* – that is, when we move from Aristotle's concept of *dunamis* to the Spinozan concept of *potentia* – we further understand how this productive force cannot be alienated from the individual – it is not a property but a nature. The means of its

full deployment is given by its relational capacity. It is here that capital operates an expropriation: an external power – external from that nature – inserts
itself in the relation of value, in the production of this relational capacity which
is value, and extracts from that relation of production its productive nature, its
dunamis, up to extracting this very productive force from the body/mind of the
single individual. The litmus test for checking this expropriation is the principle of reciprocity, where the production of value defined by the relation of
production increases both terms of the relation.} This is the basic knowledge
of the relation of production, indicated by the commodity as common notion.
Common notions are common, and I would add mutual, knowledge of the relation. The third stage, the equivalent of choosing the joyful encounter, means
to make the commodity a poetic object – to find, that is, that relation of production which incentivises its proper *dunamis*, its proper productive capacity,
whose product and property is not value as equality, as equivalence, but virtue
as the power of procuring for oneself one's own good.

This passage commodity – abstract thing → commodity known as relative
being (that is, being in a relation of production; the production as a being in
relation) → commodity whose property is virtue (power of procuring oneself
one's own good), can occur only by understanding the role of *dunamis* – of
this *dunamis* property, force, expression of the substance which can be at once
value and virtue but which, certainly on the plane of knowledge, on the plane
individuated by itself, is freedom of creation.

Poverty is *potentia* because it is constituted by that relation of production of
which the *dunamis* is the first *in nuce* expression. Poverty is the place where the
virtuality of the *dunamis* – at once its power of being, virtue of achieving what
is good for oneself, and property of being exchanged, of being equal to, of making things commensurable in as much as it is itself the constituent element of
the relation – is caught.

It is the place where freedom is necessary to become productive capacity. It
is the place where the relation of production (commodity at its second stage
of knowledge) should be clear and distinct, knowable and known; where the
productive capacity of each one should be expressed and recognised in this
expression, let be and implemented; to which the concept of the self should be
given back, its being relation, bridge, cipher of composition, productive force.

Poverty is free from possession because it knows that the being relative is
common. It knows that the common cannot be appropriated and it is not privation, but it is an explosive expression of itself.[58]

---

58   See Souilhé 1919, p. 74 and p. 109.

The property designated by *dunamis* is, in this case, an expression of mutual belonging, not of individual appropriation; it is an increase of potentia, not its suppression.[59]

3.5.1   *The Four Songs of Poverty: The Ancient Concept; Politics of Poverty; potentia of Poverty, Ultimate Poverty*[60]

Let us briefly go through the ancient Western concept of poverty, to see how it is delineated according to these two lines, value and virtue.

3.5.2   *Ancient Poverty*

It was between the tenth and eighth centuries BCE that poverty as a concept and as a social condition started to be produced within the Western world. Majid Rahnema[61] dates the birth of the concept of poverty to the establishment of monarchy (in Israel, in the tenth century BCE) and the advent of merchant civilisation (Greece, seventh-eighth century BCE). This formulated two main opposed conditions: on the one hand, destruction of the ties of social solidarity, and on the other, a choice in favour of virtue.

In this same period, we have the birth of coinage. Money, already present in Oriental societies since the thirteenth century BCE, originated as a concept and expression of the common medium of exchange with the Greek coins of the seventh century BCE. In Greece at this time, naturalistic philosophy took on the features of abstract thought. This passage sanctioned the birth of Western metaphysics.

The production of the concept of poverty can thus be read in relation to money and to abstract thought. In relation to money, poverty is the expression of a relational lack: it is the rupture in the equivalence established by the economy of exchange, the expression of the breaking of the social tie. It is the improper element inside the commensurability, inside the 'common' established by value. In relation to abstract thought, poverty is the material expression of the operation of abstraction produced by the first philosophers of metaphysics.[62]

---

59   See Souilhé 1919, p. 89.
60   I addressed these aspects in the entries 'Ancient Thought', 'Poverty politics'; 'Empowerment of the poor', 'Ultimate poverty' in Odekon 2006. What you find here is a re-elaboration of those themes.
61   Rahnema 2003.
62   Here, I mean the definition of a concept of virtue which finds its roots in the notion of '*dunamis*'. The *dunamis* in its pre-Aristotelian meaning means at once value and virtue, but, in both cases, it is a material expression of the substance. Further down, we will see

Poverty thus expresses at once a relational lack and the material side of knowledge.[63] The concept of poverty would undergo various different trans-formations[64] but would remain defined mainly in terms of these two para-digms:[65] poverty as an expression of the breaking of the social bond (value) and poverty as a material expression of an abstraction (virtue).

A concrete expression of the breaking of the social bond is the slave,[66] indicating the breakdown of the collectivity, the fracture between single and collective labour, between manual and intellectual labour. This fracture can also be read in light of the Aristotelian relation *dunamis-energeia*, potency-actualisation: the slave is he whose own potency is taken away, he whose *duna-mis* is possessed by someone else. The virtue of the slave, his capacity of produ-cing his own life, as well as his reason, belongs to someone else (Aristotle, *Pol.* 1260 a 33–b5). Being an article of property, his value is that of being an instru-ment for action, separable from his owner.

From the point of view of the praxis of the management of the collectivity, the figure of the slave is a clear example of the substitution of virtue for value.

A second instance of the substitution of virtue for value is the birth of money. By creating a common measure coinage makes possible an equivalence between things of a different nature, which allows for their exchange. In order to be exchanged, or set in a relation of equivalence, things have to be meas-ured according to a defined uniforming principle, a unit. For Aristotle this unit is the need [*chreia*]. The reduction of the different characters of things to a unit indicates the formation of that common on which society is based. This 'com-

---

how poverty is defined by the *dunamis*. In this sense we can say that, in a knowing system, vis-à-vis the abstract thought of metaphysics, poverty is its material expression.

63   I refer the reader to my article 'Privilegium paupertatis': Pascucci 2003b.

64   From the notion of 'love of the poor', in the late Roman Empire, and of the *isotés* in Paul, to the meaning that it takes on in the Middle Ages, before the conceptualisation of capital and value, in the different 'uses of poverty' (*usus pauper*) and in the answers given to them by figures such as Saint Francis and Saint Claire (*privilegium paupertatis*).

65   Thus, an aspect of lack of relation, in respect to the figure of value; and an aspect which expresses a choice, the search and the pursuit of virtue. This latter aspect would be developed in the deliberate choice of poverty (from Christ to the choices of medi-eval poverty, to the contemporary forms of voluntary poverty). The former aspect would instead develop in the history of thought, in parallel with the concept of value (in the Middle Ages: value and capital; in the sixteenth century the English Poor Laws; in nine-teenth-century capital and the second Poor Laws; today, immaterial labour) and will con-tribute to the continuous reinvention of the poor.

66   I take as an example the status of the slave, which clearly expresses the fracture that is established at the level of collectivity and that it is reflected in the separation of manual and intellectual labour, in a second moment of abstract and material knowledge (Alfred Sohn-Rethel).

mon' [*koinonia*] is created through an operation of abstraction which does not bear the traces of its formation, of the different natures of which it is composed.

Thus the unit through which things are made equivalent is the need (*chreia*); but the common among things, created by the relation of equivalence, occurs only thanks to an operation of abstraction and the levelling out of differences, the common measure of which is money (*nomisma*). *Nomisma*, money, replaces, by convention, *chreia*, the need. The passage from need to the equation of equivalence results in a chiasmus – that same aforementioned movement which Marx observes in the deviation in the falls of the atoms, constituting the first intuition of the mechanism of Capital, which allows for a flow between material and immaterial. But the common of the need is a material status. It is through an operation of abstraction that a new common measure, money, is arrived at, as a unit.

Aristotle makes clear that money is so called (*nomisma*) because its existence does not depend on its nature but on the fact that it has been established as 'value' (*nomos*), as index of division which allows for the proportional relation. It is in our power to change it and put it out of use. Value is established to have something separable (*nomos, geltend*) from the thing itself (the instrument from his master, for example). This allows for a relation of proportion and, later, for exchange. It is an operation that separates the attribute of a thing from the thing itself. Its practical nature lies exactly in the fact that it covers the fracture operated on the differences equating them to a universal medium.

In the case of money, this fracture is the separation of use and exchange, which reflects the fracture between the single and the whole, between single and collective labour. Ultimately, it is the fracture between the capacity of one's own definition and the definition operated by someone, of the slave. While virtue is a medium of finding accord among differences, a composition of the single with the whole, the integration of manual labour and intellectual labour, of thought into praxis, value is the expression of the fragmentation of being: the sign of property, of slavery, and of monarchy. It is the sign of political poverty.

3.5.3   *Political Poverty*

Every time that the poor is defined through lack, the impotence of poverty is established.

A different political approach to poverty addresses the fact that the real lack is not the relational lack, but rather the continuous production of its subtraction. We saw that one of capital's features is that it creates a-conceptual relations. The lack of relation with which poverty is defined indicates the theft of the possibility of the concept, the theft of one's own *dunamis*/potentia, of its own *autarchia*,[67] of those collective ways of being and of production which re-establish for each his/her own capacity of persevering in life.

The plane of the concept and of its separation from the pursuit of happiness – the real aim of politics – is the only instrument that could dismantle these systems for the reproduction of misery. Misery takes over when poverty is impotent.

Poverty is the index of the breaking off of the social composition and of the substitution of material relations of production with abstract a-conceptual relations. It is thus at the level of the material-immaterial relation that we should reconstruct a different mode of production.

In order to be able to transform value into virtue; in order to be able to dismantle the concept of money in the knowledge of a-conceptual relations that money itself creates and reproduces, we have to establish a new potentia-poverty relation, in light of an economy of joy.[68] This relation hinges on the same position of productive force of the single individual that poverty as condition and potentia as concept, share: deprived of the superstructure, of an external power which dominates them, they are the expression of the being's productive force, of the human condition of the *causa sui*. One of the first instruments of an economy of joy is the relation between knowledge and poverty.

3.5.4   *Potentia of Poverty*

To conceive of a potentia of poverty means mainly to establish, or create, that plane of knowledge where poverty can be read as a potentia without concept, a potentia from which has been taken away the concept of itself, the force of producing itself in life. We could define at least three moments for the creation of this plane: to overthrow value in virtue; to comprehend the concept of money as knowledge of the a-conceptual relations that it creates; to establish a new relation poverty-potentia.

To overthrow value in virtue means to create a concept of the common as actualisation of each one's practical potentia, where the just relation single-collectivity expresses its immanent praxis, by acknowledging each individual's composition in a multitude, and increases that practical potentia of each one

---

67   By autarchy we mean, from Aristotle, the self-government that brings oneself the good.

68   By economy of joy, we mean that economy which, according to Marx, does not renounce pleasure, but rather, based on *potentia*, produces sense. See Marx, MEGA, II. 1.2, 589. A more detailed analysis can be found in Chapter Four of my PhD thesis 'Capital and the imaginary' (Pascucci 2003a), which is about immaterial labour. Here we find a hint, and a re-elaboration in another direction, of the themes developed therein.

which is his nature: the common, the *koinonia*, is the deepest feature of human nature: its differential and its time of life. The space of construction of this differential as time of life is the virtue.[69]

If we look at these two extremes, value and virtue, from the viewpoint of time, we see that the time of value is an anticipation which homogenises differences and proceeds with a principle of self-combustion. The time of virtue is, conversely, the development of a becoming.

The first, in Marxian terms, is based on the time of labour, on the process of the transformation of living labour into dead labour; the second is its opposite, the attempt of making production, and its use, open to each time of life. The time of virtue is the struggle for the transformation of dead labour in living labour through the creative force of common being and the differential proper to each man.

If we recognise, within the relations that capital establishes, a-conceptual relations – stripped of the capacity of becoming and of the accord with the whole; relations where every trace of composition is silenced, every possibility of conceiving oneself through the other de-possessed, every effort of being cause of oneself suppressed – then we have a material knowledge of money, that knowledge which has been released from the process of abstraction. These are relations whose common productive side is violated in an abstract anticipation.

Once we have acknowledged these aspects, we see that to create a new relation between potentia and poverty is to get to the heart of the single-collectivity relationship, which is also the poverty-wealth relationship. Where do they meet?

Let us outline[70] the single-collectivity, poverty-wealth, poverty-potentia relations in a single schema:

---

69   Virtue is defined, according to pre-Socratic philosophy, as the knowledge of oneself with the aim of achieving happiness. In Socrates, virtue is a force, inseparable from the good, which brings the self-actualisation of the individual subject. Virtue produces material and spiritual richness. But it can also overthrow one into the other (true richness is happiness; see Rahnema in the passages on Xenophon, *Oeconomicus*). Later, in Aristotle, the virtuous activity is the medium through which the individuals find true happiness (*Rethoric*, I, 9, 1366 b 34 fll.). According to Aristotle, virtue is the source of beauty and of pleasure, of knowledge and practical realisation of desire (*Nicomachean Ethics*, vii, xiv, 1153b, 1–24). The virtuous activity is connected to autarchy, to the principle of self-sufficiency. Individuals acquire autarchy, independence and freedom only when they find all that is necessary to their happiness in themselves.

70   I refer the reader to Pascucci 2003a, where the Marxian distinction between productive and unproductive labour is analysed, along with their relation to material and immaterial labour.

Poverty [freedom] – virtual	*Wealth* – actualization of the anticipation
dunamis – universal hidden figure	*energeia* – singular hidden figure
(under singularity); unproductive labour	(under universality); productive labour

Productive labour is that labour which 'produces value', 'value of exchange' as 'the content of itself'.[71] This content/value has its realisation in its same disappearance:[72] it is a perpetual actualisation of the extremes, the centre of which should remain substantially empty. It is material emptying, a feature which makes it (and of money, as its general figure) the perpetual actualisation of extremes whose centre needs to remain *substantially* empty.[73] This is the actualisation of the anticipation which Capital operates: its content is nothing other than itself; it is a 'permanent metamorphosis of the substance',[74] indifferent to the isolated particularity, whose identity and form of universality are expressed by the exchange value.

Unproductive labour, instead, is a labour which produces 'sense', something which escapes its crystallisation in value. Its virtuality lies in the fact that it is labour whose content is defined by, and consists in, something else. Whereas productive labour is measured according to the time of labour, unproductive labour is measured by free time, by the time of life. But how can poverty correspond to the singularity and virtuality (whose universal figure is hidden) whereas richness corresponds to the universality and actuality (whose singular figure remains hidden)? And where is it that poverty and richness meet productive and unproductive labour?

3.5.5 *The Singular Virtuality of the Free Worker*
There is a special universality of which Marx speaks that we must today take into account. This is the universality of the singular, that 'comprehension of nature, the knowledge as practical power, which is man's real body'.[75] It is

---

71   Marx 2006, p. 186. See, moreover the *Theories of Surplus Value* on productive and unproductive labour (*'Unterscheidung von produktiver und unproduktiver Arbeit'*) (Marx 1977, pp. 438–553) and *Heft XXI* (Marx 1982, pp. 2159–84).

72   *'im beiden also ist seine Realisation eine verschwindende'*, Marx 2006, p. 184.

73   See Hans Blumenberg reading Simmel, '"Geld oder Leben". Eine metaphorologische Studie zum Konsistenz der Philosophie Georg Simmels', in Boehringer and Gruender (eds.) 1976, pp. 121–34.

74   *'eine beständige Metamorphose dieser Substanz'*, Marx 2006, p. 185.

75   Marx 2006, p. 440.

here that poverty meets its potentia: in the knowing relation that nature is a practical *potentia*, is man's real body and his universality in a state of virtuality.

Let us take as our example the free worker of the *Grundrisse*: he is a force of living labour, and as such, he is exposed to the movements of life, to the cadences proper to life. *Qua* worker he can live only inasmuch as he exchanges his labour force for that part of Capital which constitutes the 'capital' of labour. Marx defines the concept of the free worker as implying his virtual poverty: he is 'virtually poor' because for him the exchange is linked to *casual circumstances* and *does not have a relation to his organic existence.*

But what the free worker knows as 'causal circumstances' is in reality the concept, taken away from him, of the real single-collectivity relation; what he thinks of as a 'lack of relation with his organic existence' is the stolen possibility of the comprehension of his nature as practical potentia.

The universal singular is already contained, as a 'hidden figure', in the free worker as his poverty and virtuality.

That wealth based on the time of labour tries to actualise this virtuality only through its own means; it tries to make the universal singularity of the worker his own property, to make him as virtual as possible, separated from the whole and from its actualisation.

To think of poverty as potentia means to give freedom to virtuality – it is on this plane that capital can be confronted. It is here indicated, at the same time, that the worker's bond to the 'causal circumstances' is the expression of his crystallised virtuality; that the 'lack of relation to his organic existence' is his state of misery. He is poor in as much as he is removed from life; his virtuality indicates his depending on chance. In him the singular universality vacillates, while nature grows dim and the body dissolves by losing the knowledge of his potentia as common mode.

3.5.6   *Production of Sense, Liberation of Joy*

In order for the poverty-potentia to activate its virtuality as a state of freedom, it is necessary to make space for some productive processes based on a new economy of joy. The production of sense remains their main instrument.

'Unproductive labour'[76] can be an example, here: the time of life bursts out immediately as a disproportion; as a resistance to crystallisation in value; as sense against the a-conceptual relations established by capital. Unproductive

---

76   See Pascucci 2003a.

labour is the place of the cumulative time of life and of the 'free worker, virtually poor'. It is in unproductive labour that the social time released from the process of capital takes shelter, hides and produces resistance.

The real wealth is the full productive potentia of all individuals, the singular universality; for it the measure is not the time of labour but the time of life, the Marxian 'available time'.[77] It is this capacity of persevering in one's own life, at the centre of most of unproductive labour, that connects the production of the universal singularity, of the knowledge as practical potentia to that difficult space of the free worker, virtually poor.

The freedom of the worker is his strength in confronting capital with its own tools (for example, the multitude against the false universality). His virtual poverty is the confused knowledge of the practical potentia of his nature. Given the fact that Capital creates a-conceptual relations, thus depriving human nature of its concept, the free worker lacks the knowledge of his practical potentia and therefore of his universal singularity as common mode. The fact that the exchange of his labour-power is, for him, connected to causal circumstances, expresses the virtuality of this position of his – the non-actualized freedom of the concept of the self. The virtuality of the state of freedom can become 'potentia' once the worker knows his nature as practical potentia in composition with the whole.

3.5.7   Ultimate Poverty

Poverty is capital's main mistake. Let us consider this in terms of two of Capital's own properties: the *material-immaterial chiasmus* and the relation with knowledge, that is, production and abstraction. When we fail to grasp the nexus that holds them together (poverty and the property of Capital), poverty becomes ultimate poverty, misery.

The material-immaterial chiasmus. The first point that we should consider is how from a material status, need, the common of society came to be based on money, an abstraction. The ultimate mistake of capital is double: it functions through an anticipation – of the actuality of the thing over its potentiality – and lets this anticipated production, inasmuch as its core is abstract, remain unknowable.

In the market, the passage from need to money individuates a chiasmus, the material-abstract productive relation. This chiasmus is to be found again in the core mechanism of capital. In his doctoral dissertation, we saw that Marx noticed how the atom could be the cause of itself once it abstracts from its rel-

---

ative mode of being and when it relates to itself as if it were something else. But this 'relating to oneself' as if to someone else, is material (ibid.).

We thus have a passage, with the features of the chiasmus, from abstraction to material. This owes to the atom's deviation from its relative mode of being:

Material Definition   Definition of individual autonomy

Differentiation from relative mode of   Abstraction
being

We thus arrive at a material definition acquired through abstraction, a defin-ition of individual autonomy acquired through the deviation, the differenti-ation from the relative mode of being as pure form. The main agent of this differentiation, of the production of a material definition through an abstrac-tion, is time.

Time is thus the engine of the passage from material to immaterial, exactly by its being the production of a differential of being. In the deviation of the atom, the thinkable becomes sensible and the sensible becomes thinkable. The crossing is time as differential of being, of production of matter. It is here that capital's main mistake, the one which produces poverty, occurs.

A material definition (*sensible*) *is acquired through abstraction* (*thinkable*): time as definition of individual autonomy (*cause of itself*), acquired through a deviation (definition through other; relating to myself as another), *produces a differentiation* from the relative mode of being of the atom; it produces a *plus of nature, plus of being*, which does not bear the traces of virtuality, of the capacity of the sensible matter of being conceived through an other.[78]

This intuition by the young Marx would constitute the core of his later ana-lysis of the mechanism of Capital: an actualisation (a sensible reality; a putting into *energeia*) of a virtuality (a thought reality, a *dunamis*, capacity of the mat-ter of being conceived through other) which produces the continuous abuse of this actuality, in order to separate it from its virtuality.

---

78   For example: where A is the sensible and B the thinkable. $A + B = C$, where C is production
      and the sum indicates the time of becoming. In the process that we are analysing, the anti-
      cipation of capital, we have B (thinkable) + A (sensible) = Ci (production of surplus). B is
      in reality Bi, that is = $B + t$ where t is the anticipated time. The passage from the immaterial
      to the material is made of anticipated time; the thinkable which anticipates the sensible,
      $Bi = B + t$, produces Ci, the surplus. A, the sensible material from which one anticipates by
      doing abstraction, remains the same, undifferentiated. The problem rises here inasmuch
      as we use the *dunamis* of A, its expressive and productive capacity of becoming, to change
      B and C but not A itself.

3.5.8   *Poverty and the Struggle with apriori-ness*

The abuse of the actuality over virtuality as operated by capital is reflected in all the a priori forms of knowledge where a separation of manual from intellectual labour is to be registered.

If we follow Alfred Sohn-Rethel's reading,[79] the first separation of manual from intellectual labour is marked by the birth of the slave. This in turn is connected to the birth of money, to the coinage. This separation is reflected in a priori forms of knowledge, to which the first metaphysics gave expression (eighth-to-sixth century BCE, Greece). The origin of this separation and the establishment of *a priori forms* go together: the birth of money as a general *equivalent form* (680 BC) also marks the birth of *abstract thought*.

This separation – of manual from intellectual labour; of the mind from the body, of abstraction from materiality – defines the space of an appropriation. The exploitation, the act which follows the separation, carries on the *appropriation* of one of the two terms of the relation (the exploited) by the other (the exploiter). This is the birth of the concept of property. The apriori-ness of knowledge is the mark of the inner feature of this exploitation, the abstraction. The abstraction expresses the separation and gives space to the appropriation.

The slave, a concrete expression of the birth of money and a figure of the separation of intellectual from manual labour, is also the figure of the loss, on the part of labour, of its social character. *The original social character of labour becomes an individual separated 'identity'; it becomes a commodity which can be appropriated by others: the expropriation of collective labour occurs through someone's appropriation of someone's else capacity of producing being.*

The appropriation of man's capacity of producing new being, the appropriation of the definition of his life, coincides with the breaking of collective labour into individual labours. The system of abstraction allows for the separation – of intellectual from material labour; of the single from the collectivity; of the body from the mind – to remain a social separation.

At the point of insurgence of the divisions, the *exploitation expresses the decomposition of modes of the collectivity.* Insofar as it means ultimate poverty, it is perhaps the fiercest decomposition of the collective mode that we are.

If capital's poverty is the decomposition of this collective mode – the creation of new slaves; the perpetual production of an abstract knowledge incapable of expressing the traces it is made of – *our poverty is* instead *potentia, a composition of the modes of the collective. It is the appropriation, by each, of his*

---

79   See mainly Sohn-Rethel 1978, but also Sohn-Rethel 1990 and the fundamental 'Zur kritischen Liquidierung des Apriorismus' (1937) in Sohn-Rethel 1971.

or her forms of becoming; it is the effort striving to produce a material knowledge made of the compositions of bodies, minds and times of life.

From the history of the pre-Aristotelian concept of *dunamis*, clearly shines through its aspect of being at once economic and cognitive. It is a peculiar property of the *dunamis*, of the becoming nature of things, to be at once the nucleus of value (to be equivalent) and of virtue (productive capacity of one's own being).

If only the aspect of value is in force, the equivalence hides its terms and abstracts from their virtue, from their productive capacities – it is here that the concept, the bridge between the two elements, is taken away. If instead we let the productive capacity be the common element of things in relation, if we let the *dunamis* be the expression of the property of the elements, of their productive capacities – which become and cannot be anticipated – then that bridge, the relation between elements, the *dunamis* of each one, becomes potentia as common mode.

We can say that potentia and poverty meet in the presence of the concept as *dunamis*, in the productive capacity of creating further being and of procuring for oneself the good as common mode.

In the knowledge of being conceived through an other, in restoring to poverty the concept of the self as *dunamis* – as being in an other, as productive capacity and expression of the common mode – there is restored to poverty the potentia, that collective autarchy, which is the constitutive element of happiness.

3.6   The Virtuality of Our Time

Deleuze's reading of the *clinamen* in Lucretius and the last concept of virtuality elaborated in *Actuel et Virtuel*[80] can help us in understanding the central function of time for the concept of virtuality here outlined. Deleuze speaks of the theory of the *clinamen* in the Appendix to *Logic of sense*.[81] His analysis of the time should be understood in the more general analysis of the philosophy of nature in Lucretius, but here we can briefly delimit ourselves to his analysis of time. He writes that in order to understand the theory of the *clinamen* and of the simulacra we have to understand that they are based on the theory of time in Epicurus.

---

80   Deleuze 1995.
81   Deleuze 1990.

We have to hold on to two coordinates in order to comprehend the theory of time. These are Analogy (between the atom and the senses' matter) and Gradation, the passage from the 'thinkable' to the 'sensible' and from the 'sensible' to the 'thinkable'. The abstract possibility of the passage from the chance of being to the chance of thinking that we saw in the Marxian analysis, can be found again here.

Analogy. The atom, the small particle invisible to the eyes, can be thought in its smallness. We could say that the atom is made by a 'thinkable minimum'. The object of the senses (the simulacrum) is not for itself 'sensible' if not in its image (sum of the simulacra): we have a 'sensible' minimum for the object of the senses.

The analogy is here: the atom is in relation to thought that which the sensible object is in relation to the senses (the thinkable minimum and the sensible minimum).

Gradation. Through the declination, the *clinamen*, it becomes possible to proceed from the thinkability to the sensibility and from the sensibility to the thinkability.

If we consider the definition of the atoms and of the simulacra under the aspect of time, we arrive at the result that the regular movement of the atoms (the time of this movement) expresses the minimum duration possible in which the atom moves in one same direction, before it meets with another atom.

The 'thinkable minimum' is, as time, the minimum duration possible for its regular movement. This minimum, says Deleuze, is a minimum of time, a minimum of matter, which refers to the 'grasp of thought' ("the atom is fast as thought").

The same thing happens with images, as an analogy: time, in which we apprehend an image, is the minimum of sensible time.

Thus the analogy presupposes a minimum of thinkable and a minimum of sensible. This minimum is a minimum of thinkable time (atom) and a minimum of sensible time (object of senses, images). But, close to these minima, we have a time smaller than the minimum time (thinkable and sensible). Here is introduced the theory of the *clinamen* and of the simulacra.

The *clinamen* occurs in a minimum time in respect to the minimum of thinkable time, the same happens with the emission of the simulacra, which occurs in a time smaller than the minimum of the sensible time.

We have thus a minimum of the sensible time, a minimum of the thinkable time and two times, which are smaller than the minimum thinkable and the minimum sensible. In reading the analogy together with the concept of time, there surfaces as well the other theory which Deleuze calls a theory of 'gradation'. We have four elements: – a time smaller than the minimum of thinkable time (*incertus tempore* of the *clinamen*), – a minimum of the continuous thinkable time (the speed of the atom in the same direction), – a time smaller than the minimum of the sensible time (a point in time, *punctum temporis*, which is occupied by the simulacra), – a minimum of continuous, sensible time (the image, which allows for the apprehension of the object).

We have, writes Deleuze, the possibility of two illusions: the illusion of the body and the illusion of the soul. The illusion of the body is the illusion of the infinite capacity of feeling pleasure. The illusion of the soul is the illusion of an infinite duration of the same soul. It is as if these illusions were born from a break – a break of time and of matter, the 'differential' of thought and matter, which is at the centre of the philosophy of Lucretius and which Deleuze calls Naturalism.

This break is the Interim, which is given between the minimum of perception and of thought and that which escapes this minimum. Once this minimum is accepted – thinkable and sensible, and a fragment smaller than the minimum – the thought becomes sensible and the sensible becomes thought.

This occurs because the inseparable atom, existing only in thought, gives itself as sensible only in the *clinamen*, in the possibility, which is given to thought, of moving freely and necessarily. This is the production of difference, the act of nature – that which Deleuze describes when he talks of Lucretius' naturalism as affirmation of the infinite truth. 'The infinite is the absolute intelligible determination (perfection) of a sum, which does not compose its elements in a whole' and 'the finite itself is the absolute sensible determination of all that is composed'.[82]

The pure affirmation (positivity) of the finite is the object of the senses; the affirmation (positivity) of the infinite truth is the object of thought. There is no contradiction between these two points of view, which are related. It is exactly in the relation of thought, of the infinite matter, as infinite sum whose elements are not put together, with the sentiment, the feeling of the finite composites, that do not dissolve one into the other, that the multiplicity as difference is affirmed. It is through thinking the infinite and feeling the finite that multiplicity is established as 'differential' and as object of happiness: the infinite can, in the finite, be thought, felt, comprehended and lived.

This movement, the rhythm of this movement which is life, is what I call, together with Deleuze, virtuality.

82　　Ibid., p. 245.

3.6.1 Virtual Time

But what is virtuality? In *Actual and Virtual* (1995) Deleuze writes: 'They are called virtual in so far as their emission and absorption, creation and destruction, *occur in a period of time shorter than the shortest continuous period imaginable*';[83] it is this very brevity that 'keeps them subject to a principle of uncertainty or indetermination'.[84]

> But the virtual's ephemerality appears in a smaller space of time than that which marks the minimum movement in a single direction. This is why the virtual is 'ephemeral', but the virtual also preserves the past, since that ephemerality is continually making minute adjustments[85] in response to changes of direction. The period of time which is smaller than the smallest period of continuous time imaginable in one direction is also the longest time, longer than the longest unit of continuous time imaginable in all directions.[86]

The virtuality is the 'continuation' of the *clinamen*. The virtuality is the crossroad of the materiality-abstraction chiasmus. This means: the relation virtuality-actualisation is the place where materiality and abstraction can primarily be exchanged. First, we have to say that it is precisely this relation which defines the plane of immanence. That is: the difference between '*virtuel*' [virtual] and '*possible*' [possible] – as we know from Deleuze's reading of Bergson[87] – is that the 'virtual', in order to actualise itself, should create its own directions and coordinates of reality. It is a problem of creation, and the virtual can produce its actualisation only though creating. Deleuze explains further how this relation between virtual and actual is always a 'circuit':

---

83   The original French says 'thinkable': '*Ils sont dits virtuels en tant que leur émission et absorption, leur création et destruction se font en un temps plus petit que le minimum de temps continu pensable, et que cette brièveté les maintient des lors sous un principe d'incertitude ou d'indétermination*' (Deleuze 1995). My underlining.

84   Deleuze 1995, p. 148.

85   I would prefer to translate one passage differently: 'because this ephemerality does not cease to continue in the 'smaller' time which follows'. '*Mais le virtuel apparaît de son côté dans un temps plus petit que celui qui mesure le minimum de mouvement dans une direction unique. Ce pourquoi le virtuel est « éphémère ». Mais c'est dans le virtuel aussi que le passé se conserve, puisque cet éphémère ne cesse de continuer dans le "plus petit" suivant, qui renvoie à un changement de direction. Le temps plus petit que le minimum de temps continu pensable en une direction est aussi le plus long temps, plus long que le maximum de temps continu pensable dans toutes les directions*' (ibid.)

86   Deleuze 1995, p. 151.

87   Deleuze 1991.

sometimes the actual refers to the virtual as to other things in the vast circuits where the virtual is actualized; sometimes the actual refers to the virtual as its own virtual, in the smallest circuits where the virtual crystallizes
with the actual. The plane of immanence contains both actualization as
the relationship of the virtual with other terms, and even the actual as a
term with which the virtual is exchanged. ... the relationship of the actual
and the virtual forms an acting individuation or a highly specific and
remarkable singularization which needs to be determined case by case.[88]

And:

Philosophy is the theory of multiplicities, each of which is composed
of actual and virtual elements. Purely actual objects do not exist. Every
actual surrounds itself with a cloud of virtual images (...) These virtuals vary in kind as well as in their degree of proximity from the actual
particles by which they are both emitted and absorbed[89]

and what we saw earlier:

They are called virtual in so far as their emission and absorption, creation
and destruction, occur in a period of time shorter than the shortest continuous period imaginable; it is this very brevity that keeps them subject
to a principle of uncertainty or indetermination.[90]

The virtual is never independent of the singularities which cut it up and
divide it out on the plane of immanence. As Leibniz has shown, force is
as much a virtual in the process of being actualized as the space through
which it travels. The plane is therefore divided into a multiplicity of planes
according to the cuts in the continuum, and to the divisions of force which
mark the actualization of the virtuals. But all the planes merge into one
following the path which leads to the actual. The plane of immanence
includes both the virtual and its actualization simultaneously, without
there being any assignable limit between the two. The actual is the com-
plement or the product, the object of actualization, which has nothing

---

88   Deleuze 1995, p. 152. 'le rapport de l'actuel et du virtuel forme une individuation en acte ou
      une singularisation par points remarquables à déterminer dans chaque cas' (Ibid., p. 185):
      the relationship of actual and virtual forms an individuation in act.
89   Ibid., p. 148.
90   Ibid.

but the virtual as its subject. Actualization belongs to the virtual. The actualization of the virtual is singularity whereas the actual itself is individuality constituted. The actual falls from the plane like a fruit, whilst the actualization relates it back to the plane as if to that which turns the object back into a subject.[91]

We have the 'virtual', which is the subject of actualisation, and the 'actual' as fruit, product and object of this actualisation. The actualisation of the virtual is a singularity; the actual is a constituted individuality. The violation of the actualisation enters into play when the virtual singularity is masked by individuality; an individuality constituted as its own cosmos. But this cosmos, that is the ensemble of relations of which the individuality is composed, is devoid of the concept, because from this virtual singularity has been taken away the concept of its own potentia.

Its potentia is, in this sense, its cosmos, the ensemble, the composition of its relations. We have thus two directions of the relation virtuality-actualisation, which should be correctly defined: the direction of the relation singular-cosmos (the singular plurality) and the presence or absence of the concept, as *ratio* of the constitutive composition of a body. The first direction depends on the second.

In order to be able to give back to the virtual singularity the concept of one's own potentia, in order to be able to liberate the actualisation of the virtual, let us think of the relation virtuality-actualisation according to the two directions individuated above, the composition of a singular plurality and the presence or absence of the concept as composing *ratio* of the body.

3.7   Potentia and Dismeasure

Against the anticipation
is constituted the expression of the relation.
Function as mode? In its relation to the substance, it seems to be the
     same.
Poverty needs a Plusconcept.

In two texts, 'The Constitution of Time' (1980; 1987) and 'kairos, alma venus, multitudo' (2000), which should be read together, Negri shows us the two con-

---

91   Ibid., pp. 149–50.

temporary coordinates for the actualisation of the virtuality of history.[92] The first is Time, time in its constitutive metamorphosis, from the time of materialist atomism, Epicurus, until the time of dialectical materialism, Marx ('The Constitution of Time').

This time is today more and more indicated as the 'time of life', together with an affirmative, creative, revolutionary time of labour, and against a precise time of violated labour. Poverty is the *place* of the knowledge of the violation and of the consequent, necessary, revolutionary practice. But in these texts, more is said: poverty is not a lack, it is not a status of need. It is a potentia, which can be found in the time of life and has its force exactly in its place in the cosmos ('kairos, alma venus, multitudo').

In 'The Constitution of Time' there is a passage key for our purposes

At the level at which the institutional development of the capitalistic system invests the whole of life, time is not the measure of life, but is life itself. Marx grasps the passage from time reduced to a convention derived from space, to medium [*medietà*], to measure of exploitation, up to its pure and simple general abstraction, and therefore to its total, mystified realization in the world of life in the phase of real subsumption. Therefore, Marx's tautology of time, life and production at the level of real subsumption is both the consummation of the materialist tradition (and the overcoming of its substantial deficiencies) as well as the eruption of a new horizon of reflection on time. In Marx, in the theory of capitalist development up to real subsumption, **the traditional relationship of time to space, is definitively overturned**. Space is temporalized, it becomes dynamic: it is a condition of the constitutive realization of time. With Marx, time becomes the exclusive material of the construction of life ... The originality of the **Marxian paradigm** consists in the fact that here **time is constitutive; it is time of constitution, time of composition.** So the paradigm is ontological. In Marx, time begins to come into view as the measure of labor ... but, step by step, as the course of the class struggle and the abstraction of labor asserts itself, time increasingly becomes **interior to class composition**, to the point of being the motor of its same existence and of its specific configuration. The process develops so that the maximal temporalization of the labour process (and of the production process) leads to the maximal reappropriation of all the spatial conditions of existence. When work has become mobility, pure and

---

92   Both of these are translated in Negri 2013a.

simple mobility – when, that is, it is time, pure and simple – then it is the possibility and actuality of the constitution of the world.[93]

And:

> The concept of time is immediately **epistemological**, that is, it cleaves to reality. When time is taken as productive force, in the infinite multiplicity of the effects and actions it delineates, in no circumstance will it be representable as mediation. Here mediation has become a **before** with respect to events, with respect to actions, **not an after**, it is not thought, but it is lived as such. Thought approximates reality, thought describes real composition – time is the real composition.[94]

Time is not only the horizon of thought; it is, according to Epicurean theory, its constitution, *that becomes at the same time thinkable and sensible*. If the time of thought is – and we know this from Spinoza – the idea of the body, then we know that time itself is the idea of the body. We know that this is the plane where the first confusion can come about, the first erring of knowledge; here is the first possibility of a mistake, and thus of being deceived by Capital.

We also know that the expression 'time is the idea of the body' simply explains how time is the structure of an encounter, of a relation, the structure of the constitution, or decomposition, of the same body. In other terms, it is the heart of the relation singular-cosmos and of its comprehension.

The two directions – the direction of the singular-cosmos relation, the singular plurality, and the presence or absence of the concept as *ratio* of the composition of the body constitution – are united, meet, as a hinge: the time of the body-thought. And since the first direction depends on the second, since, that is, the relation singular-cosmos depends on the presence or absence of the concept as composition of the body, we see how important it is first to analyse this time as presence or theft of the concept (of the concept of itself, the potentia of becoming many bodies); then to see how the presence or the disempowering of this concept affects the singular-cosmos relation.[95]

---

93   Negri 2013a, pp. 34–5.
94   Ibid., p. 36.
95   To be more precise, we can maybe think of an economic example. Permit me to refer to the concept of 'localizing surplus value' [*plusvalore localizzativo*], present in Umberto Pascucci's laureate thesis in Political Economy (Faculty of Economics and Business, Florence, April 2003). Pascucci writes: 'A "process of real development" is thus generated from the encounter of these two dimensions: local-global, endogenous-exogenous, internal-

The confused knowledge is the plane of imagination, the plane where to the singular is given an aspect of the whole which does not belong to him, which he cannot grasp, which does not belong to his constitution (or rather, which makes of a relation no longer present, his constitution).

An inadequate relation is thus created between the singular and the cosmos, the local and the global. A clear and adequate knowledge is not only that knowledge where the singular-cosmos, local-global relation is comprehended and realised, but also that for which the singular comprehends himself, conceives himself and produces, as cosmos, the local thanks to the global. Here the 'decalage' [gap] between the two dimensions reaches its productive function: we have understood what time is, that time of the first direction (relation singular-cosmos), which looks for the second (presence of the concept) in order to realise itself.

Time as dismeasure, which capital uses a priori, in *advance* (and there it becomes a 'surplus-violation') finds its productive, affirmative role in the singular-cosmos, local-global, vertical-horizontal, internal-external relation.[96]

Thus here from its own 'body' – and thanks to the *chance* of the encounter (local meets global, vertical meets horizontal, internal meets external) – time realises that practical potentia, common mode and collective element of our constitution.

The *concept and capital* thus individuate one of the two dimensions: the productive time is there abused; the relation local-global is 'beheaded', deprived of potentia. It can be reconstructed only in true knowledge.

The *virtual time* is the other dimension: time is the structure of the relation local-global, singular-cosmos. The time of life, of labour which produces itself in life, is the rhythm of the happy development of the thought-body which

external, vertical-horizontal'. Further along in the text he defines this encounter as 'localizing surplus-value', an economic concept that can help us, in a synthetic but effective way, to comprehend the paradigm that I would like to propose here. In the 'localizing surplus-value' the dimension – which I called 'direction' – local-global (singular-cosmos) not only links itself to the features endogenous-exogenous, internal-external, vertical-horizontal, but exposes also what today composes the 'plusvalue': knowledge has become fixed capital, and the meridian and parallel, so to say, of economy, are intertwined in the 'decalage' between local and global (endogenous-exogenous, internal-external, vertical-horizontal) – they cross there and in the exchange they mix. At the moment when we look at this paradigm in a counter-light we see that *the local-global dimension* is coloured throughout by the *commodity-knowledge dimension*. The *local-global* dimension is, in the terms we saw thus far, the *singular-cosmos which is thus coloured throughout by* a knowledge which can be true, adequate (example of the common notions) or inadequate and confused (abused commodity).

96   See previous note.

can be produced only as composition. When it is depotentiated, when, that is, this aggregate is separated from the concept of the self as 'practical potentia', as becoming 'singular-cosmos', it is set as process of decomposition of its elements.

To understand the virtuality of the relations of production, to understand the productive capacity of each being in relation inasmuch as expression of itself, to know there the freedom, necessary for every life, to procure oneself one's own good, these are the elements to make of poverty a revolutionary action, *umwälzende Praxis*, our potentia.

The Production of Subjectivity: Labour, Poverty and the Free Man: Or, the 'potentia' of Labour

The thread in reading this chapter is the following: there is an initial excursus on virtuality and the *causa sui*, in order then to explain what we mean by production of subjectivity [the virtual of subjectivity].

The labour-poverty relation has, at its core, the virtuality of the *causa sui*. The life force of which labour is partly the expression – the expropriation of which comes to be exposed in poverty – here shows its texture. It is the core of subjectivity, our capacity to produce life (ideas, objects, relations, in a word: to create the new).

Immaterial labour, one of today's main forms of labour, also has subjectivity at its core: a part of it is a tool of Capital (informational and cultural content of communication, for example, with Lazzarato), whereas another escapes it (what I call the production of sense). [Labour and poverty].

The theoretical point is how to articulate the self-productive capacity of the subject in a relation of production, and a relation of value-production, different from the one which Capital continues to impose upon us and to cast us into. That is, how to let the virtuality of the cause of ourselves express and produce freely. [Potentia and the intensive].

For the virtuality of the cause of ourselves to be able to express itself and produce freely means to *produce ourselves*, to transform the process of labour into an increasing transformation of our being – that is, to make labour the motor of the affirmative production of our subjectivity and not of its alienation from itself, of the separation from its own life-force.

This is what Marx, and Gorz after him, called the real richness, the production of *wahre Reichtum*.

The aim of our reflection is to understand how the core of subjectivity, the virtuality of the cause of itself, the intensive as excess, can go back, through new relations of production, to the subject and affirm a different path for the production of value and for valorisation [The plus[1] of being].

---

1   The 'plus' of being is different from the 'surplus' of value. The distinction which runs throughout the text is this: there is a surplus (a 'surplus' which can be, and is, stolen) and there is a plus (a 'plus', an augmentation of our being, an increase, an intensity reached through labour) which cannot be reduced to a 'surplus', cannot be stolen. The 'plus' is a more, the plus sign,

4.1   The Virtuality of Subjectivity

In this last chapter, I want to summarise the result of the study after *La Potenza della povertà*, published in *Causa sui*,[2] which explores the mechanism of *causa sui* in relation to the virtual of capital and to subjectivity.

There is a lineage of thought that I have already reconstructed in *Causa sui* which holds together poverty, potentia, the virtual and capital. There, I showed how poverty is the expropriation of life and of its capacities – of its time. I did so by investigating how this expropriation is a discourse not limited to the relations of production but rather extended to the concept of substance as such.

This is a new path for thinking the substance, to counter-pose it to Capital. This is a conceptualisation that can be found already in philosophers like Spinoza, Marx, Deleuze, and Negri in his readings of Spinoza and Marx, by indicating that there exists an adequate way of relations which serves life and posits itself radically against all abuse of the substance. Poverty is the place which most indicates the mistake of money, of value and of capital as a mechanism of production. It expresses the mistaken knowledge and use (abuse) of the substance. In indicating this mistake, poverty is *potentia*; in *Causa sui* I uncovered the ontological and ethical explanation for this.

In order to show the full theoretical trajectory of this mistake, I detected, in the history of thought, a mistaken conceptualisation – and consequent use – of the substance as separable from itself. The concept of the virtual proved to be an important warning light which indicated this separation.

The lineage tracks one of the first[3] conceptualisations of Capital in the scholastic tradition, with the Franciscan economists (Peter John Olivi, *'rationem seminalem lucrosi quam capitale vocamus'*). Together with the first conceptualisation of Capital, there is a debate on poverty, on how to think the substance, and the first insurgencies of the concept of the virtual. Virtual is both the *knowledge of the relation of cause and effect* – or, the relation of cause and effect in knowledge – and the *immaterial aspect of matter* which allows for

---

what is new, that adds to but is intrinsic to its nature, and its nature is intensity, its nature is to increase. As distinct from this, the surplus is additional to what is needed, somehow extrinsic to its nature. We saw that the surplus of surplus value is an anticipated *surplus of being*, which, because it is being anticipated, lacks the potentia (chap. 2). The plus of being gives back to the subject that surplus of being anticipated which was stolen from him (here chap. 2).

2   Allow me to refer to Pascucci 2009 for the analysis of what we here only hint at.

3   Not being an historian of thought, this is just an indication for further theoretical investigation.

self-production and movement. In this conceptualisation, Capital is the *ratio seminale*, a sort of eminent cause ante litteram. Its 'movement' is traced, and caught in knowledge, by the virtual.

Poverty is the space of suspension, in the subject, of the use of his properties as separated from him; that is, the place of a disowning of oneself.

There is thus a conceptualisation of the substance, cast in the 'economic': the substance is measurable, separable from its 'properties', from itself. And the virtual can function as a litmus-test of this separation of the property from the substance.

In the seventeenth century, this separation was traceable in Descartes' eminent cause, to which Spinoza would oppose his concept of immanence, the objective = formal coincidence – indeed, his entire theoretical production. In Spinoza there is no mention of the virtual, but the *Ethics* is full of the actual (and the concept of virtual as somehow an expression of the eminent cause was used and referred to by Cartesian scholars, for example, Adrian Heereboord, whom Spinoza read and opposed in his early writings *Korte Verhandeling* and in the *Cogitata Metaphysica*.)[4]

In the nineteenth century, in Marx, the virtual was the core of the mechanism of production of Capital: the figure of the virtual appears in Volume II of *Capital*,[5] where Marx spoke of the process of the circulation of Capital, and zeroed in on the relation of the material and the immaterial (the principle of production). To understand this properly, it is important to follow a trail indicated by Engels in a footnote, which he again stressed in his notes from D'Alembert, *Traité de dynamique*.[6] Here, he said that Marx takes the notion of potential (potential capital, latent capital, later virtual capital) from potential energy and from the virtual velocities in D'Alembert. In Volume II, it would be more and more the invisible trait of the production of excess, the core of both surplus value and crisis. It is as if the virtual core of Capital in Marx were the direct heir of Olivi's 'ratio seminale,' on the one hand, but also, on the other, the 'adequate' knowledge of the principle of production of excess, of the 'theft' per-

---

4   I believe that we can see, in Spinoza's concept of time and virtue, the notion of the virtual – the *sub specie aeternitatis*, for instance. Allow me to refer to Pascucci 2009, chapter 2.

5   Some references to the virtual in *Capital*, Volume II, *The metamorphoses of capital and their circuits*: in chapter 1 and chap. 2 the function of **productive capital** [1], in chap. 3, the commodity capital; mainly chap. 5, **time of circulation** [2]; and chap. 6, **costs of circulation** [3]; *Turnover of capital*: (indirectly), *The reproduction and circulation of the aggregate social capital*: chap. 20, simple reproduction; mainly chap. 21, **accumulation and reproduction on an extended scale** [4].

6   MEGA, Bd. 31, *Naturwissenschaftliche Exzerpte und Notizen Mitte 1877 bis Anfang 1883*, Berlin: Akademie Verlag, 1999.

petrated by the extraction of surplus value. Thus somehow the virtual appears as another aspect of the actual, the knowledge of an adequate self-production of the substance in Spinoza.

If in the thirteenth century the substance was cast into the economic, and the figure of the virtual expressed it (in its being the knowledge of the relation of cause and effect and that immaterial aspect of matter which renders it capable of self-production and movement); if in the seventeenth century the question of knowledge of the substance and its relation of cause and effect surfaced again and one of its examples was the eminent cause, whose place was taken by the figure of the virtual (as in the case of Heereboord); then, in the ninteenth century, with Marx, we find both these aspects of the virtual: the virtual *of* capital (virtual capital, *Capital*, Volume II) and its knowledge (the crisis – in my paradigm: poverty as potentia).

It is here that we meet Deleuze's concept of the virtual, which can texture for us the passage from his reading of Spinoza's potentia to his notion of the intensive, and traces the notion of adequate production which I want to aim at: production of our subjectivity as free men and women and, in that, production of *wahre Reichtum*, true wealth.[7]

The passage in Marx's *Grundrisse* (Notebook III) on Esau and primogeniture is explanatory: the worker exchanges labour as objectified labour and capital receives it as living labour, as capacity of producing wealth, as activity which multiplies wealth. That the worker cannot enrich himself through the exchange is clear: as Esau exchanges a lentil stew for his primogeniture, thus the worker gives away his creative force in exchange for a capacity of labour already fixed in a certain measure. It is here that he is destined to impoverish himself, because the creative force of his labour sets itself in front of him as force of Capital, as alien labour to him. He deprives himself of labour as capacity of producing wealth; Capital appropriates it as such. The separation between labour and property of the product of labour, between labour and richness, is thus already set in this act of exchange. What seems paradoxically a result, writes Marx, is already implicit in the same premise.

Theoretically this is the point on which we will insist for constructing the adequate production of wealth: there is a radical difference between the real-possible paradigm proper of Capital and the virtual-actual of *wahre Reichtum*,

---

7 'Reichtum ist *verfügbare Zeit*, und sonst nichts', d. h. der wahre Reichtum ist '*disposable time, freie Zeit für ihre Entwicklung*' (Marx 1968, pp. 251 f.). 'Aber free time, *disposable time*, ist der Reichtum selbst – teils zum Genuß der Produkte, teils zur free activity, die nicht wie die labour durch den Zwang eines äußren Zwecks bestimmt ist ...' (Ibid., p. 253). Man needs 'Zeit zur Befriedigung geistiger und sozialer Bedürfnisse' (Marx 1962, p. 246).

true wealth, the former reproducing the same premises of the relation of power which Capital is, the latter embodying the force of rupture, the force of radical innovation which the free worker is.

The productivity of the worker's work becomes for him an alien power, continues Marx, as it becomes his own labour, inasmuch as it is not working capacity but movement, an effective labour; Capital instead valorises itself through the appropriation of the other's work.

The first act of conceiving a process of adequate production should be, at once, to prevent the worker from separating himself from his creative force, that is, in other terms, to understand the fictitious nature of Capital as such: by exchanging his own labour force the worker in fact concedes that part of creative force which Capital takes on as its own productive nature. Capital's productive nature is the theft of our free production of subjectivity.

Today the productive mechanism is so stretched to its limit that the past process, the objectified labour seems to have been blown up, not to constitute the framework anymore: dead labour is no longer the basis for the exchange, there is only living labour totally subjugated. This is what it means that living labour has become 'fixed capital', on which we will pause later. Measure is no longer fixed, neither the salary, nor labour itself. Division between effect (effective work, movement) and cause (working capacity), between living and dead labour, between appropriation of work of others and expression of one's own work – everything is blurred. The crucial point of the production of true wealth is here: to start over with conceiving and perceiving the creative force of labour as *causa sui*, as endogenous, inalienable power. To foster, increase the property of the self as knowledge of the self-productive principle: production allows us to create ourselves, to enhance and actualise that difference of the matter that our life is, our time incarnates. It makes us new everyday. And to produce our free subjectivities, which is the production of our true wealth, means to free this power of creation, that creative force which is our core of living being, and which constantly composes the 'conception of the self' – virtue – with the 'definition *ab alio*' [per other] – the principle of value, of the commodity, and basis of commensurability for the exchange. Through production we have the possibility to let the *causa sui* deploy itself, to let this creative force which we are endowed with by nature to enhance life, increasing it with a surplus of being. This is what we mean by true wealth, an adequate production which can occur only by virtue of the free production of our subjectivities.

In *Causa sui* I thus individuated some theoretical threads in the history of thought where the relation between the virtual of capital and the virtual of subjectivity comes particularly into relief. Within these moments I find a theoretical continuum through Peter John Olivi's conceptualisation of Capital and of the *usus pauper* (thirteenth century), the Cartesian eminency of the substance (seventeenth century), up to the arrival at the virtual of Capital in Marx (ninteenth century). I call this theoretical thread the 'virtual of capital'.

On the other hand, we have, in the same period of the Middle Ages, St Claire and her request for the *privilegium paupertatis*[8] – this I consider to belong to the theoretical thread of the *causa sui* whose full expression would be given to us by Spinoza's ethics in the seventeenth century. I see the sixteenth-century Shakespeare's depiction of money and poverty against the first poor laws [*causa sui* vs. the virtual of capital] as somehow belonging to this same conceptual continuum. Spinoza's concept of virtue, in its aspect of prospective virtue, virtuality as you find it explained here, shows us the core of the *causa sui*. In the history of thought I find in Spinoza the highest point of the univocity of the substance wherein virtuality and actuality are not modalities that can be separated from the substance but one single being expressed in two different ways, as with the attributes {virtual could be the attribute Thought, actual could be the attribute Extension}. Deleuze explained this wonderfully.

In the nineteenth century, with Marx, we have both the virtual of capital and the indication of production of *wahre Reichtum*, which is for me the *causa sui*: the true wealth in Marx is the alternative to the virtual of capital, it belongs to the virtual as core of adequate production which, together with an adequate knowledge of relations, comes to be freed from alienation and exploitation. Production becomes, in true wealth, the adequate expression of our [working] lives.

In the "*frei arbeiter, virtueller Pauper*" the cycle is closed. The "*frei arbeiter, virtueller pauper*" is[9] the body and mind of that production of surplus of being, of that value of being, which is always excess as production of further life.

---

8 The study of Saint Claire's *privilegium paupertatis* and its constituting an alternative to Peter Olivi's concept of *usus pauper* was first set in the manuscript 'Margaritae paupertatis I and II', working papers, Collège de France, Paris, 2004 (now both available online at Academia.edu, Margherita Pascucci). Giorgio Agamben would also address the topic in a later text, *Altissima povertà* (Agamben 2011), but from a different point of view. For a more detailed analysis of Olivi's *usus pauper*, as the 'virtual of capital', to which a line of the 'virtual of the *causa sui*' counter-poses itself, I refer to *Causa sui*. Pascucci 2009, pp. 21–40.

9 Please allow me to refer to my article 'Il sogno di Marx' (Pascucci 2001). What we referred to there as Carnot's fourth phase is this notion of production of 'plus of being'. For the relation between surplus of being and plus of being, see the section 'The plus of being' in the present text.

4.2   On Labour and Poverty

4.2.1   *Labour of true wealth*

The relation between labour and poverty has, at its core, virtuality, the capacity of producing oneself in life.

Labour is that life force from which there is constantly subtracted, by the exploitation mechanism of Capital, its own *potentia*, qua force of producing itself in being. *Poverty* is the status of this deprivation but, if understood simply as a product of Capital, as deprivation, it remains a condition of impotence; if it is, further, understood as an exposure of the ontological mistake which Capital establishes with the structure of its relations of production, of its economic power mechanism, there it becomes a force, it regains – to use Spinoza's term – the adequate knowledge of itself and of the relations of production, thus striving to become also the adequate cause of itself and of this relation of production.

The theoretical hypothesis which underlines the trajectory we saw in the previous chapters sees: **a) labour** as the **life force** *used, by the machine Capital, to extract surplus value.* In order to do so, labour as life-force is constantly divided, by the mechanism of Capital, from its own *potentia*, i.e. from its own capacity of producing itself in being, from its own *causa sui*. Poverty is the condition (we could say, with Deleuze and Guattari, the plane of immanence) where this *theft of subjectivity*, the theft of the life force is **exposed** *ontologically* and *ethically* in the theft of labour, as it happens – to maintain the parallel – with the adequate/inadequate knowledge and cause in Spinoza.

The virtuality of the *causa sui* – the innermost core of our capacity of producing ourselves in life – is the 'invisible' element that reveals this theft, this expropriation.

This exposure occurs, ontologically and ethically, through the following mechanism: **b) poverty** is the **condition** which *reveals the violent expropriation of the life force for the extraction of surplus value*, it embodies the stealing of the life force of the subject and, in that, it constitutes the plane from which the force of life can expose the ontological and ethical mistake of Capital's mechanism. **c)** From the condition of poverty – where the violent expropriation of the life force is exposed in its infringement of the basic human right, the human right to be in such condition as to live one's own life – we should devise **new ways of producing oneself in being according to an adequate knowledge of power relations** and following the adequate actions originating from this knowledge. This is what it means to think poverty as potentia.

It means to denounce, through its own condition, the power relation that is capitalist production – a power relation which violently expropriates our life force in the extraction of surplus value from our labour, and in that, from our life. What is encroached upon, violated, is the bulk of our life, that invisible implication of the essence within the existence, as Spinoza would have put it. Or, as we might translate it, the more visible relation constantly at work, between our minds and our bodies (the substance and the modes, the attribute Extension and the attribute Thought) in the wonderful and difficult production of the intensive difference from ourselves that everyday life is. One of the sites of this violation, the one we are concerned with here, is labour.

Because today in all its expressions (we can call it the indebted man, cognitive capitalism, financial capital, immaterial labour, etc.) Capital's mechanism of production is still, and globally, inscribed in the theoretical framework of exploitation: in order to produce a surplus which goes to enrich a few, too many have their lifetime stolen from them, through labour, the absence of it, its exploitation, annihilation, the emptying of sense.

Marx writes in the *Grundrisse* that as long as the worker is capable of work, work is the new source of exchange ['*solange der Arbeiter arbeitsfähig ist*'], and explains that labour finds itself in the same definition of the concept ['*Begriffs-bestimmung selbst*'], 'that he, the worker, sells only his temporal disposition on his labour capacity' ['*dass er (der Arbeiter) nur zeitliche Disposition über seine Arbeitsfähigkeit verkauft*'] – in order to be able to reproduce his own life conditions ['*Lebensäußerung reproduzieren zu können*'].

We are now in the extreme advancement of this relation of production, beyond this paradigm: the time of labour is no longer the measure of the relation of production but it is our life; value is substituted by dismeasure (storage, one of Capital's mechanisms of surplus-value extraction, has now invested our bodies and minds in the annihilation of labour itself, in the deprivation of sense from it, in *us being stored*). Yet, we are still in the theoretical paradigm that Marx bequeathed to us.

There is a clear nexus which links the capacity to labour, the definition of its concept and the temporal disposition – the relation, that is, between the time of a [able-working] life and the production of the conditions for its reproduction, expressed by labour as source of exchange. So long as the worker is capable of labour, this is his source of exchange, this capacity is his time of [able-working] life and this activity his 'conceptual' definition – that is, his defining himself in that relation of production, his being able to conceive, and create, his relations of production.

The relation between the time of [an able-working] life and the production of the conditions for its reproduction, as implemented by labour, plays out along the thread of the composition, or decomposition, of the capacity of man's labour with the definition of his concept, that is, his definition in a relation of production. It plays out through Capital's use of the worker's virtuality (our capacity for producing, the seed and force of creation) for its own actualisation:[10] this is what defines the capitalist relation of production, a relation of ontological power, which hides and manipulates an ethical mistake: I, capitalist, extract the core of your being (potentia) as a productive force and make it into the content of my power over you.

Labour, and its conditions, are the litmus-test of an impoverishment, of a pauperization that crushes the subject into his own capacity for living, for producing his conditions for a good living, in his conceptual definition as a producer, as an active element in a relation of production. This pauperization is traced in our bodies and our minds and can be detected theoretically in the mistaken relation between the virtual at the core of Capital's mechanism and our subjectivity.

This is the plane where the relation of production is played out. The plane of the composition of our force of living (*causa sui*), of labour (relation of production) and the concept, the adequate knowledge of their conditions of actualisation.

And this is why it is necessary that a discourse on the potentia of poverty[11] should go together with a reflection on the cause of itself [*causa sui*], the

---

10   In his reading of Tarde, Maurizio Lazzarato highlights this same point but with another perspective. See further below.

11   The reading of the poor as powerful has a long history. In Western culture it starts from Christ and St Francis but dates back earlier in other cultures (see Richard Seaford's works for what concerns ancient Greece and India). My interest has always been focused on the idea of poverty as a force, a litmus test of the mistake of Capital's mechanism of production, or, said another way, on the attempt to deconstruct money as concept. I thus tried to detect focal moments in time when these two – value and poverty – were theoretically at a climax and where the crisis of value was revealing the force of poverty. The broader theoretical debate on the conceptualisation of money and poverty in the history of ideas is a rich one, and should take into account all different approaches, from the historical approach which goes back to the European Middle Ages and the Franciscan reflection on poverty and the privilege of poverty (Todeschini 1999; Piron 1999; Todeschini 2004), to the literary focus on the European representation of money and poverty in Renaissance literature (Goldberg 1989; Shell 1992; Carroll 1996); from the study on nineteenth-century popular literature and the governmental techniques of poverty management (Brundage 1978; Poovey 1995) to the sociological approach (Simmel 1906), taken up and developed by twentieth-century European philosophy (Lukács 1912; Heidegger 1998; Benjamin 1991, Catucci 2003) and the economic-philosophical discourse on it (Marx 1993; Foucault 1975, 1969, 1999). These approaches read poverty, both as an experience and as an economic status, as a result of the capitalist mode of production. Another approach, different from the above-mentioned ones, which reads poverty as force is starting to take place in other disciplines: mainly in economics (Yunus, 1997; Stiglitz, 2006), and in philosophy, political philosophy and law (Negri 2000; de Bernard 2002; Rahnema 2003; Catucci 2003; Azzoni

Spinozan concept that we can read today as defining the production of our subjectivity. Potentia of poverty is in fact the exposure of the force of resistance, on the part of the 'causa sui', to being expropriated, alienated, emptied of sense, and means the necessity of the causa sui to develop, to produce itself freely.

This is the 'theoretical' scheme from which our research started out. Today we need to look again at these premises and see how labour has changed and what poverty is – what the relation is today between labour and poverty.

We are interested in detecting that virtual core of our subjectivity, the mechanism of production of our lives which has been captured by Capital's self-referential, and destructive, mechanism. I call this the plane of the 'causa sui'.

We see today in all of us who are poor, unemployed, precarious, migrants, refugees, that the core of our lives, our virtuality – as the capacity to continue producing further life, persevering in being – is reduced to the real-possible cage, instead of belonging to the creative and natural relation between each single virtuality and its actualisation (what we can call, with Spinoza, potentia).

Two clarifications ought to be made: a) the virtuality-actualisation paradigm is in the Deleuzean perspective and has to be read against the real-possible which remains the coordinate of Capital, leaving out another modality and relation of production which has at its core the free invention of the new and the worker's self-augmenting capacity. (Here, Tarde and Lazzarato's reading of him could take the discourse further).

b) the virtual-actual relation is different from Aristotle's *energeia-dunamis* paradigm because it has been complicated, and transformed, by many other conceptual somersaults, from the 'seminal' of the Middle Ages [a self-augmenting virtue], to Duns Scotus' principle of individualisation, by the 'Gradus' in Kant[12] to our century's own readings of the Spinozan potentia (from Deleuze to Negri, from Giancotti to Balibar).

The virtual-actual relation has to do with creation, with the jump of innovation to the real. It has to do with what we will see in the following pages: the intensive as the differential of matter, the capacity of the living to augment being, to produce further life, as their own nature, of being producers, through adequate labour, of their own and of others' self-augmenting capacity

2006). See also the works of Pogge, of Academics Against Poverty, and the seminars, conferences, volume series that are occurring now in many countries (for instance the conference 'Poverty, Solidarity and Justice', Uludag University, Bursa, Turkey, October 2016; Springer-Salzburg www.workshop-poverty-philosophy.org).

12   See the very important study Maier 1968.

to live. Let me introduce here the notion of adequate labour as that work which empowers workers and, at the same time, others in a relation of production with them. This is the labour of *wahre Reichtum*, of true wealth.

So, labour today has to do with the virtual and the actual. There is a side of labour which cannot be inscribed into Capital's real-possible paradigm. This side is that of our subject, the core of our being as, also, workers. It is what I call the 'virtual of the *causa sui*'.

The second side is what I call the 'virtual of capital' and is what today's mechanism of production still captures from, and of, our lives.[13] In order to understand this better, here I will touch briefly on the discussions on immaterial labour, the expression of today's labour which best tells us of this ambiguity. Poverty is connected to this, to today's labour which expresses itself as such, inasmuch as it is its litmus test: the virtual of Capital has captured the virtual of our subject, to the point of making it – the virtuality of our subject, our force for producing life – its own 'fixed capital'. In this move, furthermore, it even further separates our capacities from our own disposal of this capacity (i.e. precariousness as blackmailing, in terms of the virtual of the subject, not only because we become more and more indebted, but also because we experience the reduction of our own force of innovation, of invention, of *causa sui*, to a sterile eminency, a temporary surplus of our lives sold to the mimicry of the real/possible coordinate, which does not transform, does not innovate, but simply reproduces itself.)

4.2.2   *Considered to lack, considered as force*

How can we say that poverty is the life force? Isn't labour the life force and poverty the site of the struggle?

The theoretical hypothesis that underlies this book sees labour as the life force used to extract surplus value, constantly divided by the mechanism of capital from its own *potentia*, that is, from its own capacity of producing itself in being, from its own *causa sui* (to continue holding together both Spinoza's and Marx's conceptualisations). {Maintaning the difference between *dunamis* and *potentia*, we could find a similarity in the definition of the slave in Aris-

---

13   We could find in Lazzarato (see here the section 'The plus of being') the core of subjectiv-
        ity as the content of immaterial labour, one of today's forms of labour, in both aspects as
        referred to above, even though his analysis reads this place of subjectivity in the 'commu-
        nicative' nature of today's labour. Conversely, I read virtuality in its double expression (the
        virtual of *causa sui* and the virtual of Capital) and as anticipating the content/product of
        labour. Virtuality is the core of our life as engine of creation, expression of the new which
        urges into being.

totle, i.e. as the one whose *dunamis* is in the hands of someone else. Capital's exploitation is the continuous re-proposition, in relations of production, of the slave paradigm}.

Poverty is the status, the site (and we could say, with Deleuze, the plane of immanence) where this theft of subjectivity, the theft of the life force, the theft of labour is exposed ontologically and ethically, as it happens – to maintain the parallel – with adequate/inadequate knowledge and cause paradigm in Spinoza.

To a certain extent, poverty is to Capital what, in Spinoza's *Ethics* (with Deleuze), sadness is to joy, the litmus test of the bad encounter, of the inadequate knowledge and of the inadequate cause of a relation – in our case, a relation of production (being the good encounter, the joyful one, Marx's *wahre Reichtum*). In this sense, it is not out of place, in my view, to say that poverty is the life force misplaced, in that it is the condition of a stolen, subtracted *potentia* (*qua* force of producing adequately oneself in life). Poverty is the condition which cries out this theft – or appropriation by someone else – of one's own life force (of labour, but not only).

Poverty is the condition which reveals the violent expropriation of the life force for the extraction of surplus value. It embodies the stealing of the life force of the subject and, in that, it constitutes the plane from where the force of life can expose the ontological and ethical mistake of Capital's mechanism.

The origin of *La Potenza della povertà* was the intuition that Capital's mechanism in Marx and the imagination in Spinoza use time in a similar way, by anticipating and abstracting (traced also in the analysis of Marx's *Heft Spinoza*), thus not allowing for the correct knowledge of the relation of production (Capital), of the trace of an encounter (imagination). (My contribution in *Causa sui* adds that it does not allow for our own adequate production of ourselves.)

But whereas the anticipation that Capital operates serves alienation and exploitation, the anticipation of the imagination in Spinoza can become an instrument of material knowledge. Thus the theoretical operation of conceiving poverty as *potentia* in the framework of Spinoza and Marx can be exemplified in Spinoza's concept of imagination: imagination makes present things that are absent or not yet present, and if conceived as such is an abstract false knowledge, prey to impotence and mistake. But if it is understood as that force which makes absent things present, it becomes affirmative and can be transformed into a common notion and adequate knowledge (*Ethics*, II, P 17, Scholium).[14]

---

14   'At this point, to begin my analysis of error I should like you to note that the imaginations of the mind, looked at in themselves, contain no error; i.e. the mind does not err from the

Then, it is not only knowledge of one's own nature, or condition; rather, it is adequate knowledge of a relation, of its privation, and of what our nature, in fact, can do.

With poverty, it is the same: if considered as a simple product of Capital, it is misery, an impotent condition of exploitation. If it is considered as a litmus test of a mistaken mode of production, of a mistaken relation of production, it becomes a force of – allow me this term – revolution, of transformation.

Poverty today indicates three major junctions, turning points: a) **how surplus value is born of a mistake in the relation between virtual and actual.** This point expresses how a mistake of 'expression' of the one into the other becomes the possibility of private property and how this could be detected, in history, from the figure of the slave (his *dunamis* is in the hands of someone else) to medieval usury (*'quandam capitale vocamus'*, Olivi), to the definition of the 'usus pauper' (the space left empty in the chiasm between knowledge and praxis, which allows for the appropriation of richness which is really a common essence). The explanation of this 'mistake' can be exemplified in describing money as a relation between virtual and formal in the expression, or production, of an equivalence. b) **How this mistake leads to the unfair appropriation** (slave-usury-social relations: debt/credit) **of each person's own conatus, of the living force, of labour force** (called variously *dunamis* by Aristotle, use of the self by Chiara in the *privilegium paupertatis*; virtue in Leibniz as read by Marx). This undue appropriation is not only alienation but it is the annihilation of the principle of conservation of life. It is the annihilation both of virtuality and actuality in the usury of life: the use value of labour power, of *us* as labour power, has been nullified, made the usurer's coin. It has been taken away from living exchange to become fictitious capital (anticipation, put into

---

fact that it imagines, but only insofar as it is considered to lack the idea which excludes the existence of those things which it imagines to be present to itself. For if the mind, in imagining non-existing things to be present to it, knew at the same time that those things did not exist in fact, it would surely impute this power of imagining not to the defect but to the strength of its own nature, especially if this faculty of imagining were to depend solely on its own nature; that is, (Def. 7, 1), if this faculty of imagining were free' (Spinoza, *Ethics*, II, P 17, Scholium). Poverty, if considered according to Capital, is impotent, a condition of continuous exploitation (if considered lacking the idea which excludes the possibility of its free production of being, of its own wealth). If considered instead as the force from which life has been taken, that is, if considered according to the strength of its nature (persevering in being notwithstanding the ontological theft), it can radically change this condition, because its nature is powerful in creating new conditions of production when it gains adequate knowledge of itself and of what it *can*. It is here that poverty is *potentia*, capacity – from that place of 'lack' of oneself, of theft – of producing the adequate relations of production.

latency, *Überschuss*). **In this process – which, in short, I call the 'usury of life' – the mechanism of capital is deployed:** profit, the *Überschuss*, does not come from circulation, from exchange, but is intrinsic to the concept of capital inasmuch as its heart (labour power) is virtual, it is thought as virtual – and as virtual of capital, not understood as virtual of causa sui – as something of which the vital part should be put into latency to then come back into circulation with another value; not inasmuch as it is increased in value but because, in being put into latency, a substitution occurs: the use value becomes exchange value, value, from being potentia of labour power, from being virtue, which sets itself in a relation of production – it even sells itself – becomes the 'thought' of Capital, its structure, its flesh, its possible pounds of flesh in the hands of Shylock. It is a sequence, anticipation-put into latency-profit: labour power becomes only the channel through which the passage occurs. c) To revolutionise the **relation between value and virtue** we need **an economy founded in Spinozan sense**, with the concept of adequate production at its core.

4.3   Potentia and the Intensive

In Gilles Deleuze's *Difference and Repetition*, there are two concepts that help us in tracing, or imagining, a new modality of production. These are the virtual and actual paradigm and the notion of the intensive.[15]

The virtual-actual relation – which he would again explain in 'L'Actuel et le Virtuel' – is here clearly described in relation to the real-possible paradigm. We should not confuse, he says, the virtual with the possible: the virtual has a full reality, whereas the possible does not. The possible comes to be by 'realising' itself; the virtual by a process of actualisation. The difference between the two lies in the nature of production, or creation: the possible is already inscribed in the concept that reality gives it, of the possible. The virtual, conversely, is the 'feature of the idea, and from its reality the existence is produced, according to time and space immanent to the idea'.

---

15   What follows is just a reading of the section of the 'Asymmetric synthesis of the sensible' with the purpose of individuating what, in other works, we have called the fourth phase missing in Marx, and which is present in Carnot's cycle. We do not contextualise it within the wide and fine scholarship regarding *Difference and Repetition*, and Deleuze and the political (for instance, the works of Paul Patton, Brian Massumi, Keith Ansell-Pearson, Henry Somers-Hall, Nathan Widder, Ian Buchanan, Nicholas Thoburn, Isabelle Garo, Jason Read and others; see Buchanan and Thoborn (eds.) 2008).

For us this is fundamentally important: Capital in fact operates within the real-possible paradigm, whereas the virtual of the *causa sui* operates with its own lines of actualisation.

This latter is invention, production, creation of the new and, in the main, cannot be owned adequately except by the one who conceives it.

The former is what 'the concept gives it as possibility' – that is, what is foreseen by the one who manages that concept (see section '"Ideal" synthesis of the difference').

We thus understand that in order to have a free production of our own capacity of conceiving the new, we have to move along the virtual-actual paradigm and not along the mimicry represented by the real-possible paradigm.

The notion of intensive is the other term that helps us contextualise the force of potentia in terms of production and of the production of the self, that is, that construction of the plus of being, which is the first building block of the production of the free man.

I believe that the intensive is the warning signal to tell us when there is the illusion of production (production of the possible by Capital) and the real production of the new (the expression of the virtual of the *causa sui*).

The intensive indicates the production of sense, the 'work' that goes back to the subject and cannot be taken away from him. It is the expression of that production of the *causa sui* which is irreducibly one with ourselves.

Here, we find the solution to that fourth phase of the cycle of Capital which is missing in Marx, and which we previously investigated following the suggestion of A. Drago.[16] The fourth phase is that phase in which the 'work', the energy, the transformation done with production, comes to augment our being, the being of the worker, instead of being stored – or, today, being cast into 'fixed' capital – by Capital's mechanism of production.

Today, we find it in Deleuze's notion and elucidation of the intensive. In wonderful, breathtaking pages, in the section 'Asymmetric synthesis of the sensible', Deleuze takes us inside the constitution of the intensive, of the difference, its relation with extension, with depth, with the Idea, with individuation. A new revolutionary ontology is delineated, here. The 'Asymmetric synthesis of the sensible' moves from the definition of difference: 'everything which happens and everything which appears is correlated with orders of differences … difference … of potential, *difference of intensity*, as affirm … the principles of Carnot and Curie'.[17]

---

16   Allow me to refer to Pascucci 2011.

17   For the English translation, see Deleuze 2004, pp. 280 ff. Following the places where he quotes Carnot can provide a small guideline to trace the parabola we want to explore.

THE PRODUCTION OF SUBJECTIVITY

Intensity is difference, but this difference tends to deny or to cancel itself out in extensity and underneath quality. It is true that qualities are signs which flash across the interval of a difference. In so doing, however, they measure the time of an equalisation – in other words, the time taken by the difference to cancel itself out in the extensity in which it is distributed. This is the most general content of the principles of Carnot, Curie, Le Châtelier et al.: the difference is the sufficient reason of change only to the extent that the change tends to negate difference.[18]

This is important because it establishes a principle of causality for which 'intensity defines an objective sense for a series of irreversible states which pass, like an "arrow of time", from more to less differenciated, from a productive to a reduced difference, and ultimately to a cancelled difference'.[19] It seems paradoxical[20] that we are using Deleuze's critique of Carnot to give an answer to our search for the fourth phase in Marx. But the point lies exactly in this: Deleuze's concept of the intensive, of the difference, constitutes the element-object of the fourth phase, the plus of being which comes to be produced (in the difference, as intensive).

Let us continue to read these groundbreaking pages. The difference is thus established as 'origin of = x of the diverse: a given, but not a "value"'.[21] Deleuze takes us into the meandering folds of intensity in order to make us understand that it is not 'self-destruction', to let us comprehend the immense magnitude of the 'value' of difference. 'Even if the production of difference is by definition "inexplicable", how can we avoid *implicating* the inexplicable at the heart of thought itself? How could the unthinkable not lie at the heart of thought?'[22]

'Difference explicates itself but tends to cancel itself in the system in which it explicates itself. This means only that the difference is essentially implicated, that its being is the implication. For difference, to be explicated is to be cancelled or to dispel the inequality which constitutes it'.[23]

The fact that difference is essentially implicated explains how its movement in being is not self-destruction, or dispersal,[24] but the not-yet-thought production of transformation. In fact, it is in the fertile, productive relation of the Idea

---

18   Deleuze 2004, pp. 281–2.
19   Ibid., p. 282.
20   See the wonderful pages in this section on paradox and philosophy.
21   Ibid.
22   Ibid., pp. 286 ff.
23   Ibid., p. 287.
24   See the parts on *extensio* (extension) and *extensum* (extensity), ibid., pp. 281 ff.

and the intensive that this creation of the new will occur. It is the relation of the actual-virtual, based on the potentiality of the Idea. 'The difference, in fact, did not cease to be in itself, to be implicated in itself, when it explicates itself outside itself' (ibid.).

When L. Selme (*Principe de Carnot contre formule empirique de Clausius*) counter-poses Carnot to Clausius – writes Deleuze – he makes an acute discovery, that is, that the *increase of entropy is an illusion*. There is a transcendental form of the illusion, the paradox of entropy. 'Of all extensions, entropy is the only one which is not directly or indirectly measurable with a procedure independent from the energetic',

> The paradox of entropy can so be pronounced: entropy is an extensive factor, but, differently from all other extensive factors, it is an extension, an 'explication' that, as such, finds itself implicated in the intensity, which does not exist if not implicated, it does not exist outside the implication, and this *because it has the function of making possible the general movement through which the implicated explicates or distends itself*. There is therefore a transcendental illusion, essentially tied to the *qualitas* Heat and the extension Entropy.[25]

Understanding that the increase of entropy is an illusion or, in other terms, to understand the transcendental form of this illusion, is key for us: it seems to us that our fourth phase, by counter-posing the virtual (of the *causa sui*) to the possible of the entropy (virtual of capital), could solve the paradox and give an affirmative answer to the transcendental form of the illusion.

That entropy is an extension *implicated* in the intensity; that it does not exist *if not in this implication* – and this, because *it makes possible* the *movement through which* the *implicated explicates itself* – shows the transcendental illusion of the 'increase' of entropy. It is the same transcendental illusion of Capital's mechanism of production.

The transformation is inside: it is the making-possible of the movement of explication, it is *the implication* itself. (The transformation is at the level of the *causa sui*). Its fruits are the individuations that derive 'from a "deeper" instance, the depth, which is not extension but an implex'.[26]

Depth is thus the further dimension which explains the individuation, the transformation within the implication-explication movement. Depth is an ex-

---

25   Deleuze, my translation and emphasis. For the English edition, see Deleuze 2004, pp. 287 ff.
26   Ibid.

tensive quantity, the last dimension of the extension (and the individuating factors express exactly this original depth).

Indeed, connected to the intensive is *depth, qua* the last dimension of the extension, but also in a manner original to it: 'Depth is the intensity of being, or vice-versa'. The description of the synthesis of depth reminds us of the 'virtual': 'This synthesis of depth, which endows the object with its shadow, but makes it emerge from that shadow, bears witness to the furthest past and to the coexistence of the past with the present'.[27]

Through the entire chapter, we follow the dynamic of intensity, the relation extension-extensity, implication and explication at once of the relation with the self inasmuch as it is always differing:

> Intensity, which envelops the distances, is explicated in extensity, while extensity develops, exteriorises and homogenises these very distances. At the same time, a quality occupies this extensity, either in the form of a *qualitas* which defines the milieu of a direction, or in the form of a *quale* which characterises a given object in relation to that direction. Intensity is simultaneously the imperceptible and that which can only be sensed.[28]

> The strangest alliance is formed between intensity and depth, which carries each faculty to its own limit and allows it to communicate only at the peak of its particular solitude: an alliance between Being and itself in difference. Depth and intensity are the Same at the level of being, but the same in so far as this is said of difference. Depth is the intensity of being, or vice versa.[29]

Three are the characteristics of intensity:

> According to the first, intensive quantity includes the unequal[30] in itself. It represents difference in quantity, that which cannot be cancelled in difference in quantity or that which is unequalisable in quantity itself: it is therefore the quality which belongs to quantity. It appears less as a spe-

---

27 Ibid., p. 289.
28 Ibid., p. 290.
29 Ibid.
30 Could not this be the concept of *dismisura* [dismeasure] in Negri's reading of Marx? The point of this entire analysis is in fact to counter-pose the concept of intensity to that of value, as it has been reduced by Capital.

cies of the genus quantity than as the figure of a fundamental or original moment present in every quantity.[31]

'Intensity is the uncancellable in difference of quantity, but this difference of quantity is cancelled by extension, extension being precisely the process by which intensive difference is turned inside out and distributed in such a way as to be dispelled, compensated, equalised and suppressed in the extensity which it creates'.[32] *Extension as the intensive process which poses the intensive differ- ence outside itself, but so as to neutralize, equate, suppress it in the extension that it creates*, finds its answer in the second feature of intensity.[33]

The second characteristic is in fact the following: by comprising the unequal in itself, being already difference, the intensity *affirms* difference: 'intensity *affirms* difference. It makes difference an object of affirmation'.[34] 'Intensity affirms even the *lowest*, it makes the lowest an object of affirmation. The power of a waterfall or a very deep descent is required to go that far and make an affirmation even of descent. Everything is like the flight of an eagle, overflight, suspension and descent. Everything goes from high to low, and by that move- ment affirms the lowest: asymmetrical synthesis'.[35]

As against the political task of representation, which always refers difference to the identical, and begins the process of the negative, we are powerful by vir- tue of the potentia of the lowest. '*We disquiet as the waterfall ... We know no king / nor any king's laws, / We submit to no rule or regulation, / We are born free with the mind / open as the blossoming lotus. / We are the murmuring flood tide of the sea*' writes Nazrul Islam, Bangladeshi poet, in 'Song of the Mountain', *Panari Gan*.[36]

---

31   Ibid., p. 291.
32   Ibid., p. 292.
33   A wonderful page on Plato's *Timeus* and the third hypothesis of the *Parmenides*, the hypo- thesis of the differential or intensive instant.
34   Deleuze 2004, p. 293.
35   Ibid., p. 294.
36   The entire poem is breathtaking: 'We are wild as the storm / We are restless as the spring / We are fearless like god and generous like nature. / We are as free as the sky / We are Bedouin, the deserts wandering tribe. / We know no king/nor any king's laws, / We submit to no rule or regulation, / We are born free with the mind / open as the blossoming lotus. / We are the murmuring flood tide of the sea and the warbling waters of the mountain spring / We are generous hearted wide open meadows ... / We are mighty invincible hills / We are flying birds with outstretched wings / We are bubbling laughter and gay songs. / We eat wild fruits and drink rain water / We sleep under trees in the depth of green forests / We are the gushing river of life. / We are the flowing waters of mountain brooks warbling singing roaring / always restless and ever on the move. / *kol kol kol, chol chol chol chol chol chol*', Nazrul Islam, A Mountain Song, *Panari Gan*.

Faced with the illusion of the negative, the differentiation of the difference affirms in intensity:

> every field of forces refers back to a potential energy, every opposition refers to a deeper 'disparateness', and oppositions are resolved in time and extensity only to the extent that the disparates have first invented their order of communication in depth and rediscovered that dimension in which they envelop one another, tracing hardly recognizable intensive paths through the ulterior world of qualified extensity.[37]

This breathtaking path in the depth of creation, in the intensive, in the implication of being in life – the entire dynamic of the intensity and of the difference – is the most wonderful explanation of that production whose ultimate object is us, our being.

This is what we define as the 'plus of being', the product of affirmation, constantly implicated in life by life itself. The illusion implicit in the intensive quantities is *not* intensity, but that movement through which the difference of intensity annuls itself outside itself, in extension and quality. But now we know that this annulling, cancelling, is an illusion, as is the increase in entropy; we know that something remains, which is the intensity, 'that which cannot be cancelled in difference in quantity', 'that which is unequalisable in quantity itself ... the quality which belongs to quantity'. The quality of the quantity.

The third characteristic of intensity which brings together the other two, writes Deleuze, is the fact that 'intensity is an implicated quantity, enveloped, reduced to embryo. To the extent in which it is not implied in quality if not secondarily, it is above all implicated in itself: implicating and implicated. The implication should be conceived as a form of being perfectly determined. Within intensity, we call difference that which is really implicating and enveloping; we call distance that which is really implicated or enveloped'.[38]

Here, we have intensity as implicating and implicated. Again, it seems to be a description of the movement of the *causa sui*.

Deleuze further asks:

> We asked how a transcendental principle might be extracted from the empirical principles of Carnot or Curie. When we seek to define *energy* in general, either we take account of the extensive and qualified factors

37   Ibid.
38   Translation slightly altered.

of extensity – in which case we are reduced to saying 'there is something which remains constant', thereby formulating the great but flat tautology of the Identical – or, on the contrary, *we consider pure intensity in so far as it is implicated in that deep region where no quality is developed, or any extensity deployed. In this case, we define energy in terms of the difference buried in this pure intensity and it is the formula 'difference of intensity' which bears the tautology, but this time the beautiful and profound tautology of the Different.*[39]

'However energy in general or intensive quantity is the *spatium*, the theatre of all metamorphosis or difference in itself which envelops all its degrees in the production of each. In this sense energy or intensive quantity, is a transcendental principle, and not a scientific concept'. The eternal return expresses this: 'It is said of a world the very ground of which is difference, in which everything rests upon disparities, upon differences of differences which reverberate to infinity (world of intensity)'.[40]

'Thus the two themes most profoundly linked to eternal return, that of qualitative metamorphosis and that of quantitative inequality'.

When Deleuze writes that 'the eternal return is neither qualitatively nor extensive, but intensive, purely intensive. In other words, it is said of difference',[41] it makes us think of the potency/power reversibility of Carnot's machine. To this we could apply – to explain what we meant with the 'fourth phase missing in Marx' – the intensity-idea relation (of production, if I may), which explains how the virtual invents its lines of actualisation, i.e. how all this occurs: 'A whole flow of exchange occurs between intensity and Ideas, as though between two corresponding figures of difference. *Ideas are problematic or 'perplexed' virtual multiplicities, made up of relations between differential elements. Intensities are implicated multiplicities, 'implexes', made up of relations between asymmetrical elements which direct the course of the actualisation of Ideas and determine the cases of solution for problems.* The aesthetic of intensities thus develops each of its moments in correspondence with the dialectic of Ideas: *the power of intensity (depth) is grounded on the potentiality of the Idea*'.[42]

---

39   Ibid., my emphasis.
40   Ibid., p. 302. See these wonderful pages on eternal return and will to power.
41   The 'eternal return as intensive' is reminiscent of Deleuze's quote from Pascal: to 'make of chaos an object of affirmation'.
42   My italics. Ibid.

How can the reversibility of Carnot be understood as eternal return, will to power, the potentia of poverty? How can the construction of the plus of being come about?

Deleuze's 'power of intensity (depth) [that] is grounded on the potentiality of the Idea', together with the parallel drawn by Spinoza – 'the order and connection of ideas is the same as the order and connection of things' (*Ethics*, II, P 7), 'By virtue and potentia I mean the same thing' (*Ethics*, IV, Def. 8) – sets free our comprehension, and with it, our becoming adequate cause of ourselves: 'the *conatus*, with which each thing endeavors to persist in its own being is nothing but the actual essence of the thing itself' (*Ethics*, III, P 7).

The movement of the idea, the movement-idea, is inseparable from actualisation. But how does it actualise itself? By the process of individuation:

> The essential process of intensive quantities is individuation. Intensity is individuating, and intensive quantities are individuating factors. Individuals are signal-sign systems ... *Individuation emerges like the act of solving such a problem, or – what amounts to the same thing – like the actualization of a potential and the establishing of communication between disparates.* The act of individuation consists not in suppressing the problem, but in integrating the elements of the disparateness into a state of coupling which ensures its internal resonance. The individual thus finds itself attached to a pre-individual half which is not the impersonal within it so much as the reservoir of its singularities. In all these respects, we believe that individuation is essentially intensive, and the pre-individual field is a virtual-ideal field, made up of differential relations. Individuation is what responds to the question 'Who?', just as the Idea responds to the questions 'how much?' and 'How?'. 'Who?' is always an intensity ... Individuation is the act by which intensity determines differential relations to become actualised along the lines of differentiation and within the qualities and extensities that it creates in the quality and in the extensions that it creates.

Individuation 'does not presuppose any differenciation; it gives rise to it. Qualities and extensities, forms and matters, species and parts are not primary; they are imprisoned in individuals as though in a crystal. Moreover, the entire world may be read, as though in a crystal ball, in the moving depth of individuating differences or differences intensity'.[43]

---

43   See the beautiful pages on Leibniz and the order of implication toward the end of the chapter.

Every body, every thing, thinks and is a thought to the extent that, reduced to its intensive reasons, it expresses an Idea the actualisation of which it determines. ... The thinker, undoubtedly the thinker of eternal return, is the individual, the universal individual. It is he who makes use of all the power of the clear and the confused, of the clear-confused, in order to think Ideas in all their power as the distinct-obscure. The multiple, mobile and communicating character of individuality, its implicated character, must therefore be constantly recalled. The indivisibility of the individual pertains solely to the property of intensive quantities not to divide without changing nature. We are made of all these depths and distances, of these intensive souls which develop and are re-enveloped.

Individuality is not a characteristic of the Self, but, on the contrary, forms and sustains the system of the dissolved Self.[44]

In the moment in which difference ceases to be thought, it dissolves in non-being.

'To create is equal to produce lines and figures of differentiation, even though it remains true that intensity does not explicate itself without annulling itself in the differentiated system that it creates'.[45] This is the transformation principle and the principle of the plus of being that we look for to oppose to Capital's entropic mechanism, in which dispersal and putting-into-latency are fuels for the process.

4.4   The Plus of Being

We saw that today's forms of labour have, at their core, subjectivity and the encroachment upon it by a mechanism of production, that of Capital, which is essentially a constant reproduction of a relation of power. This was detected both at the beginning of the last century, by Walter Benjamin, in his reading of Marx and Grandville, and, at its end, by Gilles Deleuze and Félix Guattari's work. The Konvolut X of Benjamin's *Passagen-Werk* on Marx, together with Konvolut G, on Grandville, which can be considered its 'figuration', give us a fundamental insight into the knowledge of the mystery of commodity and Capital's mechanism at the level of its encroachment upon our subjectivity.

---

44   Ibid.
45   Ibid.

As both Maurizio Lazzarato (*Signs and Machines*) and Ubaldo Fadini (*Divenire Corpo*) highlight, in Deleuze and Guattari's work (*Anti-Oedipus* and *Mille plateaux*), we find the main element of this encroachment: the infrastructure of desire.

The virtual of the causa sui is the structure of desire.[46]

Thus, keeping Walter Benjamin's reading of Marx and Deleuze's work in the background, I now want briefly to address the work of Maurizio Lazzarato[47] and Ubaldo Fadini, who, in the wake of the works of Benjamin and Deleuze, push the reflection further. On the one hand Maurizio Lazzarato did this with regard to reflection on immaterial labour and the production of subjectivity. On the other hand, Ubaldo Fadini did so for capitalist valorisation's 'interiorisation' of all that is creative/inventive.

Taking a step back, Benjamin's reading of Marx and his figuration in J.I.I. Grandville[48] gives us a thorough understanding of the construction of the commodity as a poetic object: that part hidden by material labour comes to be unmasked and shown in the experience of the phantasmagoria and its 'affirmative' side, which we could call the construction of sense.[49] Maurizio Lazzarato refers to the importance of Benjamin's works for the genealogy of immaterial

---

46   My conceptualisation throughout the entire book can appear an abstract, almost metaphysical, reflection. For instance, Deleuze and Guattari talk about the infrastructure of desire as machinic, plunged into our everyday reality with its mechanism, its machinic enslavement and subjectivation. I talk of the virtual of the causa sui, which seems almost pre-structural, as if I were talking at the level of an essence, and they at that of existence. This is not so. The virtual of the causa sui is as much the same consistency of this desire plunged into life as the Spinozan essence is involved in the existence. It is crucial for me to talk of it as such, because it is that core of resistance of the affirmation within the same machinic enslavement and subjectivation. It is the same difference in understanding of the virtual that we have with respect to a Cartesian like Heereboord, for example. For him, the virtual is the place of eternity as separated from the existence – it is the place of the eminency of the substance (the surplus of Capital, I would dare to say). To understand virtue, and the invisible virtual as prospective virtue, in Spinoza, is to understand the *sub specie aeternitatis*: not separated from existence, from reality, it is in fact its deepest understanding, the most adequate understanding of life. To understand virtue is thus to understand and conceive the essence as that force which constantly produces the new.

47   We refer here to the works of Maurizio Lazzarato on immaterial labour (Lazzarato 1997; Lazzarato 1998); (with Toni Negri and Paolo Virno) Lazzarato 2004; Lazzarato 2006; Lazzarato 1992; Lazzarato 1994; Lazzarato 1995; on Tarde (Lazzarato 2002); on debt (Lazzarato 2012; Lazzarato 2015); on production of subjectivity (Lazzarato 2014)

48   See Benjamin 2002, Konvolut G, X, K.

49   I analysed Benjamin's work and the construction of commodity as poetical object in my PhD thesis (Pascucci 2003a). I refer to that work for a deepening of the theme.

labour.[50] Indeed, the experience of phantasmagoria, and the consequent 'disclosure' of the mystery of the commodity is, I believe, at the centre of what we experience today with immaterial labour.

Benjamin's notion of phantasmagoria – the experience of the commodity as collective intoxication which at the same time opens to the 'absolute imaginal space' ['*hunderprozentigen Bildraum*'[51]] – are themes also central to Fadini's research. I read phantasmagoria, our experience of images and of the commodity, not only as the disclosure of Marx's concept of fetishism (that is, the possibility of knowing the mystery of the market) but also as our capacity of conceiving, constructing and producing sense as exactly that alternative to Capital's value. In the terms of 'Capital and Imaginary',[52] sense is the composition of the concept and of life, the seed content of the *nicht-materielle Produktion*, of that part of immaterial labour which affirms, so to say, the *causa sui* of the subject.

What, I believe, the works of Lazzarato and Fadini point to, is that part of our subjectivity which cannot be taken, stored, stolen by today's mechanism of power production, but which instead resists through its irreducible unity with itself in the production of difference,[53] thus constituting the lever of change.

Lazzarato's work, with his attention to, and inheritance from, Benjamin, Deleuze-Guattari, and Tarde, is important for our discourse with regard to three main theoretical points: immaterial labour, the dynamic of invention, and debt. All these converge in his recent important work on capitalism and the production of subjectivity (*Signs and Machines*).

He defines immaterial labour as labour that 'produces the informational and cultural content of the commodity'. The centrality of living labour within post-Fordist production lies in the fact that it exhibits subjectivity at its core.[54]

---

50   Lazzarato 2006, pp. 146–7.

51   See Fadini 2015, pp. 35 ff. Here Fadini refers to the reading that Ferruccio Masini did of Benjamin's '*hunderprozentigen Bildraum*'.

52   See note 113.

53   What we saw in the previous section of Deleuze's *Difference and Repetition* goes in this direction.

54   Together with the works of Benjamin, the reading of Marx, of Tarde, the theoretical background for this was also prepared by the work of Guattari and Deleuze-Guattari in *Anti-Oedipus* and *Mille plateaux* as well as Deleuze's reading of Nietzsche. The theoretical insights there are elaborated upon by Lazzarato in his works and developed up to the investigation of the semiotic structure of the Machine Capital (Lazzarato 2012, 2014, 2015).

Subjectivity is codified within production: immaterial labour is at the cross-roads of a new relationship between production and consumption;[55] it 'produces a social relationship (a relation of innovation, production and consumption)', it 'produces the capital relation': 'production of subjectivity as the content of valorization',[56] 'immaterial labour constitutes itself immediately in collective forms'; 'productive is the "whole" of social relation ... brings into play the "meaning"'.[57]

This production of subjectivity as the content of valorisation would be further elaborated in *Signs and Machines* with the articulation of Deleuze and Guattari's analysis of machinic enslavement and subjectivation. For me it is important, in this paradigm, to still keep a core of resistance which, like Tarde's virtual, can constitute those escape lines which break constitutively with this same paradigm.

To focus on the concept of immaterial production helps us to detect the element which produces sense, that which is not directly captured by the machine of Capital – that is, that which is no longer appropriable from the substance. In terms of production, this is labour; in terms of the production of the self, it is the *causa sui*. This also helps us to better understand what a discourse on potentia of poverty means in relation to the production of the free man.

With Lazzarato's work,[58] in immaterial labour the core of labour is subjectivity, how 'the capitalist encroaches on processes of subjectivity'.

The status of this subjectivity encroached upon by capitalist power is the status of pure virtuality: 'in the precarious worker, the unemployed youth we are dealing with pure virtuality'.[59] Here we find what we touched on already in *Causa sui* – something which the 'work paradigm' of our century has been making clear to us: namely that capitalist production aims at capturing the pure virtuality of our self. Marx understood the role of virtuality in the production process, even if he analysed it only from the side of Capital, that is, as an internal factor of production, whereas virtuality is the 'innovation' (creation/production) principle itself inside us that Capital has since its birth been using as its own hidden mechanism: the *ratio seminale*, which produces more than what it is, and which does so because of the virtuality of which it is made.[60]

---

55   It transforms the consumer, who becomes equal to the producer. See also Benjamin's work
       (Benjamin 2002, but also 'Author as Producer').
56   Deleuze 2004, pp. 142–43.
57   Ibid.
58   And Negri, Virno, on the one hand, on the other hand with Gorz, Marazzi, Fadini.
59   Lazzarato 2006, p. 135.
60   On the virtuality of money, see Lazzarato 2004, p. 196; and Lazzarato 2002, p. 85 (see here
       below).

In this last chapter, we want to see how the pure virtuality of today's precarious worker/unemployed youth – whose litmus test within the production
mechanism[61] is immaterial labour – could be turned into the explosion, from
the inside, of the thieving mechanism of Capital.

Where are the traces of this pure virtuality in immaterial labour?

We saw that for Lazzarato immaterial labour 'appears as a mutation of living labour', 'finds itself at the crossroad (or rather, it is the interface) of a new
relationship between production and consumption'.[62]

The particularity of immaterial labour, he explains, lies in the fact that the
commodity which it produces 'is not destroyed in the act of consumption' but
rather 'enlarges, transforms and creates the "ideological" and cultural content'
and transforms the person who uses it. So, the consumer is transformed (as it
is in the knowledge economy, and as the producer is, too).

Furthermore, immaterial labour produces a 'social relationship', a 'relationship of innovation, production and consumption' – most importantly in that
'it shows thus what material production had "hidden", namely that labour produces not only commodities but, first and foremost, it produces the capital
relation'.[63]

So, immaterial labour produces a 'social relationship', the 'capital relationship', while simultaneously transforming the person who uses it; that is, it
encroaches directly on subjectivity.

Of interest for our own discourse on poverty and virtuality is how this immaterial labour transforms the subject who does it – how it arrives at expressing,
enhancing or exploiting that virtuality of the precarious unemployed, Marx's
'free worker, virtually poor'. Because it is in this nexus that the production of
real richness, *der wahre Reichtum*, comes to be unwrapped.

The second point important for us is Lazzarato's work on Tarde, *Puissances
de l'invention*. This is fundamental for understanding both the dynamic of capital and of invention, which has at its core the virtual-actual dialectic:

> For Marx and Tarde, the specificity of the immanent dynamic of eco-
> nomic movement in modernity sticks to the act of the infinity within
> finitude, but Marx affirms the primacy of the capital/labour relation over

---

61   Immaterial labour bears the traces of this pure virtuality: the unemployed youth as pure
      virtuality, that 'undetermined capacity that already shares all the characteristics of post-
      industrial productive subjectivity', the 'basin of immaterial labour' (Lazzarato 2006, ibid.).
62   Lazzarato 2006, pp. 133–4.
63   Ibid.

the invention and imitation of social forces, whereas the economic psychology of Tarde sets the ontological priority of invention and cooperation over the capitalist relation.[64]

Tarde defines, like *Mille plateaux*, the surplus as differential relation between flows. Invention is the relation (dx/dy) of heterogeneous and infinitesimal currents of knowledges, wills and affects which flow on the body without organs from the collective brain, real *socius* of psychological forces ... In Deleuze and Guattari's definition, money expresses a potency of nature higher than that of labour because it is a force of creative destruction (creation and destruction of money), that is, a force of junction and disjunction, of differentiation and composition of flows. In Tarde, this potency of composition is that of invention which expresses a heterogeneous potency higher than simple reproduction.[65]

It is only when the collective brain and the intercerebral relations express themselves as 'production of knowledges' – that is, that they do not manifest themselves anymore in the form of labour, but as a differential composition of invention and imitation – that money-capital shows itself to be a poor and inhibited form of organisation of economic relations. We can maybe draw from the *Psychologie économique* a theory of emancipation of the social brain from the grip of the division of labour, a theory of exodus, of flight of the psychological forces captured in labour toward the intercerebral cooperation. To complete successfully this project, we have to follow another suggestion of Tarde: to disconnect labour from capital and connect it to invention.

These pages explain with great clarity the possibility of another modality of production, radically alternative to capital, which is embedded in invention. In his fundamentally important pages on the virtual, Lazzarato explains how this occurs in the actual-virtual dynamic:

The virtual, which represents the conditional existence of every thing, constitutes, according to a very beautiful definition of Tarde's, 'above life and the chain of relations, a silent life, a peaceful chain of possibilities. This infinite crowd of conditional certainties ... advances a step toward

---

64   Lazzarato 2002, p. 51, my translation.
65   Ibid., pp. 52–3.

existence every time that a new element of this entire complex comes to be realized, or it gets away every time that one of the elements already assembled die; and nothing is more agitated than the destiny of these shadows that populate the kingdom of void'.[66]

Tarde's rupture, Lazzarato highlights throughout the book, is to 'put at the centre of the economic phenomenon neither labour nor utility but *life as difference, heterogeneity*, and its *power of invention* in as much as *dynamic of cooperation between brains*'.[67] Also extremely important is the discourse on money as force, as infinite virtuality: 'Money is a force in the sense in which it is a "possibility, an infinite virtuality" which tends to its actualisation. If political economy resembles a social physics, it does so … in virtue of the exchange between virtual and actual which money makes possible'.[68]

Here we can find in filigree our discourse on the virtual of capital, which should be kept distinct, in my contention, from the virtual of the *causa sui*, which in Tarde's and Lazzarato's terms is the virtual of invention.

The third point is Lazzarato's work on debt, whose two hypotheses are: i) the social lies in credit not in exchange; the debtor-creditor paradigm comes before the one of production and wage. ii) Debt represents an economic relationship inseparable from the production of the debtor subject and his 'morality'.[69]

In *Governing by Debt*, Lazzarato highlights how it is the very concept of production to have to be subverted. Here, he recalls Guattari's 'economy of the possibles': 'Capitalism (and its power) is above all defined as absolute control over what is possible and what is impossible'.[70] 'What is expropriated by credit/debt is not only wealth, knowledge, and the "future", but more fundamentally the possible. Desire neither strictly refers to libido nor simply to urges but to the possible (Deleuze-Guattari). There is desire when, out of a rupture in past equilibriums, relations emerge which had previously been impossible. Desire can always be identified by the impossible it eliminates and by the new

66   Ibid., p. 66; and pp. 67 ff.
67   Ibid., p. 74, my emphasis.
68   Ibid, p. 85, my translation. 'Money is at the same time a *force* in the sense in which it is one of the main ways of action on men. There exist three big 'categories of virtuality which are social forces par excellence: Power, Right and Money' (Lazzarato 2002, p. 85). See also the following pages: 'The power of money is a power of relation of which Marx decrypts the hieroglyphs which it draws on the social body through the relations of production' (ibid., p. 88).
69   Lazzarato 2012. See the reading of Nietzsche by Deleuze and his work with Guattari, which prepare this.
70   Lazzarato 2015, p. 22.

possibilities it creates. Desire is the fact that, where the world was once closed, a process secreting other systems of reference breaks through'. 'Capital is a social machine', 'a semiotic operator'.

In *Signs and Machines. Capitalism and the production of subjectivity*, Lazzarato thoroughly explains how the production of subjectivity is connected to Capital as a semiotic operator, as a social machine:

> Today the weakness of capitalism lies in the production of subjectivity. As a consequence, systemic crisis and the crisis in the production of subjectivity are strictly interlinked. It is impossible to separate economic, political, and social processes from the processes of subjectivation occurring within them.[71]

Let me quote a series of passages to give the theoretical paradigm which Lazzarato exposes:

> In capitalism, the production of subjectivity works in two ways through what Deleuze and Guattari call apparatuses [*dispositifs*] of social subjection and machinic enslavement. Social subjection equips us with a subjectivity, assigning us an identity, a sex, a body, a profession, a nationality, and so on. In response to the needs of the social division of labor, it in this way manufactures individuated subjects, their consciousness, representations and behaviour.[72]

It is at the level of fixed capital that the exploitation is most exposed:

> ... seem to have lost sight of what Marx had to say about the essentially machinic nature of capitalism: "machinery appears as the most adequate form of fixed capital; and the latter, in so far as capital can be considered as being related to itself, is the most adequate form of capital in general".[73]

The articulation of the machinic nature of Capital is to be detected in its capacity as a 'semiotic operator'.[74] Now, we can see how subjectivity, which in imma-

---

71   Lazzarato, 2014, p. 8.
72   Ibid., p. 12.
73   Ibid., p. 13.
74   'Capital is not only a linguistic but also a "semiotic operator". The distinction is fundamental because it establishes that flows of signs, as much as labor and money flows, are the conditions of "production"' (ibid., p. 39); 'Attentive to the tremendous increase in

terial labour starts to become fixed capital, is the terrain where the machinic nature of Capital finds its hold.

The book, as Lazzarato himself states, is the investigation of the 'difference between apparatuses of "social subjection" and "machinic enslavement", for it is at the point of their intersection that the production of subjectivity occurs'.[75] It is a 'cartography of the modalities of subjection and enslavement, those with which we will have to break in order to begin a process of subjectivation independent and autonomous of capitalism's hold on subjectivity, its modalities of production and forms of life'.[76] Important for us is how the production of subjectivity is connected to the production of wealth:

> Guattari and Deleuze bring to fulfilment the discoveries of Marx and classical political economy: *the production of wealth depends on abstract, unqualified, subjective activity irreducible to the domain of either political or linguistic representation.* The production of wealth (and production, period) operates at the *intersection of two heterogeneous power apparatuses – social subjection and machinic enslavement.* What is called economy is the assemblage of this dual investment of subjectivity such that, as Guattari puts it, 'one must enter the field of subjective economy and stop concentrating only on political economy', which was incapable of realizing the full ramifications of its discoveries.[77]

> We are thus subject to a dual regime. We are, on the one hand, enslaved to the machinic apparatuses of business, communications, the welfare state, and finance; on the other hand, we are subjected to a stratification of power that assign us roles and social and productive functions as users, producers, television viewers, and so on.[78]

And how this encounters desire:

> Recognizing the consequences of capital's socialization, Deleuze and Guattari argue for the univocity of the concept of production. If production and the social overlap, then the 'field of desire' and the 'field of

---

"constant fixed capital" (of machinery), Deleuze and Guattari introduce the concept of machinic surplus value and machinic time' (ibid., p. 43).

75   Ibid., pp. 13–14.
76   Ibid., p. 14.
77   Ibid., p. 24, my emphasis.
78   Ibid.

labor', the 'economy' and the production of subjectivity, infrastructure and superstructure, can no longer be taken separately. The question of production is inseparable from that of desire (Guattari) such that political economy is no more than a 'subjective economy'.[79]

In *Anti-Oedipus*, Deleuze and Guattari advance a fundamentally new concept of desire appropriate to the new nature of 'economy' wherein 'labor' and 'work on the self', production and subjectivation, coalesce and desire serves to define economy as the 'production of the possible'.[80]

Lazzarato warns us that:

deterritorialized desire has nothing to do with 'drives' or 'conatus'. It is a question instead of the possible, of the creation of new potentialities, of the emergence of what appears possible within the framework of capitalist domination ... Deterritorialized desire, machinic desire, bears with it an 'economy of possibilities' and an autopoietic (self-productive) subjectivity which explains the nature of modern-day capitalism and above all its crisis. Capitalism can no longer contain them within the limits of private property or the subjective figure of the entrepreneur of the self.[81]

Holding that desire and production are inseparable, the virtual of the *causa sui* constitutes the alternative to this deterritorialised desire inasmuch as the virtual-actual relation in Tarde, Bergson, and Deleuze, is radically different from the real-possible paradigm. The *causa sui* of subjectivity is what Capital cannot hold onto but rather tries to appropriate and mimic, by reproducing it. That its capture, techniques of power, produces in us the two subjections, 'machinic enslavement' and 'social subjection' could be read as the continuation of Benjamin's phantasmagoria.

Ubaldo Fadini's work is also central for deepening our discourse, here.

In *Divenire corpo*, there are two poles of reflection important for us: one on Gorz and Marazzi, the other on Benjamin and Deleuze-Guattari. Fadini writes regarding Gorz's[82] analysis of the *basis of production of wealth as production of the self*: 'A practice of appropriation/suppression of work which expresses

---

79   Ibid., pp. 50–1.
80   Ibid., p. 51.
81   Ibid, p. 52.
82   Within Gorz's discourse of knowledge economy as belonging to collectivity, the exit from work, from the merchandise. See the critique that Toni Negri subjects Gorz to in 'Recen-

itself in the connection production of the self-production of wealth, able to indicate an exit from capitalism'.[83] With Marazzi, Fadini highlights the partial resolution of fixed capital in the variable, that is the transfer of the productive functions in the living body of the labour force.[84] This is the centrality of immaterial labour.[85]

Fadini introduces labour power's becoming 'fixed capital' with an articulation of Deleuze and Guattari's analysis of the variable relation between the human and the machinic with relation to the realisation of surplus value. Here, we have machinic surplus value as the constant capital and the human surplus value as the variable capital.

In the organic composition of Capital, the variable capital is the regime of subjection of the worker (human surplus value). Constant capital grows in automation and finds new subjection within the context of the factory or the enterprise. The surplus value becomes machinic and the framework extends itself to the entire society (Deleuze-Guattari, *Mille plateaux*).[86]

Important for the discourse we proposed in *Causa sui* is the following passage:

> To the idea of the living body of the labour force as container (of the faculties of work, of specific functions of fixed capital ...) should be linked the idea of an articulation of a phase of the logic of capitalistic valorization characterised under the guise of 'interiorization/internalisation' of all that appear creative/inventive, even in the proliferation of the different forms of social life.[87]

In *Causa sui* we tried to explain this 'interiorization' in its (metaphysical) original mechanism: it is the theft of the virtual of subjectivity.

---

sion *Misère du présent, richesses du possibles'* [http://www.multitudes.net/Recension-Mi seres-du-present/ (access November 2016)].

83   Fadini 2015, pp. 106–7, my translation.
84   We use the terms 'labour force' and 'labour power' without distinction.
85   This transfer of labour power into, and as, fixed capital was also underlined by Negri and Lazzarato in an article which appeared in *Derive & Approdi*, number 0, 1992, 'Lavoro immateriale e soggettività' (Lazzarato 1992).
86   In *Anti-Oedipus*, in the parts on desire as element of anti-production, it seems that the subject is produced as a remainder along the desiring machines, as an intersection between machinic and human surplus value, the incommensurability of which is that element of anti-production within Capital. Is this element of anti-production desire, the discovery of a "subjective abstract essence of wealth" in labour, in production?
87   Ibid., p. 43.

Further, Fadini introduces Marazzi's notion, following Marx, of the endowment of nature (*'dote di natura'*): the conservation of value through an increase of value, intended as an 'endowment of nature of the labour force in act, of the living labour', natural potency under human guise, that is, something that does not lose its use value not working for Capital. This is the excess which I call the 'plus of being' (see here further below).

Fadini remarks how this is the centrality of the conflict between living and dead labour. He highlights the importance of focusing on the fixed part of living labour 'fixed' productively – read from a Deleuzian and Guattarian perspective: the variable-fixed relation is even more incisive for the relation between 'machine' and 'essence' of desire. Capital enters into the subject through the machinic subjection.[88]

Shown again, here, is how the core of immaterial labour is subjectivity, both as production of new lines of actualisation (the virtuality of the free man, let's say) and as object of the subjection of Capital (virtual of capital). And since getting out of subjection is a matter of the *Ethics*, we should investigate how affect[89] is the building block of the construction of the self, of the *causa sui*; how we can start anew from the construction of the social relation of production to realise the 'adequate production', the productive motor at once of our own production of ourselves and of collective wealth. It would be interesting, that is, to explore how affect is that 'economic' element that can turn value into virtue, into production of the plus of being that could be the basis of the production of true wealth. With this, we mean that that core part (virtual of *causa sui*) of the production of subjectivity, which is captured neither in machinic enslavement nor in social subjectivation, can become productive of a 'virtue-value' through another modality of production whose content is no longer self-augmenting money but an increase in living capacity, in the capacity of life.

Capital operates by reproducing within the paradigm of the real-possible.

Beyond this, and also as its origin, there is a being, a subject, who expresses his capacity for production through labour, and whose 'virtue' – whose living, productive core – is the principle of virtuality. His adequate production is the actualisation of his, her, *potentia*. It cannot be sold entirely to the mimicry of Capital, of its real-possible paradigm. Where is the difference between the two?

It is in the very notion of creation, or, if we like, of production. Capital produces by making the life force of the subject its own and proceeding within the

---

88   It is important, once again, to revisit Fadini's reading of Deleuze and Guattari in *Divenire Corpo*, together with Lazzarato 2014.

89   See A. Negri–M. Hardt 1999, pp. 77–88. See also Negri 2012 and his preface to this book.

possible-real paradigm: it does not really innovate, it does not adequately produce, but rather it steals the plane of the Idea in which the virtual is embedded and makes its own that concept on which it inscribes the possible.

The worker is thus cast into the tracks of the realisation of this possible, of which he does not have the concept, of which he does not hold the Idea. In the moment in which the worker holds the idea, possesses the concept, and can transform it, become with it, he is outside of Capital's mechanism, he is increasing his own being.

This is why the economy of knowledge (Rullani, équipe Matisse, etc.)[90] has shown us its potential: knowledge is what cannot be possessed (Rullani) but shared, and transforms the subject who owns it. At the same time (at different levels in different ages) we witness how knowledge is indeed a factor of economic production and of surplus value – that is, how it can be taken away from the one who produced it anew.

4.4.1   True Wealth

But what is 'true wealth', and how can we produce it? And what would these same authors' work suggest? *Wahre Reichtum* is the *causa sui* liberated from the separation from its own *potentia* – that is, the *causa sui* where the virtual (the concept, the 'essence') and the actual (life, the existence) are composed with one another in the production of adequate life conditions.

Let us now try to sketch out a framework for the construction of what I want to call adequate production, moving from the discourse on immaterial labour ebbing into the actual-virtual relation, on the one hand, to the question of how to build an ontology of labour and an economy of affects, based on potentia, on the other.

To construct the concept of adequate production means, for me, to deepen the theoretical trajectory: potentia of poverty-causa sui-production of true wealth.

What does 'potentia of poverty-causa sui-construction of true wealth' mean?

We have already seen the following constellation:[91] Lazzarato's analysis of immaterial labour, the production of subjectivity, the indebted man from the one side, and on the other the dynamic of invention. Fadini's interiorisation

---

90   See Rullani 2004a; 2004b; 2002; Moulier Boutang (ed.) 2002; Vercellone (ed.) 2006.
91   This is an outline which does not take into account many other fundamentally important works on this and similar subjects (Marazzi, Revelli, Virno, Vercellone, Corsani, Fumagalli, etc.) because our focus is on the virtual element of the production of subjectivity. We are interested in those readings that hold together Walter Benjamin's reading of Marx and Deleuze and Guattari's analysis of Capital.

by capital, and the endowment of nature. Deleuze and Guattari's machinic enslavement and social subjectivation, and desire as an element of anti-production.

Benjamin's analysis of the commodity, of the phantasmagoria, of commodity as poetical object as genealogy of immaterial labour (Lazzarato) has to be added to the above constellation as the first indicator of that 'production of sense' which is Marx's distinction between '*materielle und nichtmaterielle Produktion*'; the first direct producer of value, the second producer of sense, which, in turn, can produce value or refuse to produce something that can be stored as value, in that it produces something which goes to increase being.

As for the production of wealth, Lazzarato in *Puissances de l'invention* focuses on its meaning and its relation to subjectivity:

> At the end of the 18th century and at the beginning of the 19th century, political economy experienced a theoretical revolution through the works of Adam Smith and David Ricardo. The essence of wealth was no longer searched for on the side of the properties of the object but on the side of the activity of the subject ... It is Marx who directs us on this path affirming that with the development of capitalism, political economy enlarged scientific progress when it located the source of wealth in the subjective activity. Capitalism allows us to think of a form of *production in general*, a form of *abstract* production, without any privilege of a kind of activity over another ... Deleuze in this respect talks very pertinently of the Kantian conversion of political economy, because the essence of wealth is defined by the relation that subjectivity maintains with time.[92]

The following two pages are central for understanding the assignation of the power of production to subjectivity but also, at the same time, its mystification. For it is still 'caged' within the capital/labour relation: 'Classical political economy and Marxism reduce *any action* expressed by *subjectivity* to labour and the force of labour. Thus the production of wealth is assigned to the productive subjects who operate inside the capital/labour relation'.[93]

Allow me to quote the following passage at length, given its importance for our discourse on subjectivity and *causa sui*:

---

92   Lazzarato 2002, op. cit., p. 109, my translation.
93   Ibid., pp. 109–10.

The mutilation which political economy and Marxism make subjectivity endure finds its foundation in the concept of *force* which, explicitly or implicitly, these theories take on in order to define the subjective and active which operates in production. The definition of labour (and of labour power) *qua* economic power, is strictly linked to the debate which started during the Renaissance between philosophers, physicians and engineers around the concept of force. In an ambiguous way, the concept of economic activity has long been tied to the concept of muscular effort and physical-physiological expenditure. Political economy and Marxist critique, notwithstanding their will to differentiate themselves from an energetic-mechanical theory of labour, have long reinforced these hesitations ... Being inspired by the concept of force in Leibniz (which is somehow an 'average between faculty and action') and by the concept of voluntary effort (conatus) of Maine de Biran, Tarde develops a concept of force which is reducible neither to the effort which, by meeting a resistance, produces a movement or energy, nor to force understood as a simple *transformation of sensation*. Tarde gets rid of any energetic-mechanical ambiguities accompanying the notion of labour. He highlights a virtual subjective force underlying pleasures and pains, through which the utilitarians explain the productivity of economical actor and the underlying abstract activity, through which the theories of labour-value take account of the productivity of the labour force. The use of the idea of force in Tarde is always synonymous with *virtual* force which 'merges and sinks, like a drop of water into the sea, in the infinite totality of possible phenomena of the entire nature, that is, in the full and true force'. Tarde's force gets out of the pre-constituted and transcendental measure of theories of value. These latter define a measure which does not emerge, in an immanent way, from the relations of creation between forces. On the contrary, they annul the virtuality, the outside-measure, the force invention of economic action by reducing the unknown to the known, creation to reproduction.[94]

For us, the Deleuzian definition highlighted here is central: the Kantian conversion in political economy for which the essence of wealth is defined by the relation that subjectivity has with time and Tarde's notion of force, emancipated from labour power and very close to our concept of the virtual of the *causa sui*.

---

94   Ibid., p. 111.

This force, the virtual, the relation of subjectivity with time – which is constitution[95] – is wonderfully described:

> Tarde has some images which, in order to talk about the unity of each phe-
> nomenon, refer to the variation, to the fluctuation, or more to a chaotic
> temporal regime: a mobile equilibrium coming back on itself, as a musical
> refrain or an harmonious sequence of movements or, rather, the whirl-
> winds of a river. The *whole*, whatever it will be, is like a fold, like a wave
> which, being part of the movements of the sea, singularises them. What
> we grasp as substance, as being is but a whirlwind, in reality, a fold which
> functions as a relay, an exchanger of unstable relations, fluctuating, which
> circulate in the intercerebral cooperation according to a temporal, non-
> linear, Brownian regime. The force of this thought lies in that the indi-
> vidual is not produced from above ... but rather from below, 'at the infin-
> itesimal level of beliefs and desires that imitate themselves and by imitat-
> ing combine themselves or disagree, neutralize or strengthen themselves'
> [Bruno Karsenti, introduction to *Les lois de l'imitation* ...].[96]

The relation between time and subjectivity is the condition for the process
of subjectivation, and it is this production which defines the dynamic of the
economic phenomenon:[97] '[the production] is the attractor of the process
of creative destruction of capitalism. It is in the metamorphoses and variations of the action of subjectivation, and not in the metamorphoses and
variations of value, that we should look for the immanent dynamic of capitalism'.[98]

Lazzarato highlights how for Tarde capital reproduces and does not invent
the new – and that his revolutionary trait lies exactly in making invention,
the 'incommensurable of creation ... the measure of the world and of economy':[99] 'the theory of knowledges and the theory of art explain *value* by the
outside-value of the invention and cooperation, by reversing the relation of sub-
ordination of creation to reproduction which Marxist and economic theories

95   See for this A. Negri, *La costituzione del tempo*, manifesto libri, 1997.
96   Lazzarato, 2002, p. 132. On the notion of force, the transcendental illusion, and the 'exit'
      which could be a theory of affects, the following pages (pp. 135–7) are important (see also
      pp. 10–11, 15–16).
97   Ibid., p. 142.
98   Ibid.
99   Ibid., pp. 148, 149.

suppose'.[100] 'In short, economic psychology is a theory of creation and constitution of values, whereas economics and Marxism are theories of the *measure
of value'*.[101]

Regarding the essence of wealth and the relation between subjectivity and
time, the section on memory and living labour is also important:[102]

> The Kantian reconversion operated by political economy identified the
> source of cumulative character of wealth in the relation of the subjective
> activity to time. But subjectivity refers now to memory and its capacity to
> incarnate the cumulative process with the help of material supports. Time
> is no longer reduced to the homogenous measure of labour but becomes
> duration, multiplicity, time which means 'invention, creation of forms,
> continuous elaboration of the absolutely new'.[103]

To explain the radical act of creation which is the actual-virtual dynamic, Lazzarato here marvellously notes: 'The Aristotelian concepts of potency and act
which Marx uses to take account of living labour do not serve to give form to
the new. The *Economic Psychology* made us move up in this direction, by renew-
ing the description of the process of creation, by substituting the categories of
potency and act with those of actual and virtual'.[104]

The entire book is a dive into the act of creation and into a theory of affects.
This is the keystone of the production of a free subjectivity, which finds its first
building block, if I may, in Spinoza: 'Invention is for Tarde the social incarn-
ation of a "system of difference"'[105] – this system of difference is played out
along what Spinoza defined as adequate knowledge, adequate action, and inadequate knowledge, inadequate action.

It is the affect which constitutes the differential among the two. And for our
economic ethics, it is the affect which constitutes the engine of creation of the
new, of the invention, expression of the free subject.

Indeed, Lazzarato cites him: 'In parallel to the succession of ideas, it operates in us a "variation, increase-decrease of the force of existing or the potentia
to act" which expresses the passage from one state to another. The affect thus
continues a kind of "melodic line" of variation of the *vis existendi* or *poten-*

---

100   Ibid.
101   Ibid., p. 50.
102   Ibid., p. 176.
103   Ibid., p. 178.
104   Ibid., p. 76.
105   Ibid.

tia agendi. For Tarde ... there is always in them [expressions of subjectivity] an affective and differential element, the pure feeling [*sentir*] which plays the principal and active role'.[106] Here Tarde's *Economic Psychology* and Spinoza's *Ethics* compose what we could call an 'economic ethics' for the adequate production of the self.

Virtuality is the 'power of variation and constant differentiation of the *vis existendi* or *potentia agendi*' and time is this absolute difference, existence as differing, and feeling as differentiating.[107] The virtual is not representative, it is the force of invention. In that, it differs from the real-possible of Capital, which reproduces instead of really producing: 'It is a question of two different ways of considering the becoming and the change. The dialectic conceives a becoming *possible* which contains since the beginning its result: identity and representation. The virtual introduces in the social dynamic an absolute novelty which undoes identity and representation'.[108]

'The Tardian conception of life as virtual, as creative difference, shows us an ontological, social and political power which is positive and in constitution';[109] 'the refusal of labour criticises the slavery of reproductive labour and shows the will to take away virtuality and the creation of cooperation from the division of labour ... Production and life identify as expressions of time of creation, of difference, of the force-invention, of cooperation and sympathy'.[110]

> Suddenly we are in 'another population', in 'another world', in 'another man'. The big transformation contains, from its very genealogy, this virtuality, this temporality of a new beginning ... It is not a question of affirming, in front of the second big transformation, which we are now living, the end of labour, nor the primacy of intellectual labour over manual labour, nor the end of history, all expressions which perpetuate the old categories of thought. Tarde proposes that we measure the world in light of invention and cooperation, to distribute categories and concepts differently and to arrange the active forces according to the difference and repetition of the time of creation. It is an infinitesimal displacement which opens to the change of paradigm, to other possibilities of life.[111]

---

106   Ibid, p. 215.
107   Ibid, pp. 217 ff.
108   Ibid., p. 340; see also p. 339 and p. 396.
109   Ibid., p. 396.
110   Ibid., pp. 398–9.
111   Ibid., pp. 400–1.

Fadini's work also touches upon the construction of true wealth. He quotes the work of Berta: it is the general intellect as a social general knowledge, transferred in immediate productive force, the concrete possibility of the 'creation of true wealth' which no longer depends on the 'immediate time of labour' but from 'the general status of production and from the progress of technology, or of the application of this science to production'; 'collective knowledge transfers entirely its creative potency to the production', and to insert this perspective in the architecture of Capital makes it explode.[112]

Fadini keeps as his reference Gorz's notion of the exit from work, his and Marazzi's focus on human fixed capital, and Deleuze and Guattari's analysis on the variable relation between man and the machine based on the infrastructural position of desire and the notion of 'creative plusvalue'. In so doing, he articulates a reflection at three levels, where our labour power's becoming fixed capital (Marazzi, Gorz), Benjamin's *hunderprozentigen Bildraum* [absolute imaginal space] and Deleuze and Guattari's understanding of the machine Capital as a capture of desire also substantially traversed by it (cracked to the point of overthrow), together build a plane where it is possible to postulate a new horizon of human productive capacity, no longer subject to the destructive mechanism at the core of Capital.

It is thus with, on the one hand, Lazzarato's discourse on immaterial labour and its genealogy (Benjamin), on the production of subjectivity (Deleuze-Guattari), and, on the other, Fadini's discourse on 'creative plusvalue'-infrastructure of desire (Deleuze-Guattari), labour force as fixed capital (Gorz-Marazzi), Benjamin's 'body collective' that we can look for that revolutionary point of overthrow which will give an account of one of the levers to exit from Capital.

I find this revolutionary point of overthrow in Benjamin's reading of Marx, that is, on his discourse on commodity as a poetical object.[113]

---

112   Fadini 2015, p. 50, my translation.
113   Please allow me to refer, here too, to my first doctoral thesis, 'Capital and Imaginary: A Study of the Commodity as a Poetical Object' (Pascucci 2003a), where this theme was discussed at length. The commodity as a poetic object indicates the production of sense. By sense I mean what Marx called the content of the *nicht-materielle Produktion* (the wider category to which also immaterial labour belongs). 'Sense' is that 'surplus' which cannot be owned and managed by capital but remains in the worker. It is the residue of the social relation: knowledge, for example, which increases the subject and in that cannot be owned but by him-herself; or love, another affect, expression of a relation, which cannot be owned if not being mutual – the maximum expression of common good; common goods are also another element, external this time to the subject, but whose property is that of *being* the social relation: it cannot entirely be expropriated or captured, extrapolated from a body, from nature, which is our collective substance.

It can be found also, with Lazzarato, in the work of Gabriel Tarde, with his crucial, and liberating, reading of the actual-virtual axis.

It can be found hinted at in that residual element of anti-production (man's virtuality, his capacity of producing his further life, his pleasure in life, etc.): the exceptional increase of immaterial labour, of precariousness, of poverty, of wars, of indebted men and women, of despair is yet liberating huge transformations which are overwhelmingly teeming, traversing spaces, mixing societies, differentiating from within, making 'of chaos an object of affirmation' (Deleuze quoting Pascal).

Virtuality is powerfully looking for lines of actualisation, for its own freedom. It is an index, an arrow of innovation, of the new. If we do not understand its cipher, its signal, we will be as blind to an adequate production as those who, in Spinoza's letter 12, try to capture and understand substance by dividing it into pieces[114] and thus remain blind to the true, adequate knowledge.

Immaterial labour, or *nicht-materielle Produktion*, not only produces a social, capital relationship but it produces something that is not immediately, or not only, storable as surplus value. For it is also a residue for transformation in the subjectivity of both the consumer (Lazzarato) and the producer (somehow already in Benjamin's reading of Marx).

This transformation in the producer concerns me because it detects the point at which that 'pure virtuality' of the free worker – subject to being stolen, manipulated, trapped, thus coming to make him poor – finds its transformative power.

Seen from another angle: it is from the position of the poor that this theft, this manipulation of one's own subjectivity as a virtual capacity of producing one's own life (Spinoza's *causa sui*) is mostly understood.

This 'social relationship' which immaterial labour exposes and material labour hides – that is, that production is always (also) a capital production, production of capital, of a power relation – also exposes the pure virtuality which is the core of what is violated and hidden: our capacity of producing (life, commodities, relations, etc.) – our potentia. Labour force has become a life force.

---

114   With Spinoza the destructive nature of a mechanism of production like the one embodied by Capital was sensed, I believe, in what I would like to call the mistake of infinity: in letter 12 he wonderfully explains how we cannot understand the substance if we cut it, if we separate it from its attributes, from its modes. Capital does so – its mechanism of production did not, and never will, understand adequately the capacity of life of producing further life, that is, our infinity. It will just appropriate it, separating it from its producers, our bodies and minds.

The first element of the adequate production is thus the life force: not appropriable by anyone (principle of reciprocity), not separable from our mind and body (principle of adequate knowledge and adequate cause), not dividing us from our collectivity (principle of democracy).

To transform, to subvert the capital relation means, at once, to expose that core of each one's production of subjectivity – what I call the *'causa sui'* – which, in the capital relation, comes to be violated.

The force of poverty is the blatant exposure of this violence perpetrated against our life.

Immaterial labour is not only the producer of capital relations, for in so doing it is also their revolving door. This relation of capital production in fact 'intersects' with the discourse of *causa sui*: living labour is the labour power of the free worker, it is that 'pure virtuality' which still owns itself, and remains inside the worker as his own transformation, forced as he is to confront *inside* himself the alienation from his own force, the dispossession of his own *dunamis*. He, she, come to be separated from their own life force in that primary tool of producing life (conditions) which is work.[115]

It is in this connection, in this gear – in how a relation of production can enhance our own potentia (again as in Spinoza's terms) or de-potentiate us in alienating, in separating us from ourselves – that today's poverty brings us to question the radicality of the economy's encroachment upon subjectivity. Subjectivity is the product and the content of immaterial labour but does not exhaust itself in it: our capacity of striving in life, of producing further life, when reduced to what can be separated from us, belongs indeed to others (I have called this mechanism the 'virtuality of Capital'). This occurs inasmuch as we conceive our capacity to labour as detachable from us, its substance. But potentia is neither detached nor detachable from it. Potentia is the body and mind of the worker: what has been taken from him is only the knowledge of this inseparability, of this substantial univocity of being and work (being a worker) as self-productive forces (forces of multifaceted unicum which is our own life) – what is given to him/her (the subject) is the mistaken, manipulated knowledge of a substance which can be separated from itself, a body from its mind, intellectual from manual labour, material from immaterial production. We should conceive our political economy as an economic ethics, taking labour

---

115 All the contradictions we find (immaterial labour as producer of capital's relation but also as pure virtuality, crisis – something which capital constantly produces but also possibility of revolution, etc.) are the expression of this fundamental dualism of the production process: separated inside ourselves as much as separated from our own work as a life expression.

away from a Cartesian paradigm and understanding it in a radically different way. The worker's living labour cannot be taken from him, for this would mean a misunderstanding of the substance and his economic capacity: an economy of joy in the Spinozan sense means to understand how to liberate potentia from its false misconceptions and manipulations, how to produce true wealth, our common essence.

Not only will it freely produce value, but a value which goes to increase the 'surplus of being', the composition of the subject into a happy time of life, his, her capacity of increasing his/her life through production.

The 'potentia of labour' means that the content of production should remain within the subject, as force. That is the source of actualisation that Tarde was referring to.

If we deprive man of that expression of his capacity which is labour – his own force as that capacity of productivity – we deprive him not only of his product (the discrepancy between objectified labour/necessary time-salary; today the virtuality of the unemployed), but of his very capacity for being the free cause of himself. The process of inner separation which makes him, as worker, the subject of that 'labour objectified as domination, the power to dominate living labour'[116] (which is Capital), is prolonged in the process of social subjectivation and machinic enslavement that goes to encroach upon desire. It develops a part within the worker where he has to confront Capital, in the form of that subjected part of himself as producer which is under domination, under power.[117] Yet the process goes further still: man is deprived of his own free capacity of producing himself – that is, his potentia, the same core of this force is separated from him. It is objectified and starts to be divided, separated from within.

A potentia divided, separated from itself is the field of all dispossession, violence, depredation, deprivation. In a word: it is reduced to the state of subjection to enslavement (be it machinic enslavement or social subjectivation).

The substance, our life, the constant fluctuation of essence (the virtual) into existence (the actual), in its adjustments, compositions, decompositions, re-compositions, if misunderstood (and used, managed) as made up of parts, as separable from itself, cannot be adequately conceived. And therefore it cannot develop itself fully, cannot act correctly. The risk is that, being separated

---

116   See Mandel 2015, p. 160.
117   It is here that the indebted man falls back to be trapped in Plato's cavern. Allow me, for this, to refer to chap. 6, Timon of Athens, in my *Philosophical Readings of Shakespeare* (Pascucci 2013).

from itself, life remains 'without substance', that is without that compositional force of its own self, and 'confronted with the alienated reality, which does not belong to it but to others'.[118]

The production of subjectivity which Capital, in today's forms of labour, establishes, is the infinite reproduction of this alienation within ourselves (mirroring the outside alienation in the form of labour). And this latter has overflowed from labour to life, inundating the very texture of our singular and collective being.

118   Mandel 2015, p. 160, referring to Marx, *Grundrisse*, pp. 357–8.

Selected Bibliography

Alliez, E. 1991, *Les temps capitaux, Tome I. Récits de la conquête du temps*, Paris: Cerf

Alliez, E.- Stengers, I. 1988, 'Énergie et valeur: Le problème de la conservation chez Engels et Marx', in *Contretemps, Les pouvoirs de l'argent*, in collaboration with M. Féher, D. Gill, I. Stengers, Paris: Michel de Maule.

Althusser, L. and Balibar, E. 1970, *Reading Capital*, translated by Ben Brewster, London: NLB.

Balibar, E. 1993, 'Le politique, la politique: De Rousseau à Marx, de Marx à Spinoza', *Studia Spinozana*, 9.

Becker, I. 1993, *Spinoza und die Defizite der Marxschen Theorie, I. Becker im Gespräch mit H. Seidel und M. Walthe, Studia Spinozana*, 9.

Benjamin, W. 2002, *The Arcades Project*, tr. By Howard Eiland and Kevin McLaughlin, Cambridge MA: Harvard University Press.

Bieling, R. 1979, *Spinozas im Urteil von Marx und Engels*, Berlin, Freie Universität Fachbereich 11-Philosophie u. Sozialwissenschaft Dissertation.

Boehringer, H. and Gruender, K. (eds.) 1976, *Ästhetik und Soziologie um die Jahrhundertwende: Georg Simmel*, Frankfurt am Main: V. Klosterman.

Bongiovanni, B. 1987. *Quaderno Spinoza*, Torino: Bollati Boringhieri.

Buchanan, I. and Thoburn, N. (eds.) 2008, *Deleuze and Politics*, Edinburgh: Edinburgh University Press.

De Golyer, M. 1992. 'The Greek Accent of the Marxian Matrix', in *Marx and Aristotle, Nineteenth-century German Social Theory and Classical Antiquity*, edited by by G.E. McCarthy, New York: Rowman & Littlefield.

Deleuze, G. 1969, *Spinoza et le problème de l'expression*, Paris: Les Éditions de Minuit; 1992, *Expressionism in Philosophy: Spinoza*, New York: Zone Books.

Deleuze, G. 1984, 'La grandeur de Yasser Arafat', *Revue d'études palestiniennes*, Beirut: Institute des études palestiniennes, n. 10.

Deleuze, G. 1990, 'Simulacrum and ancient philosophy', Appendix to *Logic of sense*, New York: Columbia University Press, translated by M. Lester and C. Stivale.

Deleuze, G. 1991, *Bergsonism*, translated by Hugh Tomlinson and Barbara Habberjam, New York: Zone Books.

Deleuze, G. 1995, 'L'actuel et le virtuel', in Gilles Deleuze-Claire Parnet, *Dialogues II*, translated by E. Ross Albert.

Deleuze, G. 2001, *Spinoza. Practical philosophy*, translated by Robert Hurley, San Francisco: City Lights Publishers.

Deleuze, G. 2004, *Difference and Repetition*, translated by P. Patton, London: A&C Black.

Deleuze, G. 1998, 'The Grandeur of Yasser Arafat', translated by T. Murphy, *Discourse*, 20, 3 (Fall).

Deleuze, G. 2006, 'Spoilers of Peace', in *Two Regimes of Madness*, New York: Semiotexte.

Deleuze, G. and Guattari, F. 1983, *Anti-Oedipus*. Capitalism and Schizophrenia, translated by Robert Hurley, Mark Seem, and Helen R. Lane, Minneapolis: University of Minnesota Press.

Deleuze, G. and Guattari, F. 1987, *A thousand Plateaus: Capitalism and Schizophrenia 2*, translated by Brian Massumi, Minneapolis: University of Minnesota Press.

Di Vona, P. 1960, 1969, *Studi sull'ontologia di Spinoza*, Firenze: La Nuova Italia, vols. I, II.

Euclid, 2002, *Elements*, edited by D. Densmore, translated by L. Heath, vol. 1, Santa Fe: Green Lion Press.

Fadini, U. 2015, *Divenire corpo*, Verona: ombre corte, Verona.

Fischbach, F. 2005, *La production des hommes. Marx avec Spinoza*, Paris: Presses Universitaires de France.

Hardt, M. and Negri, A. 1999, 'Value and Affect', *boundary 2*, 26: 2 (Summer)

Hardt, M. 2012, *The procedures of love/Die Verfahren der Liebe*, dOCUMENTA (13), n. o68, Hatje Cantz.

Heinrich, M. 2005, *Kritik der politischen Ökonomie. Eine Einführung*, Stuttgart: Schmetterling Verlag.

Hull, G. 2000–1, *Marx's Anomalous reading of Spinoza, Interpretation* 28, 2.

Igoin, A. 1977, *De l'ellipse de la théorie politique de Spinoza chez le jeune Marx*, in *Cahiers Spinoza*, 1, Eté 1977, Paris: Editions Réplique.

Il'enkov, E.V. 1977, *Denken als Attribut der Substanz*, in *Wissenschaftliche Zeitschrift*, 1, Leipzig: Karl-Marx-Universität.

Lazzarato, M. 1997, *Lavoro immateriale e produzione di soggettività*, Verona: ombre corte.

Lazzarato, M. 2004, 'From Capital-Labour to Capital-Life', *Ephemera*, 4:3.

Lazzarato, M. 2006, 'Immaterial labour', in *Radical Thought in Italy: A Potential Politics*, edited by Paolo Virno and Michael Hardt, 135, University of Minnesota Press.

Lazzarato, M. 1992, 'Lavoro immateriale e soggettivita' (with Toni Negri), *Derive e approdi*, 0.

Lazzarato, M. 1994, 'Il ciclo della produzione immateriale', *Derive e Approdi*.

Lazzarato, M. 1995, *Futur antérieur*, n. 10 e 16; *Futuro anteriore*, 2.

Lazzarato, M. 2002, *Puissances l'invention. La psychologie économique de Gabriel Tarde contro l'économie politique*, Les Empêcheurs des penser en rond, Paris: Le Seuil.

Lazzarato, M. 2012, *The Making of the indebted man. An essay on the liberal condition*, semiotexte interventions, series 13.

Lazzarato, M. 2015, *Governing by debt*, semiotexte, series 17.

Lazzarato, M. 2014, *Signs and machines. Capitalism and the production of subjectivity*, semiotexte.

Lazzarato, M., with Negri, T. and Virno, P. 1998, *Umherschweifende Produzenten, Immaterielle Arbeit und Subversion*, ID Verlag, Berlin.

Maier, A. 1968, *Zwei Grundprobleme der Scholastischen Naturphilosophie*, Roma.

Mandel, E. 2015, *The formation of the economic thought of Karl Marx, 1843 to Capital*, translated by B. Pearce, London: Verso

Marx, K. 1962, *Marx Engels Werke*, Volume 23, *Kapital I*, Berlin: Dietz.

Marx, K. 1968, *Marx Engels Werke*, Volume 26, Part 3, *Theorien über Mehrwert*, Berlin: Dietz.

Marx, K. 1975a, *Capital*, vol. 1, unabridged, edited by Frederick Engels, New York: International Publishers.

Marx, K. 1975b, *Differenz der demokritischen und epikureischen Naturphilosophie*, in MEGA I/1, Artikel, Literarische Versuche bis März 1843, Berlin: Dietz Verlag.

Marx, K. 1975c, *Capital*, vol. 2, in *Marx and Engels Collected Works*, vol. 36, London: Lawrence and Wishart.

Marx, K. 1976, *Exzerpte aus Benedictus de Spinoza: Opera*, edited by Paulus, 'Theologisch-politischer Traktat, Briefe in *Exzerpte bis 1842*', MEGA IV, 1, Berlin: Dietz Verlag.

Marx, K. 1976. *Grundrisse der Kritik der politischen Oekonomie*, 1857–8 (III, 2), MEGA II/1.1.

Marx, K. 1977, *Zur Kritik der politischen Ökonomie (Manuskript 1861–1863)*, Teil 2. Berlin.

Marx, K. 1982, *Zur Kritik der politischen Ökonomie (Manuskript 1861–1863)*, Teil 6. Berlin.

Marx, K. 2006, *Grundrisse der Kritik der politischen Oekonomie*, in *Ökonomische Manuskripte 1857/58*, Berlin: Akademie.

Matheron, A. 1977, 'The "Theological-political treatise" seen from the young Marx', *Cahiers Spinoza*, Numéro 1, Eté 1977, Paris: Editions Réplique.

Matheron, A. 1969, *Individu et communauté chez Spinoza*, Paris: Editions de Minuit.

Moreau, P.F. 1975, *Spinoza*, Paris: Seuil.

Moreau, P.F. 1978, *Marx und Spinoza*, Positionen 4, Hamburg: VSA.

Moulier Boutang, Y. (ed.) 2002, *L'età del capitalismo cognitivo. Invenzione, proprietà e cooperazione delle moltitudini*, Verona: ombre corte.

Negri, A. 1991, *The Savage Anomaly. The power of Spinoza's metaphysics and politics*, translated by Michael Hardt, University of Minnesota Press, Minneapolis Oxford.

Negri, A. 1992, *Marx beyond Marx*, Pluto Press.

Negri, A. 2013, *Time for revolution*, translated by M. Mandarini, London: Bloomsbury Academic.

Negri, A. 2012. *Spinoza e Noi*, Milan: Mimesis Edizioni.

Negri, A. 2017, *Spinoza then and now*, Cambridge: Polity Press.

Negri, A. 2013a, *Time for revolution*, tr. M. Mandarini, London: Bloomsbury Academic.

Negri, A. 2013b, *Spinoza for our time: politics and postmodernity*, tr. W. McCuaig, CUP 2013b.

Negri A. and Hardt, M. 2009, *Commonwealth*, Cambridge MA: Harvard University Press.

Odekon, Mehmet A. 2006, *Encyclopedia of World Poverty*, New York: Sage Golson Books.

Pascucci, M. 2011, 'Il sogno di Marx', *Millepiani*, n. 37, Milano: Mimesis.

Pascucci, M. 2003a, 'Capital and the Imaginary: A Study of the Commodity as a Poetical Object', Phd diss., New York University.

Pasucci, M. 2003b, 'Privilegium paupertatis', *Millepiani*, n. 26, Milano: Mimesis.

Pascucci, M. 2009, *Causa sui. Saggio sul capitale e il virtuale*, ombre corte.

Pascucci, M. 2013, *Philosophical Readings of Shakespeare*, London: Palgrave.

Rahnema, M. 2003, *Quand la misère chasse la pauvreté*, Babel, Fayard.

Rubel, M. 1977, '*Marx à la rencontre de Spinoza*', introduction, *Cahier Spinoza*, Numéro 1, Eté 1977, Paris: Editions Réplique.

Rubel, M. 1957, *Les Cahiers de lecture de Karl Marx*, in *International Revue of Social History* (2) Cambridge: Cambridge University Press.

Rubel, M. 1982, *Marx à l'ecole de Spinoza. Contribution à l'etiologie de l'alienation politique*, in *Spinoza nel 350 anniversario della nascita*, Atti del convegno, ed. E. Giancotti, Urbino 4–8 ottobre.

Rullani, E. 2002, *Multitudes* n. 2, Paris: Exils.

Rullani, E. 2004a, *L'economia della conoscenza. Creatività e valore nel capitalismo delle reti*, Roma: Carocci.

Rullani, E. 2004b, *La fabbrica dell'immateriale. Produrre valore con la conoscenza*, Roma: Carocci

Schrader, F.E. 1985, *Substanz und Begriff: Zur Spinoza-Rezeption Marxens*, in *Mededelingen* XLVII Vanwege Het Spinozahuis, E.J. Brill.

Seidel, H. 1977, *Karl Marx und Baruch Spinoza*, in *Wissenschaftliche Zeitschrift*, Leipzig: Karl-Marx-Universität, 1, 1977; and 2, 1977.

Seidel, H. 1978, *Zum Verhältnis des Marxismus zur Philosophie Spinozas*, in *Leipziger Universitätsreden*, Neue Folge Heft 48, Leipzig: Karl-Marx-Universität.

Seidel, H. 1981, *Marxismus und Spinozismus, Materialen einer wissenschaftlichen Konferenz*. Leipzig: Karl-Marx Universität.

Seidel, H. 1993, *Spinoza und Marx über Entfremdung*, in *Studia Spinozana*.

Sohn-Rethel, A. 1978, *Intellectual and manual labour. A critique of epistemology*, Humanities Press, New Jersey.

Sohn-Rethel, A. 1990, *Das Geld*, die bare Münze des *Apriori*, Berlin: Wagenbach.

Sohn-Rethel, A. 1971, 'Zur kritischen Liquidierung des Apriorismus', in *Warenform und Denkform. Aufsaetze*, Frankfurt-Wien: Europa Verlag

Souilhé J. 1919, *Etudes sur le terme dunamis dans les dialogues de Platon*, Paris: Alcan.

Spinoza, B. 1992, *Ethics, Treatise on the Emendation of the Intellect and Selected Letters*, Indianapolis: Hackett, ed. by S. Feldman.

Spinoza, B. 1988, *Etica*, Roma: Editori Riuniti, ed. by Emilia Giancotti.

Spinoza, B. 2007, *Theological-political Treatise*, edited by J. Israel, Cambridge University Press, Cambridge.

Spinoza, B. 2014–2020, *Correspondence*, Early Modern Text, 2014–2020, Peter Millican, p. 4, http://www.earlymoderntexts.com/assets/pdfs/spinoza1661.pdf, [access November 2016]

Smith, T. 2013, 'The "General Intellect" in the Grundrisse and Beyond', *Historical Materialism*, 21, 4: 235–255.

Tosél, A. 2007, *Pour une étude systématique du rapport de Marx à Spinoza, Remarques et hypothèses*, in *Spinoza au XIX siècle*, sous la direction d'André Tosel et Jean Salem, Paris: Publication de la Sorbonne.

Vercellone, C. (ed.) 2006, *Capitalismo cognitivo. Conoscenza e finanza dell'epoca postfordista*, Roma: manifestolibri.

Vercellone, C. 2007, 'From Formal Subsumption to General Intellect: Elements for a Marxist Reading of the Thesis of Cognitive Capitalism', *Historical Materialism*, 15, 1: 13–36.

Virno, P. 2001, 'General Intellect', *Lessico Postfordista. Dizionario di idee della mutazione*, ed. by A. Zanini and U. Fadini, Milano: Feltrinelli, Milano. [Engl. tr., P. Virno, 'General Intellect', *Historical Materialism*, 15, 3: 3–8].

Yovel, Y. 1993, *Marx's Ontology and Spinoza's Philosophy of Immanence* in *Studia Spinozana*, edited by W. Manfred, editor Würzburg: Verlag Königshausen & Neumann.

Yovel, Y. 1989, *Spinoza and other Heretics, The adventure of immanence*, NJ: Princeton University Press.

Wolfson, A.H. 1934, *The Philosophy of Spinoza*, II, Cambridge, MA: Harvard University Press

Index of Names

[*] Given too many entries, I chose only some peculiar ones.

*

General Index